FUNDAMENTAL ISSUES IN TRADE THEORY

By the same author

MARX AFTER SRAFFA
TRADE AMONGST GROWING ECONOMIES

FUNDAMENTAL ISSUES IN TRADE THEORY

Edited by
Ian Steedman
Professor of Economics
University of Manchester

© Ian Steedman 1979
Softcover reprint of the hardcover 1st edition 1979
All rights reserved. No part of this publication may be
reproduced or transmitted, in any form or by any means,
without permission

First published 1979 by
THE MACMILLAN PRESS LTD
London and Basingstoke
Associated companies in Delhi
Dublin Hong Kong Johannesburg Lagos
Melbourne New York Singapore Tokyo

British Library Cataloguing in Publication Data

Fundamental issues in trade theory
1. Commerce
I. Steedman, Ian
382'.01   HF81

ISBN 978-1-349-04380-4   ISBN 978-1-349-04378-1 (eBook)
DOI 10.1007/978-1-349-04378-1

This book is sold subject
to the standard conditions
of the Net Book Agreement

Contents

Preface	vii
Acknowledgements	viii
Contributors	ix

1. INTRODUCTORY ESSAY *Ian Steedman* — 1

2. RESWITCHING AND PRIMARY INPUT USE *J. S. Metcalfe and Ian Steedman* — 15

3. RESWITCHING, PRIMARY INPUTS AND THE HECKSCHER-OHLIN-SAMUELSON THEORY OF TRADE *Ian Steedman and J. S. Metcalfe* — 38

4. A NOTE ON THE GAIN FROM TRADE *J. S. Metcalfe and Ian Steedman* — 47

5. HETEROGENEOUS CAPITAL AND THE HECKSCHER–OHLIN–SAMUELSON THEORY OF TRADE *J. S. Metcalfe and Ian Steedman* — 64

6. RELATIVE PRICES AND 'FACTOR PRICE' EQUALISATION IN A HETEROGENEOUS CAPITAL GOODS MODEL *L. Mainwaring* — 77

7. THE INTEREST RATE EQUALISATION THEOREM WITH NON-TRADED GOODS *L. Mainwaring* — 90

8. 'ON FOREIGN TRADE' *Ian Steedman and J. S. Metcalfe* — 99

9. A NEO-RICARDIAN ANALYSIS OF INTERNATIONAL TRADE *L. Mainwaring* — 110

10	THE NON-SUBSTITUTION THEOREM AND INTERNATIONAL TRADE THEORY *Ian Steedman and J. S. Metcalfe*	123
11	THE GOLDEN RULE AND THE GAIN FROM TRADE *Ian Steedman and J. S. Metcalfe*	127
12	ON THE TRANSITION FROM AUTARKY TO TRADE *L. Mainwaring*	131
13	THE VON NEUMANN ANALYSIS AND THE SMALL OPEN ECONOMY *Ian Steedman*	142
14	DISTRIBUTION, GROWTH AND INTERNATIONAL TRADE *Sergio Parrinello*	159
15	EXCHANGE RATE CHANGES AND THE CHOICE OF TECHNIQUE *L. Mainwaring*	188
16	GROWTH AND DISTRIBUTION IN AN OPEN ECONOMY *J. S. Metcalfe and Ian Steedman*	201
	Index of Names	228
	Index of Subjects	229

Preface

The capital controversies of the 1960s reminded economists that—as Wicksell, for example, had been well aware—there are intrinsic logical difficulties in the notion of 'capital' as a 'factor of production'. Since that notion has played a significant role in the dominant theory of international trade in recent decades, it is not surprising that in the late 1960s and throughout the 1970s a number of writers have sought to trace through the implications of the capital debates for orthodox trade theory and, where necessary, to provide some new trade theory. The essays brought together in this volume are addressed both to the critical task of discussing the orthodox trade theory and to sketching the outlines (no more) of an alternative approach. The four contributors are, of course, only too well aware that the criticism of existing theory will always be easier than the construction of fruitful new theory; they can only hope that the 'constructive' essays presented here will be thought sufficiently interesting to merit the same critical attention as is addressed to the orthodox theory in the more 'negative' of the following essays.

As is perhaps implied above, the contributors have had a significant, mutual influence on one another's work, so that although the respective authors all accept full responsibility for the essays under their names, many of those essays are more significantly 'joint-products' than might be apparent.

I wish to thank my fellow contributors for their patient assistance and Sheila Fenton for her excellent typing, which together have greatly lessened the editorial burden.

Manchester
July 1978

Ian Steedman

Acknowledgements

Some of the essays in this volume are versions (in some cases revised and/or translated) of previously published papers. For permission to republish in this way, we should like to thank *Australian Economic Papers* (Essays 6 and 10), *Economia Internazionale* (Essays 8 and 14), the *Economic Journal* (Essay 2), *Economic Record* (Essays 4 and 15), the *Journal of International Economics* (Essays 3 and 7), *Kyklos* (Essay 9), Longman Group Limited (Essay 5) and Presses Universitaires de Grenoble (Essay 11).

Contributors

IAN STEEDMAN	Professor of Economics, University of Manchester.
J. S. METCALFE	Senior Lecturer in Economics, University of Liverpool.
L. MAINWARING	Lecturer in Economics, University of Cardiff.
SERGIO PARRINELLO	Professor of Economics, University of Rome.

1 Introductory Essay*

IAN STEEDMAN

While the precise nature of the causal links between economic growth and international trade may be a matter of dispute, there can be little doubt that growth and trade were closely related during the period of initial development of a world capitalist economy and that they continue to be so related in the present period. Whether one considers the industrialisation of underdeveloped countries, the growth of the Eastern European economies or that of the advanced capitalist countries, trade and other international economic relationships are of considerable importance. As the overall volume of international trade has grown, its composition has, of course, changed, notable features being the increasing relative importance of trade in industrial, as opposed to primary, products and, in particular, the increasing share in world trade of intermediates and capital goods ([12], [20], [22]).

It might be expected then that growth, capital accumulation and the role of produced means of production, in both domestic production and world trade, would be *central* issues within the pure theory of international trade.

THE HECKSCHER-OHLIN-SAMUELSON THEORY

In fact, however, the dominant trade theory of recent decades—the Heckscher-Ohlin-Samuelson, or H-O-S, theory—has, until quite recently, placed relatively little emphasis on such issues. The reason for this can perhaps be found in the fact that the H-O-S model of trade is ultimately rooted in the general equilibrium model of an exchange economy, the central emphasis of the analysis thus being on the scarcity of the goods in *given* supply. It is, of course, true that that model is then elaborated to include the discussion of production but the elaboration is carried out in such a way that the essential 'vision' of the pure exchange model remains; the emphasis continues to be on the scarcity of *given* supplies, the difference being that given supplies of consumption goods have been replaced by given supplies of primary inputs which limit the possible output patterns of consumption goods. Being founded on a theory incorporating this particular vision of the economic process, it is perhaps not surprising that H–O–S theory has, until relatively recently, said rather little about the continuous expansion of the output of both consumption goods and means of production, which is one of the most striking features of world growth and trade.

As is well known, the basic H–O–S model usually starts from the following assumptions:

a) there are two countries, each of which produces the same two consumption goods;

b) these consumption goods are produced directly by the homogeneous factors land[1] and labour, with no time lag, subject to constant returns to scale production functions (exhibiting diminishing marginal products) which are the same in both countries;

c) there are no factor-intensity-reversals;

d) while the two factors are qualitatively the same in both countries, the latter are endowed with the (immobile) factors in different proportions;

e) there is perfect competition, free trade, zero transport cost, full employment of factors;

f) all consumers have identical, homothetic preferences.

In order to emphasise the close relation between H–O–S theory and the conventional micro-theory of the closed economy, we may consider first a pure exchange model before turning to the full production model. Suppose, then, that in each 'period', each country receives, as manna from heaven, a given endowment of the two consumption goods, where the two goods enter in different proportions into the endowments of the two countries. Given the assumption of identical, homothetic preferences, it follows that the autarky equilibrium price ratio would differ as between the two countries. If trade is possible within each 'period', then it is clear that it will actually take place, that the trade equilibrium price ratio will lie between the two autarky price ratios and that consumers in both countries will obtain an 'exchange gain' from trade.[2]

The analysis can now be made more complex—and this is, indeed, nearly always done—by introducing the assumptions concerning production, so that each country's endowment now consists not of consumption commodities but of homogeneous land and labour which can, unaided, produce the two consumption commodities. As was stressed above, this greater complexity does not fundamentally alter the picture of the pattern of trade being determined by the interaction of given preferences and scarce endowments. The inverse relation between relative commodity prices and the relative demand for the two consumption goods is naturally unaltered by the introduction of production. And the assumptions concerning the latter ensure that the production of commodities by factors involves in each country the same, direct functional relationships between the autarky commodity price ratio, the autarky factor price ratio and, given the identical preferences, the factor endowment ratio. The analysis is thus able to proceed in a manner little different from, though more complicated than, the pure exchange case, the emphasis now being laid, however, on factor endowments and autarky factor prices, as in the 'quantity' and 'price' forms of the basic H–O–S theorem. The closeness of the production model to the pure exchange model is well captured in the description of the former as involving 'the exchange of factors'.

Once the basic model—with its vision of a static economy transforming given factors into consumption goods and then exchanging and consuming the latter—has been established, the analysis is, of course, greatly embellished by considering how certain changes in the assumptions modify the standard conclusions concerning the pattern of trade and the gain from trade. No attempt need be made here, however, to survey the many analyses of the effects of, e.g., non-uniform or non-homothetic preferences, factor-intensity-reversal, non-constant returns to scale, imperfect competition, trade policy, transport costs, etc., etc.;[3] for such analyses are concerned with complications which do not challenge the basic vision of the H–O–S theory. It is more important here to consider further the treatment of production within that theory, for not only is that treatment open to criticism but such criticism also suggests the lines along which one can start to create a trade theory with an alternative 'vision', a theory which is concerned with growth and accumulation.

PRODUCTION IN THE H–O–S MODEL

It was stated above that the simple H–O–S model presents production as being carried out by the unassisted primary inputs, land and labour, with no role being played by produced means of production, either in the form of intermediates or in that of fixed capital goods. This issue may now be considered more closely.

It may be noted first that there has been a considerable increase in recent years in the attention paid to intermediate goods, to their role in production and to their effects on trade.[4] Their introduction does not, of itself, create difficulties for H–O–S theory; it merely complicates it somewhat. Thus if, for example, the two consumption commodities are assumed also to enter as inputs into the processes of production (so that the introduction of intermediates does not lead to any difference between the number of factors and the number of commodities and thus to all the attendant and well-known difficulties caused by such a difference)[5] then no essential changes are introduced into the standard analysis, as has been shown by, for example, Vanek [21]. However, Vanek's demonstration of the unimportance of intermediates as such does not provide a demonstration of the unimportance of *time* and of circulating *capital*, where the latter term refers to produced means of production which must be purchased before being used in production and on whose value the normal rate of profit (interest) is earned; this for the simple reason that Vanek does not allow for any such profit (interest) return. When the existence of a time lag in production and hence of such profit (interest) on the value of circulating capital is allowed for, i.e., once 'capital' is allowed to enter the analysis of production with its full significance, it is found that the standard conclusions of H–O–S analysis are radically affected. This is examined in some detail for the closed economy, or autarky, situation in Essay 2 below, while the effects on 'positive' H–O–S analysis are examined in Essay 3 and those on the H–O–S 'welfare' analysis are considered in Essay 4.

'CAPITAL' IN THE H–O–S THEORY

The preceding remarks on circulating capital lead naturally to the point, which will no doubt have struck the reader already, that 'capital' does appear to be treated in many presentations of H–O–S theory, for the two given factor endowments are commonly said to be not land and labour, as assumed above, but rather 'capital' and labour. This endowment of 'capital' merits further scrutiny.

The traditional concept of 'capital', as opposed to land and labour, is that it consists of, or at the very least is embodied in, *produced* means of production. The 'capital' endowment found in the basic H–O–S theory is, however, no such thing. It is simply given in quantity, even in long-run equilibrium:[6] it is apparently a homogeneous, malleable productive input: and it does not consist of produced means of production, for there is no productive sector to produce them. (Thus if we turn to the well-known papers of Jones [7] and of Lancaster [11], to take but two of many, many possible examples, we find that each economy has a given amount of labour, a *given* amount of the homogeneous factor 'capital', and a productive sector for each consumption good. But there is no mention of any sector which can produce 'capital', since the latter is treated as if it were a primary input.) It is, of course, no accident that the 'price' of this 'capital' is often referred to as 'rent' and not as the rate of profit (interest), for this 'capital' has no supply price to which the 'rent' could be related as a profit (interest) rate.

One way to interpret this 'capital' endowment is obviously to say outright that it is not the traditional factor 'capital' at all but is simply the traditional factor 'land', masquerading under a false name. On this reading, one should simply strike out the term 'capital' whenever it occurs and replace it by 'land'; one would then be left with an analysis which was logically flawless but which manifestly failed to deal with the crucial role of produced means of production. The limited relevance of the theory to the modern world of growth and trade would then be transparent.

There is, however, an alternative possible interpretation of the 'capital' endowment, namely as a given sum of *value*; the assumption is then that whatever concrete, physical form may be taken by the capital goods within an economy, their total value, in some standard, must be equal to the exogenously given 'capital endowment'. Such an interpretation clearly fits in well with the long-run equilibrium nature of all basic trade theory. Indeed this interpretation must be accepted implicitly by many H–O–S theorists, for it would otherwise be impossible to explain why they considered Leontief's findings concerning the 'capital/labour' intensities of United States exports and imports, which were related to *values* of capital, to have any bearing on H–O–S theory.

One may well be puzzled as to how a country can be 'endowed' with a given total of *value* and as to which standard of value it is given in terms of. (It may be noted that this last question is no mere detail. If two countries have different autarky price ratios—and such a difference is the proximate basis of trade—then their relative 'capital/labour' endowment ratios will depend on the choice of the standard of value and, indeed, their *ranking* in terms of such endowment ratios may depend on that choice. How, then, can such a ranking be thought to convey fundamental information about the two countries?) Whatever the answers to these puzzles, one must inevitably wonder whether the H–O–S theory, under this interpretation, is vulnerable to the results of the capital controversies of the 1960s. It is shown below, in Essay 5, that it is. Essays 6 and 7 then pursue some of the implications for 'factor price' equalisation.

Thus, in addition to all the well-known problems within H–O–S theory, such as that of generalising to many factors/commodities/countries whilst preserving real content in the concepts of relative factor 'intensities' and 'endowments', it may reasonably be said that H–O–S theory fails to deal at all adequately with the role of produced means of production (whether circulating or fixed capital goods), despite their evident and increasing importance. Both in the basic theory and, as will be mentioned below, in its treatment of the gain from trade and of international investment, the H–O–S tradition is flawed by an inadequate treatment of 'capital', which confuses capital as a fluid fund of finance with capital as a specified list of produced means of production.

It is, consequently, not surprising, given the links between capital, profits and growth, that, until quite recently, H–O–S theory has had relatively little to say about the persistent growth of output and of trade: H–O–S analyses of 'growth' are often concerned with comparative statics results, relating to the effects of an unexplained, once-for-all increase in some exogenously given factor, e.g. labour supply. Of course, there has been an interesting development of 'H–O–S inspired' theories of growth and trade; see, for example, Johnson [6], Kemp [9], Khang [10], Oniki and Uzawa [14] and Stiglitz [18]. Much of this more recent literature, however, is concerned with the transition to long-run equilibrium, starting from an arbitrary 'capital–labour' ratio, in models assuming a single capital good, which can be combined with labour according to a neo-classical production function. One cannot feel confident that such analyses give much insight into the long-run equilibrium properties of the multi-capital good models which must be developed to deal adequately with real-world problems of trade and accumulation. Thus it may perhaps be said that the trouble with H–O–S trade theory is not that more work needs to be done on further refining an already elaborate theoretical structure; it is that the basic vision and presuppositions of the theory render it incapable of dealing with important facts about production, trade and growth.

AN ALTERNATIVE THEORY OF TRADE

Which is the best way forward? It is inevitable that, over the next few decades, some writers will continue to make more and more 'internal' modifications to H–O–S theory, in the attempt to make it relevant to real world growth and trade. It has already been suggested above that the basic vision and emphasis of H–O–S theory are such that that attempt, while welcome, will have somewhat limited success until the 'modifications' result in the effective abandonment of the basic framework. Other writers may be expected to move in the direction of rewriting trade theory within the mould of 'Arrow-Debreu' general equilibrium theory, perhaps taking each country's endowment to be a specified list of concrete, physical assets, assuming perfect futures markets and reducing the theory of trade to a particular 'interpretation' of the static, multi-period, contingent commodity model, with any number of different 'rates of return'. Such analyses will, no doubt, be of great elegance but it is certain that they will not bear on the long-period equilibria which give meaning to the concept of comparative advantage and questionable how much they can contribute to our understanding of real world trade and growth.

An alternative approach would be to start one's theory of trade from a standpoint which does place produced means of production, profits and accumulation at the centre of the analysis. Whether the particular starting point chosen be the production oriented analysis of Adam Smith, or that of Ricardo, or of Marx, or von Neumann, or Joan Robinson or any other writer, the general framework and emphasis of the analysis will inevitably lead to a trade theory which is more concerned with growth and with the role of capital goods than is a trade theory—such as H–O–S theory—which starts from exchange and consumption (however elaborated it may subsequently become). Essays 8 to 16 below make a cautious, preliminary attempt at exploring some of the features of such a production–oriented trade theory. While it is too soon to assess the degree of success of such a line of analysis, it seems reasonable to hope that will not be entirely negligible.

TEXTBOOK 'RICARDIAN' THEORY

As might be expected, the work and ideas of Ricardo are frequently referred to, whether explicitly or implicitly, in the following essays. The analysis contained in those essays is not, however, that of the so-called 'Ricardian' theory of many textbooks and it may therefore be helpful to indicate here the nature of the essential difference involved. Despite their many (and important) differences, textbook 'Ricardian' theory and the H–O–S theory have a major common feature—their inadequate attention to the role of produced means of production and to profits. In the case of textbook 'Ricardianism' this lack of attention often takes the extreme form of reasoning as if consumption commodities were produced by unassisted labour alone. With a uniform period of production for all commodities and with wages paid at the end of that period, it naturally follows that income consists entirely of wages[7] and that autarky prices are proportional to the technically determined quantities of labour needed for the production of the respective commodities. Trade patterns are then explained solely in terms of intercountry differences in technical conditions. In general, of course, if produced means of production are introduced and/or if wages are advanced over differing production periods for different commodities, then capital and profits enter the analysis and autarky prices are *not* proportional to embodied labour quantities and, indeed, are not determined by technical conditions alone. Yet this simple fact is ignored in nearly all textbook treatments of 'Ricardian' trade theory.[8] It is not ignored in Essays 8 to 16, which all allow for the role of time in production and which also introduce some discussion of the choice between alternative techniques and of the role of growth, again by contrast with textbook 'Ricardian' theory.

THE GAIN FROM TRADE

Trade theory has, of course, traditionally included a large body of 'welfare' analysis, concerned with the 'gain' from (restricted or unrestricted) trade: this topic is considered in Essays 4, 8, 9, 11, 12, 13 and 14. For the most part, the gain from trade is considered, in those essays, in terms of comparative dynamics; in terms, that is, of a comparison between two economies, one autarkic and the other open to trade, which grow at the same (positive or zero) steady growth rate. It is then found that the 'gain' from trade can be either positive or negative.

The result that, in terms of comparative dynamics, the 'gain' from trade can be negative, appears to have become generally accepted but it also seems to be commonly felt that this result, while correct, is of limited interest, first because it does not attend to the importance for 'world Pareto optimality' of whether rates of profit (interest) are equalised throughout the world and secondly because it can be argued that the 'gain from trade' should be evaluated not in terms of comparative dynamics but in terms of actual time paths of consumption, *allowing for the transition* from autarky to trade.[9] The reader's attitude to the importance of the first of these two reasons will, no doubt, be determined by wider considerations than can appropriately be discussed here but something may be said concerning 'transitions'.

When discussing transitions, it is most important not to take it for granted that the 'old', physically specified capital stock can be costlessly transformed (through production or exchange) into the 'new', physically specified capital stock or that, if the total value of the new stock should be smaller than that of the old stock, then that difference in value can be transformed (through exchange) into consumption goods of equivalent value. Transitions will often (though not always) involve the scrapping, or 'junking', of old equipment, whose value cannot be realised on any market: to ignore these difficulties would be precisely to slip back into the very same idea of malleable, all-purpose 'capital' which has been criticised above. That the 'overall gain' from 'transition plus trade' can indeed be negative, because of the non-malleability of capital goods, is demonstrated in Essay 12. (The 'with-transition' gain is found to be non-negative in Essay 4 only because certain very special assumptions are made there.)

INTERNATIONAL INVESTMENT

It is a commonplace that international economic relations involve international flows of investment and of profits, as well as trade flows, and that the balance of trade is, consequently, only one component of the balance of payments. Nor are investment and trade flows independent of one another, most obviously because direct foreign investment often leads to changes in exports and imports, in both the country of origin and the country to which the investment flows. Yet the existing theories of international trade and of international investment and profit flows are not well integrated. Indeed, until quite recently much trade theory made no reference at all to other aspects of international economic relations.

More recently greater attention has been paid to such issues but their treatment is often vitiated by the unclear conception of 'capital' which, as noted above, lies at the root of much H–O–S trade theory. Thus some analyses of the 'international mobility of capital' proceed as if a country's endowment of 'capital' were a quantity of a homogeneous, physical input, part of which may be used in domestic production, while the remainder is 'hired out' for use in another country![10] It is, perhaps, not entirely clear to what real world process such an analysis is supposed to correspond, unless it be the leasing of ships and aircraft. In the real world, international investment flows are, in themselves, *financial* flows. The latter will, of course, often lead directly to trade flows of the specific capital goods to be used in, say, equipping a factory but it is nevertheless crucial to keep the two types of flow conceptually distinct. That distinction is, however, always in danger of being lost in an analysis based on the conception of an aggregate 'factor' called 'capital', since, as is now widely recognised, that conception has fused—and confused—the concepts of 'capital as finance' and 'capital as specific means of production'.

It cannot be claimed that the essays in this volume make much progress in integrating the trade and investment aspects of international economic relations. Indeed, in all but the final essay (Essay 16) only trade is discussed, while that final essay, which deals with certain aspects of international lending and borrowing and the corresponding interest flows, treats the traditional issues of trade theory only in (at best) an implicit way. The purpose of Essay 16 is simply to sketch how the well-known macro growth analysis of Keynesian inspiration (to be found in the work of Harrod, Kaldor, Kahn, Robinson, Pasinetti and others) might be extended to the case of an economy which is 'open' to both current account and capital account transactions with the rest of the world.

It may reasonably be hoped that a careful blending of theories giving a detailed picture of pricing and income distribution relations, within a production oriented analysis, and theories concerned with Keynesian effective demand considerations, may eventually yield a more useful and integrated account of international trade and investment than has been provided within the H–O–S framework but that account remains to be given.

A CAVEAT

It is no part of the purpose of this introductory essay to give the impression that the alternative approach to the theory of international trade and investment, which is suggested in the following essays, is either complete or free from problems. Indeed, since some of the difficulties in that approach are common to much current economic analysis and might therefore escape the reader's notice, it will be as well explicitly to draw attention to some of them here.

A common feature of several of the essays in the later part of the book is that they are concerned with economies undergoing steady-growth at a constant rate. While the assumption of a constant, positive growth rate is certainly not more restrictive than the assumption of a constant, zero growth rate which is to be found in much trade theory, it is hardly a 'realistic' assumption, being more an analytically tractable 'bench-mark' than an accurate description of the world. Such a 'reference path' is not to be too readily dismissed, however, since it may well be indispensable in the development of a more adequate growth theory. (The reader who is inclined to reject steady-growth analysis is invited to replace it by something better.)

Steady-growth analysis cannot easily incorporate fixed primary inputs such as land and it is thus no accident that land is not discussed in the later essays. One can hardly deny, however, that no matter how important manufactured products have become in world trade, primary products, and hence natural resources, continue to be of great importance. It should therefore be recognised explicitly that the type of analysis suggested in the later essays of this book places growth and the reproducibility of means of production at the centre of the picture only at the cost of ignoring other important issues. At this point the general 'vision' of H–O–S analysis becomes relevant because of its emphasis on scarcity and non-reproducible resources. This is not to say, however, that the analysis itself is of great help, for the assumption of *identical, homogeneous* land in each country completely fails to capture the role of scarce natural resources in production and trade. (The recent revival of interest in 'specific factor' theories is therefore to be welcomed, provided that it does not lead to the treatment of given, concrete capital goods as 'specific factors', thus again confusing 'capital' and 'land'.) Nor should the recognition of the phenomenon of scarcity lead one to assume that the H–O–S interpretation of wages and rents as 'indices of scarcity' is correct; see Essays 2 and 3.

It should also be noted explicitly that technical progress is not discussed in any of the following essays. Since technical progress is of such obvious importance in determining world trade patterns, international prices and economic 'welfare' and since, further, technical progress is closely linked to the accumulation of produced means of production, this may seem a strange absence. Yet it follows naturally from the use of steady-growth analysis, with which only Harrod–neutral (labour augmenting) progress is generally consistent. It would certainly be highly desirable to incorporate into trade theory *useful*, formal results on technical progress from closed economy theory but such results are scarce (those relating to 'induced' progress perhaps being potentially the most relevant). It may also be noted, in similar vein, that nothing is said below about the role of trade in creating and changing consumer preferences, although that role is undoubtedly important: formal theory has even less to say about the formation of preferences than it does about the creation of technical knowledge.[11] Again, it is important to note that little attention is paid to 'imperfections' in competition.

The above—and other—problems notwithstanding, it may be hoped that the following essays will help to focus attention on a central weakness of H–O–S theory and to suggest an alternative and potentially more fruitful way of analysing international trade and investment. Whatever the precise shape and form which will be taken by trade theory over the next few decades, there can be little doubt that a central part of that theory will have to be concerned with produced means of production, with profits and with investment (both 'domestic' and 'international') for the simple reason that they are central features of the reality which is to be understood.

NOTES

*I should like to thank L. Mainwaring, J. S. Metcalfe, P. A. Samuelson and M. A. M. Smith for helpful comments on an earlier draft of this essay; they bear no responsibility for the views expressed in the present version.
1. More precisely, the factors are taken to be land and labour in the more careful presentations, e.g., Samuelson [15]; analyses based on labour and 'capital' will be discussed below.
2. The intra-country distribution of consumption between consumers is assumed here to be the same with trade as under autarky.
3. For good discussions of these various issues see, e.g., Bhagwati [2], [3], Caves [4] and Chipman [5].
4. One manifestation of this increased attention has, of course, been the upsurge of interest in 'effective protection', a concept which has no meaning in the absence of produced means of production. That 'effective protection' has created a considerable stir among trade theorists is striking evidence of the over-simple nature of their usual model of the production process; if one always worked with a model allowing for produced means of production, then one would just take it for granted that tariffs could often have far-reaching indirect effects on prices, incomes and activity levels.
5. See, for example, the outstanding survey by Chipman [5].
6. Traditional trade theory is not, of course, concerned with short-run equilibrium, a context within which the concept of comparative advantage would be quite out of place.
7. Rent is ignored in such models, as in Essays 8 to 16 below.
8. An important exception is to be found in Taussig [19]; even though Taussig considers the effects of profits and differing capital intensities on relative autarky prices, he nevertheless suggests, rather unconvincingly, that the

Introductory Essay   13

effects of profits on relative prices may reasonably be ignored. In explicitly considering the matter and then ignoring it, Taussig's approach is similar to that of Ricardo; cf. Essay 8 below.

9. See, e.g., Samuelson [16] and Smith [17]. Samuelson would, I believe, attach major importance to the equalisation or non-equalisation of world profit (interest) rates [personal communication].

10. See, e.g., Batra [1] chapter 13, Kemp [8] chapter 9 and chapter 13 (including Appendix II), Mundell [13]. Batra makes the matter quite explicit (p. 323); 'By international mobility of capital is meant *the physical movement of the capital goods* in response to different rentals of capital in the two countries' (my emphasis).

11. It is not, of course, denied that much interesting work has been done on technical progress and changes in preferences, both by historians and by economic theorists (as in recent 'product cycle' models); it is maintained only that very limited progress has been made in incorporating the results of such work in *formal* analysis.

REFERENCES

[1] Batra, R. N. *Studies in the Pure Theory of International Trade*. Macmillan, London, 1973.
[2] Bhagwati, J. 'The pure theory of international trade: A survey'. *Economic Journal*, 1964, pp. 1–84.
[3] Bhagwati, J. (ed.) *International Trade*. Penguin, 1969.
[4] Caves, R. E. *Trade and Economic Structure*. Harvard University Press, 1960.
[5] Chipman, J. S. 'A survey of the theory of international trade'. *Econometrica*, 1965, pp. 477–519 and 685–760 and 1966, pp. 60–76.
[6] Johnson, H. G. 'Trade and growth: A geometrical exposition'. *Journal of International Economics*, 1971, pp. 83–101.
[7] Jones, R. 'Factor proportions and the Heckscher–Ohlin theorem'. *Review of Economic Studies*, 1956–57, pp. 1–10.
[8] Kemp, M. C. *The Pure Theory of International Trade and Investment*. Prentice-Hall, 1969.
[9] Kemp, M. C. 'International trade between countries with different natural rates of growth'. *Economic Record*, 1970, pp. 467–81.
[10] Khang, C. 'Equilibrium growth in the international economy, the case of unequal rates of growth'. *International Economic Review*, 1971, pp. 239–49.
[11] Lancaster, K. 'The Heckscher–Ohlin trade model: A geometric treatment'. *Economica*, 1957, pp. 19–39.
[12] Maizels, A. *Industrial Growth and World Trade*. Cambridge University Press, 1971.
[13] Mundell, R. 'International trade and factor mobility'. *American Economic Review*, 1957, pp. 321–35.
[14] Oniki, H. and H. Uzawa. 'Patterns of trade and investment in a dynamic model of international trade'. *Review of Economic Studies*, 1965, pp. 15–38.
[15] Samuelson, P. A. 'International trade and the equalization of factor prices'. *Economic Journal*, 1948, pp. 163–84.
[16] Samuelson, P. A. 'Trade pattern reversals in time-phased Ricardian systems

and intertemporal efficiency'. *Journal of International Economics*, 1975, pp. 309–63.
[17] Smith, M. A. M. 'The evaluation of intertemporal gains from trade'. London School of Economics, mimeo, 1977.
[18] Stiglitz, J. E. 'Factor price equalisation in a dynamic economy'. *Journal of Political Economy*, 1970, pp. 456–88.
[19] Taussig, F. W. *International Trade*. Macmillan, New York, 1927.
[20] UNCTAD *Review of International Trade and Development*. (Annual.)
[21] Vanek, J. 'Variable factor proportions and inter-industry flows in the theory of international trade'. *Quarterly Journal of Economics*, 1963, pp. 129–42.
[22] Yates, P. L. *Forty Years of Foreign Trade*. Allen & Unwin, London, 1959.

2 Reswitching and Primary Input Use*

J. S. METCALFE and IAN STEEDMAN

The object of this essay is to explain the consequences of the existence of a positive rate of profit in the neoclassical model of long-run general equilibrium,[1] in which two commodities are produced by means of land, labour and produced commodities.

Before we proceed to this task, we may note two points. First, we have no wish to discuss the forces which determine the level of the rate of profit (which, in long run equilibrium, is equal to the rate of interest). All we wish to do is to examine the logical outcome of its being positive. Second, in our analysis, the production of commodities takes place within an input-output framework, so that any pattern of net output in the economy requires a supporting pattern of goods in process, i.e., capital goods. That there are capital goods is, in itself, of no consequence. What is of consequence is that a positive rate of profit be earned on the value of the goods in process.[2]

To emphasise that the positive rate of profit is our only point of departure from the standard analysis, we shall employ the following assumptions throughout:

1. We consider an economy closed to foreign trade and endowed with fixed supplies of two homogeneous primary inputs, which we call land (L) and labour (l); we shall make the assumption that both are fully employed. The important property of the primary inputs is that they, unlike capital goods, cannot be *produced* by the economy's production system and so are the only constraints on production in long-run equilibrium.

2. The economy produces two commodities, each of which serves a dual role as a productive input (capital good) and as a consumption commodity. To produce the two commodities the economy can draw upon a number of fixed coefficient processes, each of which defines the

minimum quantities of the two primary inputs and of the two produced commodities needed to produce a unit of gross output of one of the commodities. To simplify matters further, we also assume that all production takes place within an annual cycle and that all capital stocks have to be replaced at the beginning of each production period.[3]

3. Whatever the technique chosen, each technique comprising one process for each commodity, the process producing commodity one is always more land-intensive than the process producing commodity two.

4. We ignore variations in the consumption patterns of the three groups of income recipients, landlords, workers and capitalists, by assuming that they have identical homothetic preference maps, so that the aggregate consumption pattern depends only upon relative commodity prices.

5. Perfect competition rules in all markets, so that each producer obtains primary inputs, commodities and money capital on identical terms with every other producer.

6. The economy has long been in a state of stationary equilibrium; with no net investment and with expectations and the composition of the annually replaced capital stock appropriate to that equilibrium position.

We need hardly add that our analysis will be solely in terms of the comparisons of different long-run equilibrium positions and will nowhere touch upon questions of the transition between such positions. To these very orthodox assumptions[4] we now add one further assumption; that the rate of profit on the value of capital goods is positive. To the well-known reswitching results we wish to add a result which seems to have important implications. It is that a higher ratio of rents to wages in the economy need not necessarily lead to the utilisation of a more labour-intensive technique of production but, on the contrary, can lead to the use of a more land-intensive technique.[5]

We shall first present, in some detail, a model with only one technique of production with which, although it automatically rules out our major conclusions by assumption, we shall develop the necessary tools for our analysis. This model is then generalised to two techniques and, finally, to an infinity of techniques.

AN ECONOMY WITH ONE TECHNIQUE

(i) *The Single Technique*

Let there be a single technique, consisting of the following processes for producing the two commodities:

$$\begin{array}{c} \\ 1 \\ 2 \\ \text{Labour} \\ \text{Land} \end{array} \begin{bmatrix} \overset{1}{a_{11}} & \overset{2}{a_{12}} \\ a_{21} & a_{22} \\ \hline a_1 & a_2 \\ A_1 & A_2 \end{bmatrix}$$

where column 1 shows the inputs of commodities one and two, labour and land needed to produce one unit of gross output of commodity one. Column 2 is interpreted in like fashion for commodity two.

We shall assume throughout that not only is commodity one always produced with a more land-intensive process than commodity two, but also that a pattern of net output exists which yields full employment of both primary inputs.

If the money prices of the two commodities are p_1 and p_2, the money wage and the money rent, which are paid at the end of the production period, are w and W and the annual rate of profit on the capital employed is r, then in competitive equilibrium we must have

$$\begin{aligned} p_1 &= (a_{11}p_1 + a_{21}p_2)(1+r) + wa_1 + WA_1 \\ p_2 &= (a_{12}p_1 + a_{22}p_2)(1+r) + wa_2 + WA_2 \end{aligned} \quad (1)$$

The first price equation, for example, says that the competitive equilibrium price of commodity one must equal primary input costs, $(wa_1 + WA_1)$, plus the replacement of capital costs, $(a_{11}p_1 + a_{21}p_2)$, plus the profit on the capital employed, $(a_{11}p_1 + a_{21}p_2)r$, where the rate of profit equals the ruling rate of interest. A similar interpretation holds for the second price equation.

(ii) *Relative Prices*

To analyse the effect of variations in primary input prices and the rate of profit on relative commodity prices, it is convenient to solve equations (1) for the relative price of commodity one, to obtain

$$\frac{p_1}{p_2} = p = \frac{(1-a_{22}v)(a_1 + A_1 z) + a_{21}v(a_2 + A_2 z)}{a_{12}v(a_1 + A_1 z) + (1-a_{11}v)(a_2 + A_2 z)} \quad (2)$$

where $v = (1+r)$ and $z = W/w$, the ratio of rents to wages.

It is obvious from equation (2) that, in general, equilibrium relative prices depend not only on the rent–wage ratio but also upon the rate of profit. It is now a relatively simple matter to show how the price ratio changes in response to notional variations in z.

By differentiating equation (2) with respect to z and calling the denominator of (2) D, we obtain, after some manipulation,

$$D^2 \frac{\partial p}{\partial z} = \det (I - vA) a_1 a_2 \left[\frac{A_1}{a_1} - \frac{A_2}{a_2} \right] \quad (3)$$

where A is the matrix of commodity input coefficients. In any meaningful economic system the determinant of $(I - vA)$ must be positive, for if it were zero, money prices would be infinite relative to the money wage and money rent while if it were negative, positive money wages and rents would imply negative money prices of the two commodities.[6] Since we have assumed that one is the more land-intensive commodity, equation (3) provides the expected result that the relative price of the land-intensive commodity rises as the ratio of rents to wages rises, whatever the value of the profit rate.[7]

It is more difficult[8] to show how relative prices vary with the rate of profit. Depending on the structure of commodity input coefficients, and in certain cases the value of z, a notional increase in r may raise, lower or leave unchanged the price ratio for a given z. Figure 2.1 illustrates these three cases, with $r_2 > r_1$.

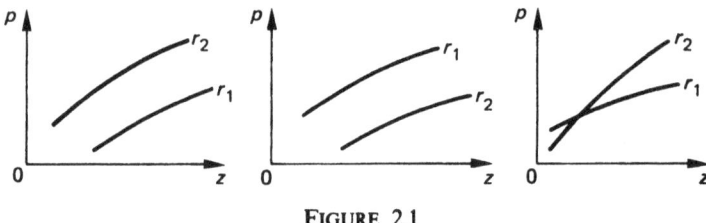

FIGURE 2.1

(iii) *The Wage–Rent Frontier*

The price equations (1) can also be used to derive the technically feasible spectrum of income distributions, between wages, rents and the rate of profit. That is, we can derive the two-primary-input analogue of the wage frontier; the wage–rent frontier. This frontier will show, for any feasible pair of values of, say, the rate of profit and the real rent, the maximum value of the real wage which the competitive economy can sustain.

If we express both the real wage rate and the real rent in terms of commodity two, w_2 and W_2, then substituting equation (2) into equations (1) and solving for the real wage rate as a function of the real rent we have,

$$w_2 = \left[\frac{\det(I - vA)}{a_2(1 - a_{11}v) + a_1 a_{12}v}\right] - \left[\frac{A_2(1 - a_{11}v) + A_1 a_{12}v}{a_2(1 - a_{11}v) + a_1 a_{12}v}\right] W_2 \quad (4)$$

a structurally similar equation holding when wages and rents are expressed in terms of commodity one.[9]

The behaviour of the wage–rent relationship as the rate of profit is notionally increased is shown in Figure 2.2. A notional increase in r reduces the maximum attainable value of both the real wage and the real rent. We note also that, for a notional increase in r, the linear wage–rent relationship (4) becomes steeper, simply as a consequence of the technological assumption that commodity one is more land-intensive than commodity two.[10]

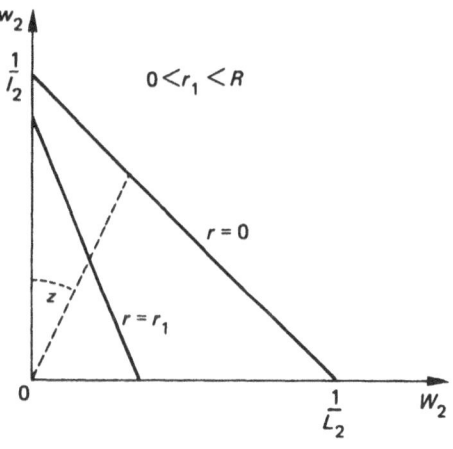

FIGURE 2.2

The behaviour of the maximum real wage, or the maximum real rent, with respect to variations in the profit rate, can be most easily seen by setting the real rent, or real wage, in equation (4) equal to zero. This yields the following two equations

$$w_2/_{W_2 = 0} = \frac{\det(I - vA)}{a_2(1 - a_{11}v) + a_1 a_{12}v}$$

$$\text{and } W_2/_{w_2 = 0} = \frac{\det(I - vA)}{A_2(1 - a_{11}v) + A_1 a_{12}v} \quad (5)$$

When the rate of profit is at its maximum, R, det $(I - vA)$ is zero and so the real wage *and* real rent are zero; as the profit rate is reduced from its maximum, the maximum wage and the maximum rent are increased to finite maxima. Possible shapes of the two frontiers are given in Figures 2.3 and 2.4. We can now draw the three-dimensional wage–rent frontier as in Figure 2.5. For any rate of profit, this shows the corresponding real

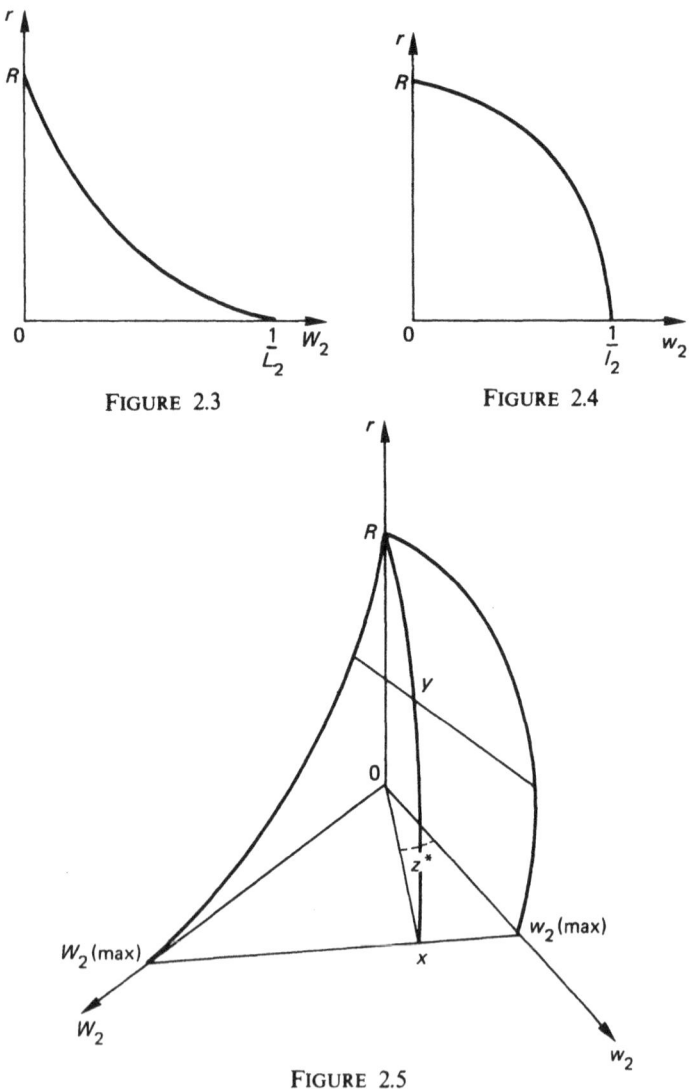

FIGURE 2.3

FIGURE 2.4

FIGURE 2.5

wage and real rent as the rent–wage ratio is varied from zero to infinity and for any rent–wage ratio, it shows the variations of wages and rents with the rate of profit. For example, with $z = z^*$ the variation of w_2 and W_2 and r is traced out by the line Ryx.

Although this specifies the technically feasible range of income distributions between wages and rents at each rate of profit, it clearly tells us nothing of the forces determining the actual equilibrium distribution. We shall assume throughout this essay that the rate of profit is given (and is independent of variations in the pattern of net output) and that the rent–wage ratio is determined in the process by which equilibrium relative prices are established.

The analysis of one technique has provided no startling conclusions, which is not surprising since there is no possibility of varying productive technique and hence input proportions. However, as soon as we introduce the possibility of a choice of techniques, the existence of a positive rate of profit on the value of the capital goods can radically change several of the relationships which hold when the profit rate is zero.

AN ECONOMY WITH TWO TECHNIQUES

(i) *Choice of Technique*

Suppose that we have two techniques (*i.e.*, two pairs of processes) which we call a and b. Let these techniques have one process in common and let technique a be more land-intensive in the production of both commodities than technique b.

The question we wish to answer is: how does the choice of technique vary as the wage–rent ratio and the rate of profit are notionally varied?

For given r and any z competition ensures that the chosen technique is the one which provides the largest possible total primary income, measured in terms of either commodity. The income generating properties of any technique are summarised by its wage–rent relationship which we know (equation 4), is a straight line, whatever the rate of profit. If, for the given r, the wage–rent relationship of technique a lies wholly outside that for technique b, Figure 2.6, then the former technique can offer more primary income at any z and so will be the technique chosen for any z. Conversely, if the wage–rent relationship of b totally dominates that of a, technique b will always be chosen.

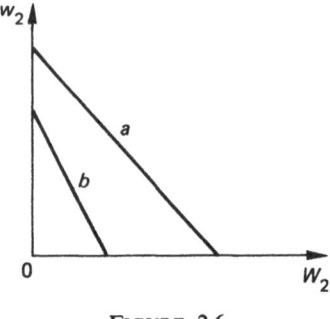

FIGURE 2.6

However, if the two wage–rent relationships intersect, then at some $z = z^*$ a switch in techniques will occur (Figure 2.7). For lower values of z, technique a is chosen; at z^* both techniques offer the same primary income and hence are equally acceptable, and at higher values of z, technique b is chosen. It will be clear, since the wage–rent relationships are straight lines, that not more than one switching z can exist for any rate of profit. Thus, *reswitching* of techniques with respect to variations in the wage–rent ratio is impossible, whatever the value of the profit rate.

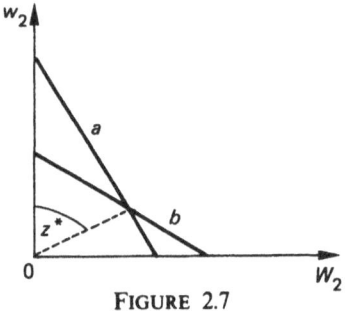

FIGURE 2.7

However, this by no means implies that the *direction* of the switch, as z is notionally varied around z^*, is of the normal neo-classical kind, *i.e.*, an increase in z yielding a switch to the more labour intensive technique.

Consider Figure 2.8, in which we have drawn the three-dimensional wage–rent frontiers for two techniques. As the rent–wage ratio is notionally varied, the rate of profit being held constant at certain specified levels, the switch of technique can be perverse, that is a notional increase in the rent–wage ratio may be associated with the choice of a more land-intensive technique.

Reswitching and Primary Input Use 23

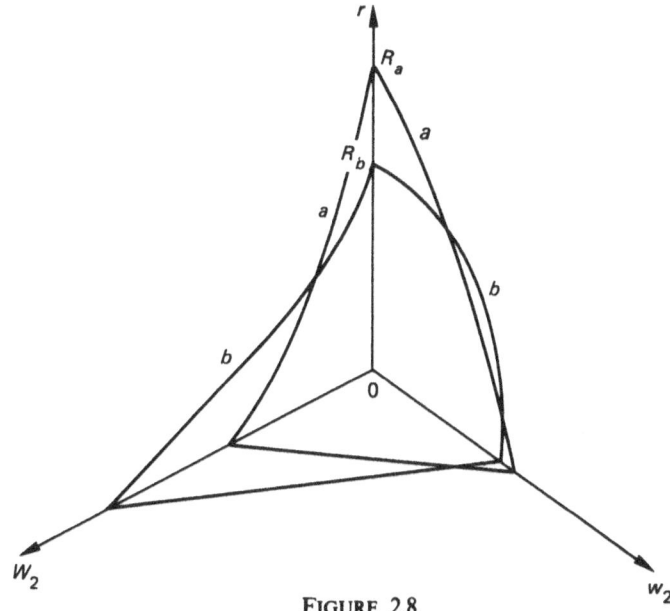

FIGURE 2.8

Perhaps the easiest way to see this is to concentrate one's attention on the intersections of the two frontiers with the zero-wage plane and the zero-rent plane and to ignore all other parts of the two frontiers. One may then rotate the wage plane, r–0–w_2, around the vertical axis, 0–r,

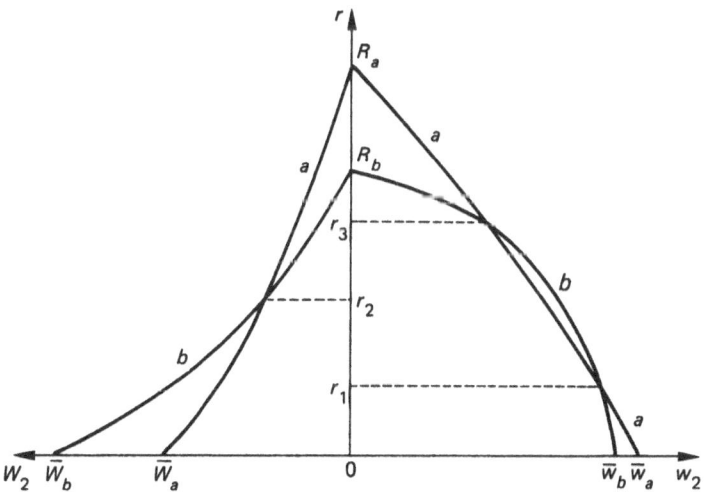

FIGURE 2.9

until it lies in the same plane as r–0–W_2. We thus obtain Figure 2.9. Concentrate for the moment on the wage plane. The wage curves, R_a – $\bar{w}_a$ and R_b–$\bar{w}_b$ show the variations of the real wage with the rate of profit, when rents are zero. As is well known, there is no reason why they should not intersect more than once so that there is reswitching of techniques with respect to r. At high rates of profit, technique a offers the higher wage and is chosen, while at middle rates of profit technique b is superior and at even lower rates, technique a re-establishes its superiority. We have drawn the wage plane with two switching profit rates, r_1 and r_3. Now, turning to the rent plane, we already know that the wage and rent curves for each individual technique will not, on our assumptions, be identical and so we are perfectly at liberty to have no reswitching in the rent plane and to have the one switching rate of profit, r_2, intermediate with respect to the switching rates in the wage plane.

It will be clear that, with two primary inputs, we cannot now speak in isolation of a switching rate of profit, or a switching value of the wage–rent ratio, we can only refer to a switching combination of these variables. A switch point is then defined as a combination of r and z for which marginal and opposite changes in one of their values, while the other is held constant, lead to a switch in technique.[11]

With the techniques given in Figure 2.9, we can now notionally vary the value of the rent–wage ratio from zero to infinity while at the same time holding the rate of profit constant at specified levels; the effect on the choice of technique is given in Table 2.1.

TABLE 2.1 *Direction of technique switch as z varies from 0 to ∞*

	$z = 0$		$z = \infty$	
$0 \leqq r < r_1$	a	→	b	'Normal' switch
$r_1 < r < r_2$	b	→	b	No switch
$r_2 < r < r_3$	b	→	a	'Perverse' switch
$r_3 < r \leqq R_a$	a	→	a	No switch

As long as the profit rate lies between zero and r_1, the switch of technique is of the normal kind; as z rises across some positive critical value, a switch is made to the more labour-intensive technique. But, contrary to this 'normal' result, there are, in addition, two ranges of the profit rate for which a single technique is chosen irrespective of the value of z and one range, $r_2 < r < r_3$, for which a 'perverse' switch to the more *land-intensive* technique takes place as z rises.

(ii) *Primary Input Intensity*

If to our assumption that technique *a* is the more land-intensive in the production of both commodities we add our assumption that commodity one is the more land-intensive commodity for each technique, then we may draw Figure 2.10, to show the variation of primary input intensity, with the rent–wage ratio, for values of the rate of profit given by $0 < r < r_1$ and $r_2 < r < r_3$ corresponding, respectively, to ranges of 'normal' and 'perverse' switching.

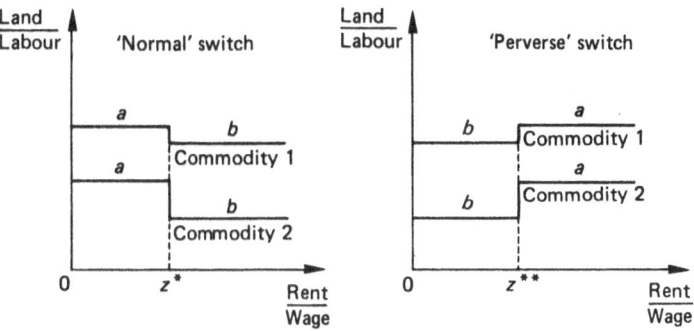

FIGURE 2.10

The implication of this is obvious; as long as the rate of profit is positive we can no longer say that a higher ratio of rents to wages will, in equilibrium, be associated with the use of a technique which economises on the use of land relative to labour. There is now no *a priori* expectation concerning the manner in which notional changes in relative primary input costs affect technique choice. We may note that remarkably little is needed to obtain this result, merely that techniques should reswitch with respect to the rate of profit for at least one non-negative value of the rent–wage ratio.

It might be worth while to give an intuitive explanation of our results. At each switching combination of r and z, the two techniques have equal unit costs with respect to the individual commodities, the same relative price ratio and the same real wage and real rent. But although the techniques produce each commodity with equal unit costs at the switch, the composition of those costs of production is, in general, different between the two techniques. Thus we can say for each commodity that, at the switch, the difference in primary input costs between the two techniques is equal and opposite to the difference in their value of capital and profits.[12] At any neighbouring, non-switching, combination of r and

z, the difference in primary input costs is no longer exactly offset by the difference in capital values and profits but which technique becomes superior it is not possible to say *a priori*.[13]

(iii) *Relative Prices*

Since, for each technique, commodity one is produced by a more land-intensive process than commodity two, p rises with z for both techniques (provided that the rate of profit is less than the technique maximum). Suppose the rate of profit is such that a switching z exists. For lower z one technique is chosen and we know that p is a rising function of z for this technique. At the switching z both techniques produce each commodity with equal unit costs and so generate the same relative prices. While at values of z greater than the switching value, the other technique is chosen for which, again, p rises with z. Hence, even with technique choice and the possibility of 'perverse' switching, the relative price of the land-intensive commodity is always increased by notional increases in the rent–wage ratio.

(iv) *Net Output*

Since we assume the existence of given, fully employed, supplies of land and labour, the use of a given technique immediately implies a particular pattern of net output. Let the net outputs be Y_1 for commodity one and Y_2 for commodity two; we shall concentrate our attention on the *ratio* Y_1/Y_2 but it should be remembered that the absolute values of Y_1 and Y_2 are also known when it is known which technique is in use. Our assumptions concerning relative land/labour intensities for techniques a and b and for commodities one and two, imply that Y_1/Y_2 will be lower when technique a is used than when b is used; recalling that p is a monotonically increasing function of z, we can now draw Figure 2.11, to show the variation of Y_1/Y_2 with p, for profit rates in the ranges which

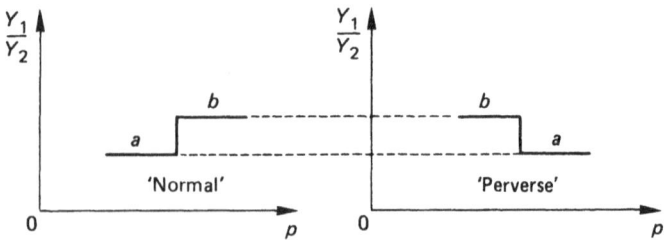

FIGURE 2.11

produce 'normal' and 'perverse' switching with respect to z. With a positive rate of profit on the value of capital goods, it is not possible to say, *a priori*, that the relative supply of two commodities will be a rising function of their relative price.

(v) *A Numerical Example*

Before proceeding to the infinity of techniques case, we present a numerical example illustrating the points made above. In this exercise, four techniques based on four processes were utilised, although it transpired that only three of the techniques were ever relevant.[14] The fourth was completely dominated by the others at a zero rate of profit and, because it also had a low maximum rate of profit, never appeared on the economy wage–rent frontier even at positive profit rates.

Table 2.2 presents the main properties of the three relevant techniques:

TABLE 2.2

Technique	Land: Labour Intensity		Net output Y_1/Y_2
	Commodity One	Commodity Two	
1	2.90	1.42	0.07
2	2.37	1.10	0.64
3	1.79	1.07	1.64

total land:labour ratios for each commodity and the full employment net output ratios.[15] Note that there is *no* primary input 'intensity reversal', commodity one always being the more land-intensive.

At a zero rate of profit the ordering of technique choice as z is notionally increased is $1-2-3$, but at higher rates of profit this 'normal' ordering can break down as Table 2.3 shows. The results are as expected,

TABLE 2.3

r \ z	0.00.	0.58.	0.84.	1.73.	2.75.
0.00	1	1	1	2	3
0.25	1	2	3	3	3
1.00	3	3	3	3	3
1.50	3	3	2	2	2
2.00	2	2	2	2	2

For the rates of profit chosen we have: 'normal' switching with respect to z, ($r = 0$ and $r = 0.25$); no switching with respect to z, ($r = 1.00$ and $r = 2.00$) and 'perverse' switching with respect to z ($r = 1.50$).[16] Furthermore it is easy to see that the response of relative outputs to changes in z, and hence p, is different for each of the positive profit rates chosen and that there are four different net output frontiers associated with these rates.

AN ECONOMY WITH INFINITELY MANY TECHNIQUES

(i) *Existence and Uniqueness of a Solution*

We are now in a position to generalise our results to a situation in which there is an infinite number of productive techniques and a given, positive rate of profit.

The behaviour of relative prices with respect to the wage–rent ratio is the first matter to be dealt with. We already know that for each individual technique p always rises with z and this must hold when we allow for an infinite number of techniques. This is shown in Figure 2.12,[17] where the price curves are simply the outer envelopes of those individual techniques curves relevant at the given rate of profit.

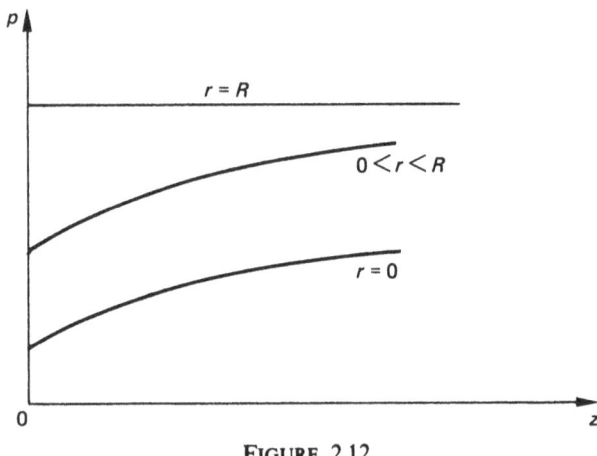

FIGURE 2.12

The variation in primary input intensity for commodities one and two, with respect to z, can be as shown in Figure 2.13. For positive r, the two land intensity curves are no longer monotonically decreasing functions

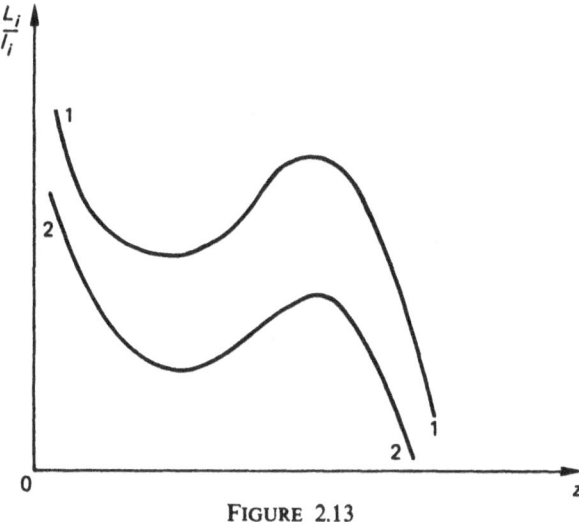

FIGURE 2.13

of the rent–wage ratio. Consequently, for several distinct values of z, the chosen techniques involves the production of *one* of the commodities with the same total primary input proportions.[18]

The existence and uniqueness of a solution, that is an intersection of the relative demand and supply curves, is considered in Figure 2.14. The

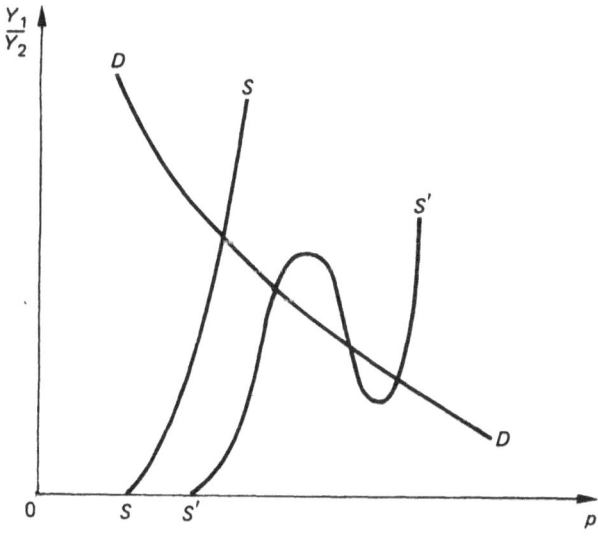

FIGURE 2.14

curve DD shows the response of the proportions in which the commodities are consumed to the price ratio. Since consumption is scale free and does not depend on distribution, the DD curve must fall monotonically as p is increased and is asymptotic to the axes. The curve SS shows the response of relative output to p for a zero rate of profit and is monotonic, with zero Y_1/Y_2 for low p and infinite Y_1/Y_2 for some higher p. Clearly, a solution exists and is unique.

For positive rates of profit we know that the 'relative supply' curve is not guaranteed to be monotonic and the curve $S'S'$ shows such a 'perverse' case for some positive rate of profit less than the system maximum. The existence of a solution is assured but multiple solutions can occur.[19]

(ii) *Comparative Statics*

We have seen that the existence of a positive rate of profit means that the 'relative supply' curve ($S'S'$ in Figure 2.14) need not be a positive, monotonic function of the commodity price ratio; this, in turn, means that important 'normal' comparative statics propositions cannot be asserted *a priori*.

Consider two stationary economies A and B, with identical technologies, supplies of land and labour and rates of profit; they have a common 'relative supply' curve, shown as SS in Figure 2.15. The proportion in which commodities one and two are demanded in A, as a

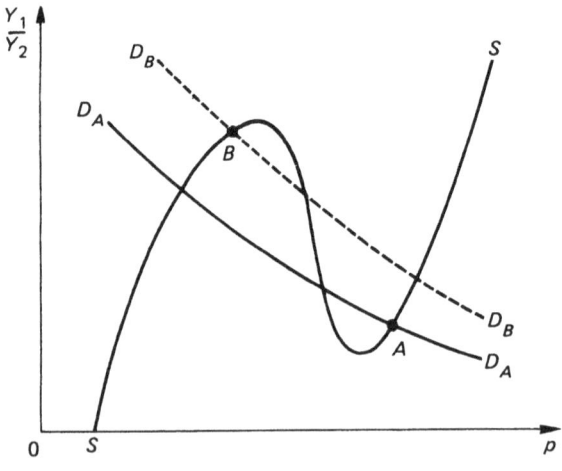

FIGURE 2.15

function of the price ratio p, is shown by the curve $D_A D_A$; the corresponding curve for B, $D_B D_B$, is higher at every price ratio, showing that demand for commodity one is 'more intense' in country B.

If economy A is at point A and economy B at point B, then the economy with the 'more intense' demand for commodity one, the land-intensive commodity, will have the *lower* price ratio, p, and thus the *lower* ratio of rents to wages.

Consider now two stationary economies A and B, with identical technologies, rates of profit and 'relative demand' curves (shown as DD in Figure 2.16). The 'relative supply' curve in economy A is shown as $S_A S_A$; the corresponding curve for B, $S_B S_B$, is higher at every price ratio, showing that economy B has a higher ratio of land to labour (commodity one is the land-intensive commodity, it will be remembered).

If economy A is at point A and economy B at point B, then the economy with the higher supply of land relative to labour (B), will have the *higher* relative price for the land-intensive commodity and thus the *higher* ratio of rents to wages.

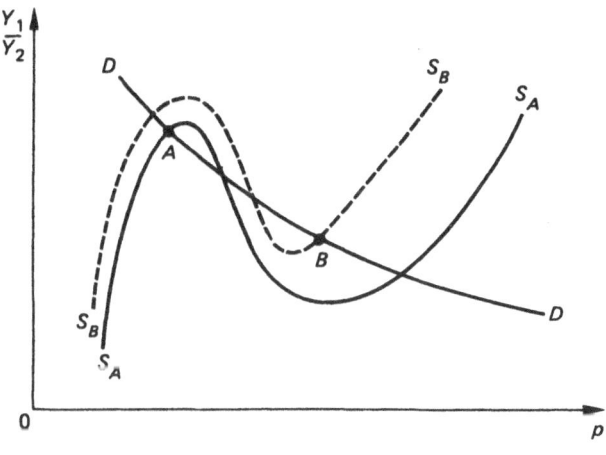

FIGURE 2.16

When there is a positive rate of profit on the value of capital goods, it is *not possible* to make any *a priori* predictions concerning the effect, on commodity prices and primary input prices, of differences in intensity of demand for commodities, or of differences in relative primary input supply.

CONCLUSION

In the well-known neo-classical analysis of a multi-technique economy, in which two commodities are produced by given supplies of land and labour, there being a uniform and zero rate of profit on the capital goods involved, one can make the following important *ceteris paribus* statements:

(i) A higher relative price of the land-intensive commodity will be associated with a higher rent–wage ratio.
(ii) A higher rent–wage ratio will be associated with the use of more labour-intensive production methods.
(iii) The relative output of a commodity will be an increasing function of its relative price.
(iv) A more intense demand for the land-intensive commodity will be associated with a higher relative price for that commodity and with a higher rent–wage ratio.
(v) A higher relative supply of land will be associated with a lower relative price for the land-intensive commodity and a lower rent–wage ratio.

When we introduce a uniform *positive* rate of profit, propositions (ii) to (v) cease to be of general validity; since there *is* a positive rate of profit in almost every economy which we wish to study, this conclusion would seem to be of some importance.[20]

APPENDIX I

The processes for producing commodities one and two, in the numerical example in the text, are as follows:

	Commodity 1		Commodity 2	
	A	B	C	D
Commodity 1	0.0	0.3	0.1	0.2
Commodity 2	0.71	0.02	0.0	0.1
Labour	0.01	0.66	1.0	0.7
Land	1.00	1.20	1.0	0.8

Reswitching and Primary Input Use

The techniques mentioned in the text consist of the following pairs of processes:

Technique	Processes
1	A, D
2	A, C
3	B, C
4	B, D

In the computations, r and z were varied over the following ranges:

r Between 0 and 2.75 by steps of 0.25.
z As follows: 0.00, 0.18, 0.36, 0.58, 0.84, 1.19, 1.73, 2.75, 5.67, 100.0. These values are (approximately) the tangents of $0°$, $10°$, $20°$, $30°$, $40°$, $50°$, $60°$, $70°$, $80°$ and $89°\,30'$.

APPENDIX II

In his *Production of Commodities by Means of Commodities*, Sraffa showed that the wage–profit-rate frontier for a given technique could be made a straight line, by measuring the wage as a fraction of an appropriately chosen 'standard national income'. The reader may well have wondered whether by measuring both wages and rents in terms of such a standard national income, we could not make our wage–rent–profit-rate frontier into a plane; the object of this brief appendix is to show that we can.

Consider a circulating capital technology with a matrix of input–output coefficients M, a row vector of labour input coefficients $\underline{a}$ and a row vector of land input coefficients $\underline{A}$. If the money wages per unit of labour and rents per unit of land, w and W respectively, are paid at the end of the year and the annual rate of profit is r, then the row vector of money prices, $\underline{p}$, must satisfy

$$\underline{p}.M(1+r) + w.\underline{a} + W.\underline{A} = \underline{p} \tag{i}$$

We now construct a standard commodity, the gross and net outputs of which are given by $\underline{q}$ and $\underline{y}$ respectively, where

$$(1+R)M.\underline{q} = \underline{q} \tag{ii}$$

$$\underline{a}.\underline{q} = 1 \tag{iii}$$
$$\underline{q} > 0$$

and
$$(1+R)\underline{y} = R\underline{q} \tag{iv}$$

R is the maximum possible value of r and equation (iii) expresses the convenient assumption that the production of the standard commodity would require the use of the total labour supply, defined as being unity.

On multiplying through equation (i) by $\underline{q}$ and taking account of (ii) and (iii), we obtain

$$\left(\frac{1+r}{1+R}\right)\underline{p}.\underline{q} + w + (\underline{A}.\underline{q})W = \underline{p}.\underline{q}$$

and thus
$$w + (\underline{A}.\underline{q})W = \left(\frac{R-r}{1+R}\right)\underline{p}.\underline{q}$$

or
$$w + (\underline{A}.\underline{q})W = \left(\frac{R-r}{R}\right)\underline{p}.\underline{y} \tag{v}$$

from (iv)

If we now define w_s and W_s as wages and rents in terms of standard national income, i.e., as $(w/\underline{p}.\underline{y})$ and $(W/\underline{p}.\underline{y})$ respectively, then we see from (v) that

$$w_s + (\underline{A}.\underline{q})W_s = \left(\frac{R-r}{R}\right) \tag{vi}$$

In equation (vi) we have a wage–rent–profit-rate frontier which is a plane. For any given feasible value of r, the trade-off between wages and rents is now not only linear but independent of the value of r; as we saw in the text, this trade-off normally depends on r when wages and rents are measured in terms of one commodity. It may also be noted that, since $\underline{a}.\underline{q} = 1$ by assumption, the coefficient of W_s in (vi) is the aggregate land/labour ratio notionally involved in the production of the standard commodity, ('notionally,' because it may not be possible actually to produce the gross output $\underline{q}$; this would be the case, e.g., if $\underline{A}.\underline{q}$ exceeded the supply of land). This coefficient may also be thought of as a weighted average of the industry land–labour ratios, the weights being the percentages of the labour force allocated to the various industries when the standard commodity is (notionally) being produced.

It will be clear that if land is not used in production, $(\underline{A} = 0)$, then (vi) becomes Sraffa's well-known wage–profit-rate frontier and that (vi) can be immediately generalised to the case of many primary inputs.

NOTES

* This essay is a slightly revised version of a paper first published in the *Economic Journal*, 1972. We should like to thank L. Mainwaring and an *Economic Journal* referee for their helpful comments on an earlier version.
1. As presented, for example, by Meade [2].
2. Cf. Samuelson [4], p. 17.
3. The assumption of uniform 'radioactive' depreciation rates different from unity would not materially affect our results; cf. Bruno et al., [1], pp. 528-31. (Of course, such a treatment of depreciation does not adequately capture the important features of fixed capital.)
4. See Meade [2], pp. 26-7 and p. 105. (Note that Meade abstracts from the problems of capital and profit.) These assumptions are made here not because they are reasonable assumptions but because they are common amongst neoclassical writers.
5. A clear statement of the 'normal' result can be found in Robinson [3], p. 299 (despite the fact that a positive rate of profits is allowed). See also Samuelson [5], pp. 408-9. One implication of this result is that market forces need not bring about full employment of land and labour; when we assume such full employment, as we do when we discuss levels of output, we are thus making a *quite arbitrary* assumption, for the purposes of argument.
6. We leave aside, it will be noted, the possibility that both the real wage and the real rent are zero. In that case det $(I - vA) = 0$.
7. Note that the ordering of commodities by direct input intensity is the same as the ordering by total input intensity, i.e.,

$$\frac{A_1}{a_1} > \frac{A_2}{a_2} \text{ implies } \frac{L_1}{l_1} > \frac{L_2}{l_2}, \text{ when } L_i \text{ and } l_i$$

are the *total* amounts of land and labour needed to produce one unit of net output of commodity i. For a proof, see the Appendix to [6].
8. By differentiating (2) with respect to v it will be found that the sign of the derivative depends on a quadratic expression in z. It can be shown that this expression is 0 for two real values of z.
9. Since the most important variable in the following analysis will be the *ratio* of wages to rents, it is clearly of no importance whether we measure real wages and real rents in terms of commodity one or in terms of commodity two.
10. This can be seen by differentiating the slope coefficient of (4), call it b, with respect to v. Calling the denominator of b, E, we obtain

$$E^2 \frac{db}{dv} = a_{12} a_1 a_2 \left[\frac{A_1}{a_1} - \frac{A_2}{a_2} \right] > 0 \text{ for } \frac{A_1}{a_1} > \frac{A_2}{a_2}$$

If all real variables are measured in terms of commodity one, then, not surprisingly, the slope of this wage-rent relationship *decreases* with each notional increase in the profit rate.
11. Cf. Robinson [3], p. 300.
12. Cf. Robinson [3], p. 301.

36 Fundamental Issues in Trade Theory

13. Professor D. G. Champernowne has kindly suggested the following intuitive explanation of our results. The choice between two techniques, a and b, at a positive rate of profit, r, is exactly equivalent to the choice between two imaginary techniques, $\bar{a}$ and $\bar{b}$, at a zero rate of profit, where each commodity input–output coefficient for the imaginary techniques is equal to $(1 + r)$ times the corresponding coefficient for the actual techniques and the corresponding direct land and labour coefficients are the same. The total land–labour intensities for $\bar{a}$ and $\bar{b}$ will, in general, depend on r; even though a is more land-intensive than b, $\bar{a}$ may for some r be *less* land-intensive than $\bar{b}$. As the rent–wage ratio is notionally increased, the switch will always be to the less land-intensive *imaginary* technique but may be to the less or to the more land-intensive *actual* technique.
14. Details of the techniques are given in Appendix I. We are indebted to S. A. Moore, who wrote the program for the technique choice exercise.
15. In the exercise the labour supply was set at 10 units and the land supply at 15 units.
16. Table 2.3 shows only a few of the r and z values for which wages and rents were actually computed. They have been chosen simply to highlight the points made above.
17. Figure 2.12, of course, shows the situation when p rises with r, for any z, for every technique, as assumed in the previous discussion. It is not the general case, cf. Figure 2.1.
18. Although the two curves must have maxima and minima for the same values of z, the curves must otherwise be of different shape. If curve 2 were a parallel contraction of curve 1, then a primary input intensity for *both* commodities together could appear more than once with respect to z, contradicting the fact that *techniques* never reswitch with respect to variations in z.
19. The solutions in Figure 2.14 will, in general, be associated with different levels of 'social utility'. It follows immediately that a solution can be *suboptimal* in welfare terms. $S'S'$ is drawn on the assumption that the 'minimum' point of curve 1 in Figure 2.13 lies above the full-employment land-labour ratio, which in turn lies above the 'maximum' point of curve 2; if this is not assumed $S'S'$ will still have two rising sections and one falling section but will not be continuous.
20. It will be clear, for example, that our conclusion has important implications for the much-used 'Heckscher–Ohlin–Samuelson' theory of trade; see Essays 3 and 4 in this volume.

REFERENCES

[1] Bruno, M., Burmeister, E. and Sheshinksi, E. 'The nature and implications of the reswitching of techniques'. *Quarterly Journal of Economics*, 1966, pp. 526–53.
[2] Meade, J. E. *The Stationary Economy*. Allen & Unwin, London, 1965.
[3] Robinson, J. V. *The Accumulation of Capital*. Macmillan, London, 1969, third edition.
[4] Samuelson, P. A. 'Prices of factors and goods in general equilibrium'. *Review of Economic Studies*, 21, 1953, pp. 1–20.

[5] Samuelson, P. A. 'A new theorem on non-substitution'. In H. Hegeland (ed.), *Money, Growth and Methodology, and Other Essays in Economics in Honour of Johan Akerman*. C. W. K. Gleerup, Lund, 1961.
[6] Vanek, J. 'Variable factor proportions and inter-industry flows in the theory of international trade'. *Quarterly Journal of Economics*, 1963, pp. 129–42.

3 Reswitching, Primary Inputs and the Heckscher–Ohlin–Samuelson Theory of Trade*

IAN STEEDMAN and J. S. METCALFE

Over recent decades the theory of trade has been dominated by the Heckscher–Ohlin–Samuelson (H–O–S) analysis which, in its most common form, deals with a two-country, two-commodity, two-factor model of trade. Since the H–O–S analysis is an application of standard general equilibrium analysis to questions concerning trade, it is to be expected that it might be affected by the recent developments in capital theory, and it can be shown (see Essay 5 below) that if the two 'factors' are taken to be labour and 'value capital' then the analysis does indeed meet difficulties. The object of the present essay is to show that the H–O–S theory also meets difficulties if the two factors are taken to be labour and land, the role of time being recognised by the inclusion in the model of a *positive* rate of profit (interest). It must, of course, be noted carefully that some writers might wish to argue that the existence of a positive profit rate implies the existence of a third factor, capital, and that the model analysed below therefore has two commodities and three factors. Since it is well known that difficulties arise for the H–O–S analysis when there are more factors than commodities (Samuelson [4]) such a writer might then argue that our analysis is redundant. Our standpoint is that the following analysis is intended for those who, like ourselves, do not regard capital (or time) as a 'factor' comparable to land and labour.[1]

It may be useful to note that this essay simply extends to the case of open economies the analysis of a closed economy which we presented in Essay 2 above and that the notation is the same in both essays.

THE ASSUMPTIONS

In order to focus attention on the effect of allowing for a positive rate of profit in H–O–S trade theory, we shall make the normal assumptions of the two-consumption-commodity, two-factor, two-country model of trade. Thus we assume that:

(a) Two countries, A and B, produce the same two consumption commodities, 1 and 2.

(b) Each country has a given endowment of factors, homogeneous land and labour, identical with respect to the quality of the factors but different with respect to relative quantities.

(c) Productive techniques are identical as between countries and exhibit constant returns to scale; for the production of each commodity there is an infinite range of alternative possible land–labour ratios.

(d) The two consumption commodities are produced with different and uniquely ordered factor intensities; there are thus no 'factor intensity reversals,' commodity 1 always being the more land-intensive.

(e) All consumers in the two-country world have identical homothetic preference maps.

(f) Perfect competition rules in all markets, transport costs are absent and there is free trade in consumption commodities (unless otherwise stated).

In the standard analysis, with a zero rate of profit, it is not important whether one assumes that the factors produce the commodities directly or that there are produced means of production (see Samuelson [4], Vanek [7]). We shall assume that all productive processes do use produced means of production as inputs, in addition to the inputs of land and labour. For simplicity, we shall also assume that all processes of production take exactly one year, that all the produced inputs are completely used up within that year and that those inputs consist of the same two commodities as are used for consumption purposes. Wages and rents will be assumed to be paid at the end of the year, so that profits are obtained only on the value of the (circulating) capital goods.

In order to keep to a minimum the differences between our assumptions and those of the standard analysis, we shall assume that the positive rate of profit is the same in both countries and less than the

40   Fundamental Issues in Trade Theory

maximum possible rate of profit. We assume, furthermore, that the level of this common profit rate is independent of the existence or nonexistence of trade.[2] The common rate of profit is obtained on the value of all capital goods, since we consider only long-period equilibrium in which the stocks of capital goods are, of course, determined endogenously, not given as data. As in the standard analysis, we assume zero net accumulation, with constant supplies of land and labour services in each country.

THE BASIC DIAGRAM

The standard analysis, with a zero rate of profit (r), is commonly presented in terms of Figure 3.1, in which p is the price of commodity 1 in terms of commodity 2, Z is the ratio of rents to wages and $L_i(l_i)$ is the amount of land (labour) used, directly and indirectly,[3] in the production of one unit of commodity $i(i = 1, 2)$. Both relative commodity prices and the land-intensity of production methods are monotonically related to the rent–wage ratio, with production of commodity 1 always being more land-intensive. Figure 3.1 applies to both countries, since each side depends only on technical conditions which, by assumption, are the same in both countries.

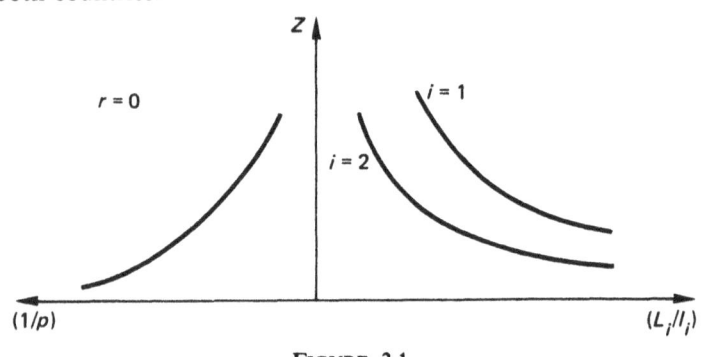

FIGURE 3.1

If the assumption of a zero rate of profit is replaced by that of a positive rate of profit less than the maximum possible rate, all the other normal assumptions being maintained, then it can be shown that the commodity price ratio will still be monotonically related to the rent–wage ratio, commodity 1, the land-intensive commodity, becoming relatively more expensive as rents rise relative to wages. It is, however, no longer possible to assert, *a priori*, that the land-intensity of production methods will be inversely related to the rent–wage ratio. (See Essay 2 above.) Thus with a positive rate of profit Figure 3.1 would, in general, have to be modified on the right-hand side, though not on the left-hand side; Figure 3.2 shows one possible example. (The broken vertical lines at (0), (i), (ii), (iii) and (iv) show alternative possible endowment ratios and will be referred to below.)[4]

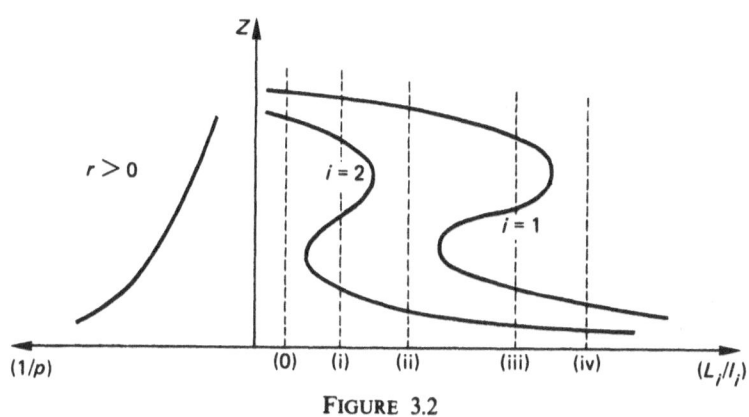

FIGURE 3.2

THE PATTERN OF TRADE

With a zero rate of profit, as in Figure 3.1, there will be patterns of net output yielding full employment of both land and labour, no matter what the endowment ratio of a country may be. It will be convenient to represent these patterns not in the form of a production possibility frontier but rather in that of a 'relative supply curve' showing how *relative* net output, with full employment of both factors, varies with *relative* commodity prices.[5] Thus, with $r = 0$, we may draw Figure 3.3(i) in which y is the full employment ratio of net output of 1 to net output of 2 and SS is the relative supply curve. If country B has a higher land–labour endowment ratio than A then its relative supply curve, $S^B S^B$ in Figure 3.3(ii), will be higher than A's, $S^A S^A$, at every price, since 1 is the land-intensive commodity. If DD shows the proportions in which the commodities are consumed, as a function of their relative price, then the no-trade price ratio will be p^B in B and p^A in A. Trade can take place only at a price lying in the interval (p^B, p^A), (for at other prices both countries have an 'excess supply' of the same commodity) and it is clear that at such a price B will export 1 and A will export 2.[6] Thus the country with the higher land–labour ratio, B, will export the land-intensive commodity 1, which is precisely the H–O–S theorem in its 'quantity' form. The theorem also holds in its 'price' form, for B, having the lower no-trade p, will have the lower no-trade rent–wage ratio and thus each country exports the commodity which uses relatively intensively the factor which is relatively cheaper, in that country, in the absence of trade.

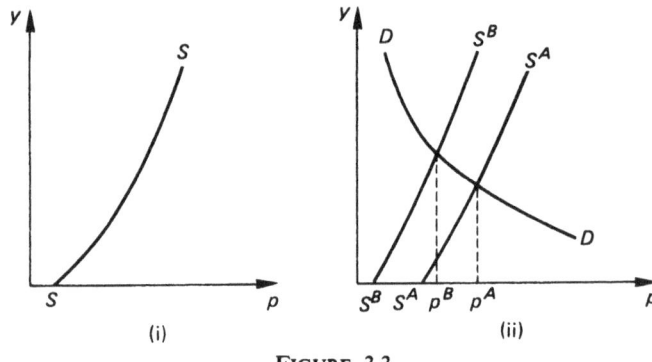

FIGURE 3.3

Suppose now that the rate of profit is positive and that the relations between Z and the factor-intensities of production methods are, for example, as shown in Figure 3.2. If the endowment ratio in a given country should be at point (0) or point (iv) in Figure 3.2, then the full-employment relative supply curve for that country will be as shown in Figure 3.3(i), i.e. it will be of the 'normal' kind despite the 'abnormal' nature of the factor-price–factor-intensity relations. If the endowment ratio should be at point (i), (ii) or (iii), however, it can be shown that the full-employment relative supply curve will be as in Figures 3.4(i), (ii) and (iii) respectively. It will be clear that if we were to superpose a relative demand curve DD, as in Figure 3.3(ii), in Figure 3.4, DD would, in each case, have either one or three intersections with the relative supply curve SS and that, if there were three intersections, two of the three would have SS cutting DD 'from below.' Thus 'stable' equilibrium in the autarkic economy may be non-unique.

Consider now the two countries A and B and assume that, as in Figure 3.3(ii), B has the higher land–labour endowment ratio. Each country will have one of the four possible types of relative supply curve (as shown in Figures 3.3(i), 3.4(i), 3.4(ii), 3.4(iii)) and thus there are sixteen possible combinations of types of relative supply curves. We shall only examine the case in which both countries have a relative supply curve of the form shown in Figure 3.4(ii) and in which the common relative demand curve,

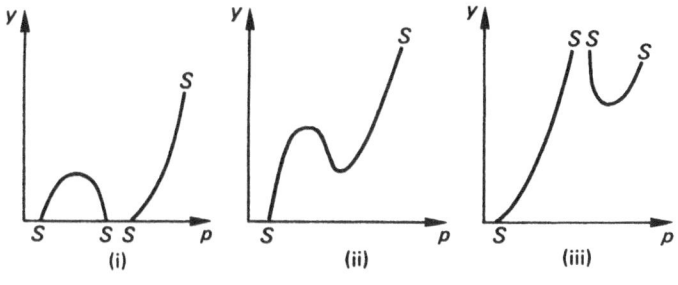

FIGURE 3.4

DD, cuts the relative supply curves as in Figure 3.5. The reader will find it easy to examine the other possible cases.

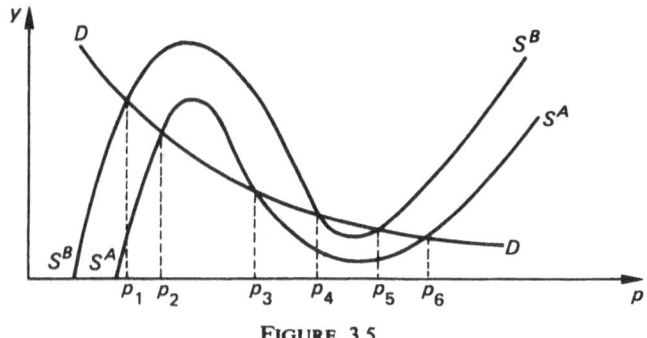

FIGURE 3.5

It will be clear that a trade equilibrium, with balanced trade and full employment of both factors in both countries, can exist only for an international price ratio, p, such that, at that price, $S^A S^A$ and $S^B S^B$ lie on opposite sides of DD. Since $S^B S^B$ lies above $S^A S^A$ at *every* p, it follows immediately that in a trade equilibrium country A exports commodity 2 and country B commodity 1 so that the country with the higher land–labour ratio, B, exports the land-intensive commodity 1. Thus the basic H–O–S theorem holds in its 'quantity' form in the presence of a *common* positive rate of profit. (With *different* rates of profit, of course, the theorem would, in general, be invalid since *different* techniques would be in use, in the two countries, at any given international price ratio, p, and thus the full-employment relative supply curve of the country with relatively more land could lie *below* that of the country with relatively more labour.)

As the reader may verify by drawing the 'intersecting offer curve' diagram, there will be three international prices consistent with balanced equilibrium trade, one in each of the price ranges p_1 to p_2, p_3 to p_4 and p_5 to p_6 (see Figure 3.5), the highest and lowest of these three prices being at 'stable' offer curve intersections and the third at an 'unstable' intersection. (The offer curve for country A is shown in Figure 3.6, where the $X_i(M_i)$ are exports (imports) of commodity i.) With a common *positive* rate of profit there is no reason to regard non-uniqueness of the equilibrium terms of trade as in any way 'abnormal' or dependent on 'peculiar' conditions. With a positive profit rate, uniqueness of equilibrium has to be regarded as a special case, even when we make all the usual assumptions about technical and demand conditions.

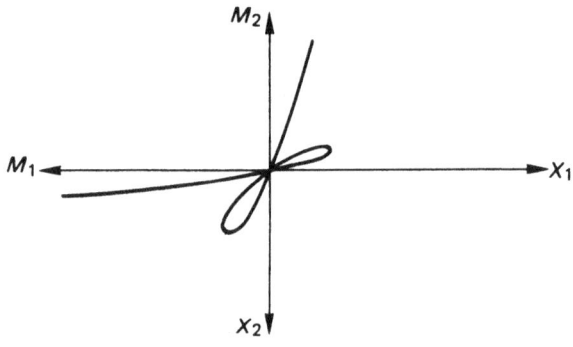

FIGURE 3.6

Suppose now that, under autarky, the equilibrium price were p^2 in A and p^5 in B (Figure 3.5). It would follow immediately, from the left-hand side of Figure 3.2, that land services were relatively more expensive under autarky in B. Yet, as we have seen above, a trade equilibrium will involve B exporting the land-intensive commodity 1, so that while the basic H–O–S theorem on the pattern of trade continues to hold in its 'quantity' form, with a positive rate of profit, it need not hold in its 'price' form. With a common positive rate of profit, the 'price' form of the theorem, far from being somewhat trivial, is, in general, invalid.

We may note, furthermore, that with autarky prices of p_2 in A and p_5 in B, neither of the international prices that can support a *stable* trade equilibrium will lie between the two autarky prices. Thus a stable trade equilibrium will yield, in one of the countries, a real return to that country's relatively scarce factor which is *higher* than the return under autarky.

THE FACTOR-PRICE EQUALISATION AND STOLPER–SAMUELSON THEOREMS

Both these theorems reduce, in essence, to the monotonicity of the commodity-price–factor-price relation which, as stated above, is not affected by the introduction of a positive rate of profit. With a positive profit rate, a tariff on an import *will* raise the real return to the factor used relatively intensively in the production of the imported commodity and free trade in commodities, between countries with a common positive rate of profit, *will* equalise real wages and real rents as between the two countries. (With *different* positive profit rates in the two countries, free trade in commodities would *not*, in general, equalise real wages and rents as between the countries.)

CONCLUSION

We have examined a version of the familiar H–O–S analysis, with two countries, two commodities and two factors; we have made *all* the normal assumptions *except that*, instead of a common zero rate of profit, we have assumed a common positive rate of profit. Since the existence of a positive profit rate does not affect the properties of the familiar relationship between commodity-prices and factor-prices it does not affect the factor-price-equalisation and Stolper–Samuelson theorems. In general, however, nothing can be said *a priori* about the relationship between factor-prices and the factor-intensity of production methods, when the profit rate is positive, and it follows that nothing can be said *a priori* about the shape of the relative supply curve. This does not prevent the H–O–S theorem about the pattern of trade from holding in its 'quantity' form, but does make the theorem invalid in its 'price' form, does mean that trade need not 'harm' a country's scarce factor, and does mean that uniqueness of international equilibrium is to be regarded as a special case when the common rate of profit is positive.

NOTES

* This essay was first published in the *Journal of International Economics*, 1977. We should like to thank Sergio Parrinello and R. B. Rowthorn for helpful comments on an earlier version.
1. See, e.g., Hicks [3], p. 39, n. 1.

2. Some writers might wish to relate this common rate of profit (interest) to a universal rate of time preference but our analysis does not depend on this or on any other theory about the rate of profit; we simply take it to be what it is. Exactly the same procedure has been adopted in recent work by Bliss [1], Burmeister [2] and Samuelson [5]. For a clear discussion of such an approach to the relation between the profit rate and one's 'primitive postulates' (in the context of comparative dynamics) see Bliss [1], pp. 71–2.
3. If M is the matrix of input-output coefficients for a given technique and $A(a)$ the associated vector of direct land (labour) use per unit of gross output, then $L = A(I - M)^{-1}$ and $l = a(I - M)^{-1}$, where I is an identity matrix.
4. This example, with an endowment ratio at point (ii), was used in Essay 2 above.
5. When trade is possible, the net output production possibility frontier can and should be extended into the second and fourth quadrants (see Warne [7]) but we shall simply assume that, in trading equilibrium, net output of each commodity is positive in each country.
6. Throughout this essay we follow the normal practice of trade theorists and write about *comparisons* in a way that might tempt the reader to think about *transitions*! The reader is asked to resist any such temptation.

REFERENCES

[1] Bliss, C. J. *Capital Theory and the Distribution of Income.* North-Holland, Amsterdam, 1975.
[2] Burmeister, E. 'Many primary factors in non-joint production economies'. *Economic Record*, 1975, pp. 486–512.
[3] Hicks, J. R. *Capital and Time: A Neo-Austrian Theory.* Clarendon Press, Oxford, 1973.
[4] Samuelson, P. A. 'Prices of factors and goods in general equilibrium'. *Review of Economic Studies*, 1953–54, pp. 1–20.
[5] Samuelson, P. A. 'Trade pattern reversals in time-phased Ricardian systems and intertemporal efficiency'. *Journal of International Economics*, 1975, pp. 309–63.
[6] Vanek, J. 'Variable factor proportions and inter-industry flows in the theory of international trade'. *Quarterly Journal of Economics*, 1963, pp. 129–42.
[7] Warne, R. D. 'Intermediate goods in international trade with variable proportions and two primary inputs'. *Quarterly Journal of Economics*, 1971, pp. 225–36.

4 A Note on the Gain from Trade*

J. S. METCALFE and IAN STEEDMAN

The object of this essay is to investigate the nature of the gain or loss from trade in capitalist economies that are in long-run stationary equilibrium.[1] The analysis may be considered an extension of recent theoretical work which has rightly emphasised the role of produced means of production in the general equilibrium analysis of trade,[2] although we depart from current analysis in allowing for the impact of a positive rate of interest upon the equilibrium properties of the economies we discuss. It must be made clear that we shall be investigating the gain from trade in two entirely different senses. First, we consider two separate economies identical in all respects, except that one is in a state of autarky while the other is engaged in international trade at given international prices; the gain from trade is derived in familiar fashion by comparing the stationary equilibrium characteristics of the two economies. Secondly, we investigate the gain from trade within the context of a single economy that is initially in a state of autarky and is then unexpectedly faced with the option of trade at given international prices. We are here investigating the gain from trade in terms of the capitalists' investment decision, weighing together the 'gains' and 'losses' of the unexpected switch from autarky to trade. The important feature of this analysis is that it takes account of the impact upon attainable consumption of the transition from autarkic to with-trade steady states.

We begin by analysing the equilibrium properties of an economy in which the rate of interest on invested capital is positive and there are distortions in the market for primary inputs. This forms a common base for the two following sections on the gain from trade.

PRICES, DISTORTIONS AND THE RATE OF INTEREST

It is well known that in the presence of factor market distortions, equilibrium relative commodity prices are, in general, not equal to the domestic marginal rate of transformation in production. We shall now demonstrate that a positive rate of interest is equivalent in its effects to a factor market distortion, in so far as they each generate a divergence between relative commodity prices and marginal rates of transformation in production. This is so even though there is no sense in which a positive rate of interest may be construed as a distortion.

To show this we consider an economy with the following properties. Preferences for current commodities may be represented by a homothetic utility function that is the same for all income recipients who, in addition, express their preference between present and future consumption through a universal and positive rate of time preference.[3] Since our concern is only with stationary economies, the rate of interest is always equal to this universal rate of time preference.

The economy is endowed with fixed amounts of primary factors, land and labour. Current and future production consists of two commodities for which inputs of land, labour and the same commodities are combined in constant returns to scale production processes.

For simplicity, technical choices are restricted to one process for the production of commodity 1 and two alternative processes for the production of commodity 2,[4] so that we may depict technical possibilities as follows:

	Process		
	(1)	(2)	(3)
Commodity 1	0	a_{12}	b_{12}
Commodity 2	a_{21}	0	0
Labour	a_1	a_2	b_2
Land	A_1	A_2	B_2

Column (1) shows the inputs of commodities 1 and 2,[5] labour and land needed to produce one unit of gross output of commodity 1. Columns (2) and (3) are interpreted in similar fashion for commodity 2.

Clearly in the closed economy at least two processes must be operated simultaneously if positive production of either commodity is to take place. It follows, therefore, that the economy has two available

A Note on the Gain from Trade

techniques of production, technique a, consisting of processes (1) and (2), and technique b, consisting of processes (1) and (3).

From this technical information and a knowledge of the endowment of primary inputs, we can draw up the economy production possibility frontier, each point on which shows the maximum possible *net* output of one commodity for a given level of *net* output of the other commodity. In Figure 4.1, this frontier is shown as $t_2 abt_1$. The points marked a and b denote the full employment patterns of net output associated with techniques a and b, respectively, while the line segment $a - b$ shows those patterns of full employment net output obtained by operating the two techniques (i.e., all three processes) simultaneously. Since, as in all analysis of the gain from trade, we are only concerned with situations where both primary inputs are fully employed, we henceforth restrict our argument to a discussion of output patterns lying on $a - b$.

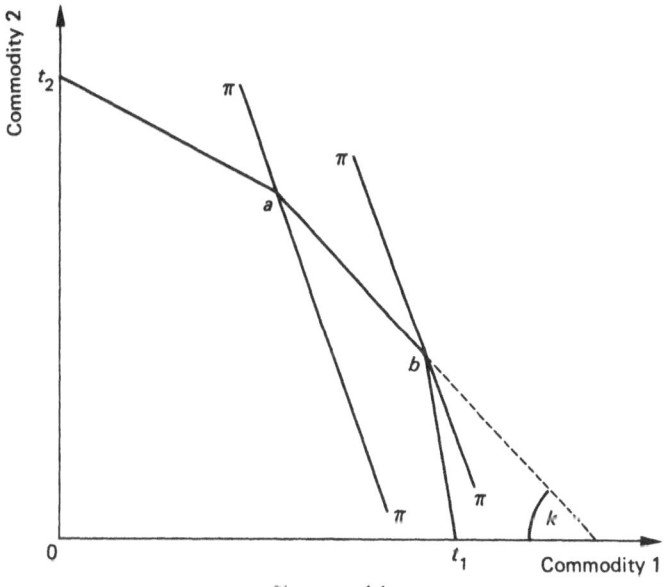

FIGURE 4.1

The slope of this segment $a - b$ is particularly important, as it indicates the domestic marginal rate of transformation in production. Elementary calculations show this to be given by[6]

$$-\left[\frac{dY_2}{dY_1}\right] = k = \frac{a_1(B_2 - A_2) + A_1(a_2 - b_2) + a_{21}(B_2 a_2 - A_2 b_2)}{(B_2 a_2 - A_2 b_2) + a_1(B_2 a_{12} - A_2 b_{12}) + A_1(b_{12} a_2 - a_{12} b_2)}.$$

(1)

We now assume that the market for land is perfectly competitive so that each industry must pay the same money rental, W, but that the market for labour services is distorted with money wage w in industry 1 and money wage $\alpha \cdot w$ in industry 2. Commodity and capital markets are also assumed to be perfect so that in long-run competitive and stationary equilibrium the following price equations must hold:[7]

and
$$p_1 = a_{21} p_2 \beta + w a_1 + W A_1 \qquad (2)$$

and/or
$$p_2 = a_{12} p_1 \beta + \alpha w a_2 + W A_2 \qquad (3)$$

$$p_2 = b_{12} p_1 \beta + \alpha w b_2 + W B_2 \qquad (4)$$

where $\beta = 1 + r$, r is the equilibrium rate of interest equal to the rate of time preference, α is the magnitude of the labour market distortion, and p_1 and p_2 are the prices of commodities 1 and 2 respectively.

The pairs of equations, (2) and (3), and (2) and (4), define relationships between relative commodity prices, relative primary input rentals, the rate of interest and the labour market distortion, which must hold when either technique a or technique b is in operation.[8] Consider, for example, technique a. For given α, β, we know that the relative price of commodity 1, $(p_1/p_2 = p)$ is a unique, monotonic function of the ratio of money rents to money wages, (W/w). If we now suppose that commodity 1 is the more land-intensive commodity and that $\alpha > 1$,[9] then clearly the commodity price ratio is an increasing function of the ratio (W/w). Furthermore, as we notionally vary this rent–wage ratio from zero through all positive values to infinity, we know that the possible values taken by the commodity price ratio are constrained to lie within the range, $0 < \underline{p}^a \leq p \leq \bar{p}^a < \infty$. We call $\underline{p}^a$ and $\bar{p}^a$ the limiting price ratios of technique a, these being defined, of course, for given values of α and β.[10] The important point is that if the commodity price ratio lies outside the range defined by the limiting price ratios, then technique a will not be operated in competitive equilibrium.

Exactly the same propositions hold with respect to technique b, which has limiting price ratios $\underline{p}^b$ and $\bar{p}^b$.

In addition to the characteristics of individual techniques, we are also interested in a situation in which techniques may be operated simultaneously, paying the common rate of interest, paying a common rental for land services and paying wages consistent with the labour market distortion. It will be clear that such a possibility is not independent of the values of α and β assumed to be in force. However, one can readily show that, if the values of α and β permit, there will be a unique value of the commodity price ratio associated with the simultaneous operation of techniques. We call this critical price ratio the switching price ratio and denote it by p^*.

For a given distortion and rate of interest, the equilibrium choice of technique will depend upon the comparison of the market clearing price ratio, p, with the switching price ratio, p^*. Now, in the closed economy, the only possible competitive equilibria involve the use of one or both of the two techniques, so that we have the following three possibilities:[11]

$\underline{p}^a \leq p < p^*$ Technique a in operation
$p = p^*$ Techniques a and b may be operated either singly or simultaneously
$p^* < p \leq \bar{p}^b$ Technique b in operation.

Associated with each of these possibilities are equilibrium patterns of net output. Thus if p satisfies $\underline{p}^a \leq p \leq \bar{p}^b$, net output must lie somewhere on the frontier t_2abt_1 of Figure 4.1; while if p satisfies $\underline{p}^a < p < \bar{p}^b$, net output must lie somewhere upon the segment $a-b$ of the production possibility frontier, all points on this segment involving full employment of both primary inputs.

Having shown the importance of the switching price ratio for the equilibrium properties of the economy, we now discuss its determinants in more detail. It can be shown from equations (2), (3) and (4) that

$$p^* = \frac{a_1(B_2 - A_2) + A_1(a_2 - b_2)\alpha + a_{21}(B_2 a_2 - A_2 b_2)\alpha\beta}{(B_2 a_2 - A_2 b_2)\alpha + a_1(B_2 a_{12} - A_2 b_{12})\beta + A_1(b_{12} a_2 - a_{12} b_2)\alpha\beta} \quad (5)$$

$$= p^*(\alpha, \beta).$$

Thus for each value of the distortion and rate of interest, a unique switching price ratio is defined and for each switching price ratio we have an infinite number of pairs, α, β, consistent with that price ratio and defined by (5).[12] Now consider the following three situations:

(a) No distortion in the labour market and a zero rate of interest. Comparing equations (1) and (5), we find $p^*(1, 1) = k$, which is the conventional result. The switching price ratio equals the domestic marginal rate of transformation.

(b) A distortion in the labour market and a zero rate of interest. Then $p^*(\alpha, 1) \gtrless k$ as $\alpha \gtrless 1$, which is the expected result from the theory of factor market distortions.

(c) No distortion in the labour market and a positive rate of interest. Again from (1) and (5), $p^*(1, \beta) \neq k$.

That is, a positive rate of interest generates a divergence between the switching price ratio and the domestic marginal rate of transformation akin to that generated by a factor market distortion.

The explanation of these results is straightforward. The domestic marginal rate of transformation is uniquely determined by the technical production coefficients of the two techniques as shown in equation (1). The switching price ratio also depends upon these same technical coefficients but in addition is influenced, as shown in equation (5), by the magnitude of the distortion and the level of the rate of interest. There is, therefore, no reason to expect that p^* will, in general, equal k.

The above analysis has demonstrated that a positive rate of interest has certain effects upon a stationary economy comparable to effects of a factor market distortion. Having established this, we may now show the consequences of a positive rate of interest for the gain from trade.

COMPARISON OF ECONOMIES AND THE GAIN FROM TRADE

In this section we compare the equilibrium properties of two separate stationary economies with identical technical possibilities, the same, given, endowments of primary inputs and identical preference patterns and rates of time preference. The only relevant difference between the two economies is that one is in a state of autarky, while the other is engaged in trade at given international prices. We know that the impact of trade upon community welfare may be decomposed into two parts:[13] the exchange effect, in which levels of net output remain in their no-trade pattern, while consumption responds to the change in relative prices; and the specialisation effect, in which the pattern of net output is allowed to respond to the change in relative prices. For a given divergence between domestic and international prices, the exchange gain depends only upon the characteristics of community preferences and is necessarily positive, while the 'specialisation gain' depends only upon the response of technique choice in the economy. However, the specialisation effect is necessarily positive only if alternative production methods are available and then only if the price ratio for current commodities is always equated with the domestic marginal rate of transformation in their production.[14]

Analysis of the impact of distortions in the markets for primary factors has shown that in the presence of distortions this last, crucial step cannot, in general, be made. That is, factor market distortions generate relative commodity prices that differ from domestic marginal rates of transformation at all possible patterns of output. So far as the gain from trade is concerned, this implies that the specialisation gain can be negative; valued at international prices, net national income may be smaller in the with-trade economy than in the no-trade economy.[15] This conclusion is, of course, perfectly straightforward and well-known. Now, as we have shown above, a positive rate of interest can also make the commodity price ratio differ from the domestic marginal rate of transformation. It is therefore to be expected that with a positive interest rate, but no distortion, the specialisation effect can be negative. This we now demonstrate.

Consider a situation in which the open economy produces both commodities and in which the international terms of trade, π, are related to the switching price ratio, p^*, and closed economy price ratio, p, by $\pi > p^* > p$. Then we know that in the closed economy production will be at point a in Figures 1 and 2 and that production in the open economy will be at point b. We wish to know under what conditions this difference in technique and associated difference in net output patterns will generate a 'specialisation loss'.

As will be readily apparent, the possibility of a loss or a gain from specialisation depends only upon the comparison of the international price ratio (the international marginal rate of transformation) with the slope of the production possibility segment (the domestic marginal rate of transformation). Three possibilities must be considered:

(1) $k > \pi > p^* > p$, for which it is readily seen (Figure 4.2) that the specialisation gain will be negative. That is, when valuation is carried out at international prices, the value of output and consumption in the trading economy will be smaller than the value of output and consumption in the autarkic economy.

(2) $k = \pi > p^* > p$, for which it is clear that, since the domestic and international marginal rates of transformation are equal, the difference in net output patterns leaves the value of net output and consumption unchanged as between the trade and no-trade economies. That is, the specialisation effect is zero.

(3) All cases in which $\pi > k$ and in which k may stand in a variety of relationships with p^* and p. In each of these cases the specialisation effect will be positive; valued at international prices, output and

consumption are greater in the with-trade than in the no-trade economy. Figure 4.1 illustrates the traditional example in which $\pi > k = p^* > p$.

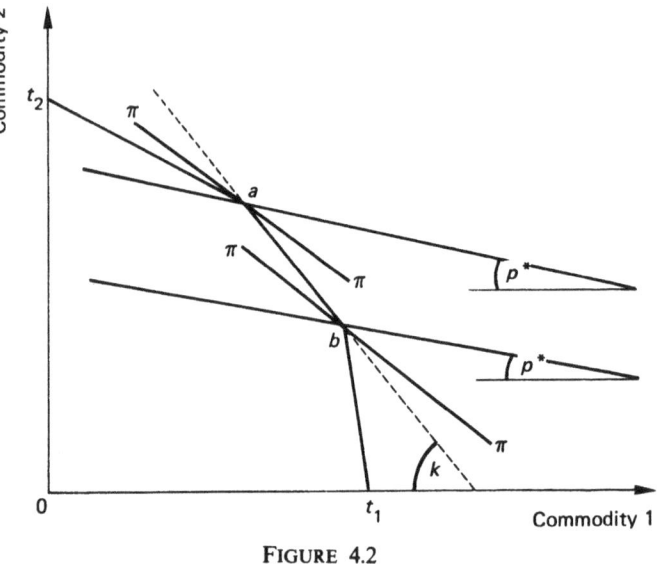

FIGURE 4.2

The source of the above 'perversities' is, of course, to be found in the fact that the switching price ratio no longer corresponds to the domestic marginal rate of transformation in production. For, this granted, it follows that trade can take place and yet at international terms of trade less than the domestic marginal rate of transformation. By producing and exchanging one more unit of commodity 1, the capitalists must, in such a situation, reduce the domestic net output of commodity 2 by more than the amount of commodity 2 which they will obtain through trade for the unit of commodity 1.

(As will be apparent, we may replace the assumption of a positive rate of interest in the above examples by the assumption of a factor market distortion and derive all the above results in a manner consistent with the distortions literature.)

We have thus demonstrated that, comparing capitalist economies in long-run stationary equilibrium, trade may generate a specialisation loss measured in terms of the values of output and consumption in the trade and no-trade situations. If we now measure the effect of trade in terms of utility, it follows that the exchange effect, which always works to increase welfare, may be more than offset by a specialisation loss so that aggregate welfare in the trading economy is less than aggregate welfare in the autarkic economy.

The possibility of an overall loss from trade should not cause surprise. For, on the one hand, a possible loss from trade is a well-known result in the theory of distortions and we have demonstrated the similarity in the effects on the economy of a positive rate of interest and a factor market distortion. On the other hand, from the golden rule, we know that when the rate of interest is greater than the rate of growth, the profit-maximising choice of technique by capitalists may not correspond to the choice of technique that maximises consumption. The result of this part of the essay is merely an extension of the golden rule principle to a comparison between autarkic and open economies with more than one primary input.

TRANSITION BETWEEN STATIONARY EQUILIBRIA AND THE GAIN FROM TRADE

We now examine the gain from trade for a single small economy, which we assume has all the properties outlined above, apart from factor market distortions which we assume to be absent ($\alpha = 1$). Our method is to begin with this economy in a state of autarkic stationary equilibrium and then to postulate that at a given point in time the option of trade unexpectedly becomes available, with the implication that prior expectations are falsified. We also assume that the newly imposed price ratio, the international terms of trade, is expected to remain unchanged over an indefinite future. As a consequence of this change in expected relative prices, the economy will switch to the pattern of output and consumption appropriate to the international terms of trade.

We shall take as our measure of the gain from trade, the difference in the present values of the consumption streams associated with the autarkic and trading situations. Needless to say, this method of analysis begs a great many questions on the meaning of equilibrium and the effects of falsified expectations—questions that could not arise in the analysis above. Before we undertake a detailed investigation of this case, some preliminary remarks are in order.

Consider first the case of an economy in which production is by means of primary inputs alone. Let production take place in an annual cycle and suppose that the economy is in a state of autarkic equilibrium. Now, at the end of a particular cycle of production, let trade unexpectedly become possible at terms of trade different from the autarky price ratio.

56 *Fundamental Issues in Trade Theory*

Because of the unexpectedness of trade, the end of the 'current' cycle of production finds the pattern of output and the allocation of primary inputs between industries inappropriate to the requirements of the with-trade equilibrium. However, in this competitive economy with no barriers to the mobility of inputs, we can imagine land and labour being immediately reallocated to produce, one year later, the equilibrium with-trade pattern of output, with the rent–wage ratio immediately taking the value dictated by the international terms of trade. Provided the terms of trade are expected to remain unchanged, the end of the next production cycle will find the composition of output in its equilibrium with-trade configuration. Thus the transition to the new output equilibrium occurs over one cycle of production. During this transitional production cycle, the net output available for consumption and trade will be that produced by the last autarkic production cycle and its value will equal the value of autarkic consumption at international prices. At the end of the transitional period, the economy will have settled into the equilibrium trade pattern and value of consumption appropriate to the trade situation.

In this economy, with no distortion and no intermediate goods, we know that in equilibrium the commodity price ratio will equal the domestic marginal rate of transformation in production. Therefore, as in the traditional case with instantaneous adjustment of output, $\pi > p$ implies $\pi > k$, so that the specialisation gain is positive. It follows that the discounted value of the with-trade consumption stream must be greater than the discounted value of the autarkic consumption stream, whatever the positive rate at which future consumption is discounted. Thus, in this sense, the gain from trade is positive.

We now return to the case of the economy in which production requires inputs of commodities as well as primary inputs. We shall find that the existence of produced means of production makes an important difference to our conclusions on the gain from trade. In such an economy, a production equilibrium requires not only an allocation of primary inputs between the two industries but also that each production period opens with the appropriate stocks of intermediate commodities to support the next cycle of production. It follows that from the gross output available at the end of each production cycle, the requisite stocks of means of production must be subtracted, so that the gross output pattern may be repeated in the next production period. The remaining net output is available to support consumption during that period.

Now assume the unexpected opening of trade and let this occur at the end of a particular autarkic production cycle. At the international terms of trade, the equilibrium output pattern will, in general, differ from the autarkic output pattern and so the economy has to pass to a new pattern of production and allocation of inputs. We shall assume that this transition can be made in one cycle of production.[16] As soon as trade becomes possible, we therefore have a situation in which land and labour are reallocated to produce the new equilibrium output pattern at wages and rents appropriate to the new terms of trade; at the same time, the stocks of commodities necessary to produce the equilibrium with-trade output pattern are subtracted from the gross outputs available at the end of the final autarkic production cycle. At the end of the transitional production period, wages and rents are paid at their new equilibrium values such that, at the ruling international prices, both industries can pay the same rate of interest (equal to the rate of time preference) upon the value of the appropriate stocks of means of production. Gross output and net output are then in equilibrium at international prices and so consumption may settle to its equilibrium with-trade value. This equilibrium state of affairs will continue indefinitely provided the terms of trade remain at their current value.

During the transitional period, however, the value of consumption is not equal to the value, at international prices, of autarkic consumption as was the case when production did not require inputs of commodities. The building up of stocks of commodities to support the with-trade production equilibrium means that the value of transitional consumption cannot, in general, equal the value of autarkic consumption. This is the important new factor created by the introduction into the analysis of produced means of production.

To formalise this, let x denote a vector of gross outputs produced in any production cycle, y the corresponding vector of net outputs, and k the vector of intermediate commodities required to support x. Then in the state of autarky, we must have

$$x_A = y_A + k_A \tag{6}$$

while in the equilibrium with-trade state, we must have

$$x_T = y_T + k_T. \tag{7}$$

To find the vector of net outputs available during the transitional period, we must subtract from x_A the vector of intermediate commodities required to support x_T. Let $\bar{y}$ denote this transitional net output vector.

Then:

$$\bar{y} = x_A - k_T$$
$$= y_A + (k_A - k_T). \tag{8}$$

The transitional net output vector is equal to the autarky net output vector plus that vector denoting the difference in physical capital requirements between the autarky and with-trade steady states. If we now denote consumption vectors by c, under autarky it must be true that $c_A = y_A$. However, in the transitional and trade equilibrium situations all we know about the relation between the respective consumption and net output vectors is that their values, at international prices, are equal. Let $q \equiv (\pi, 1)$ be the vector of international prices. Then all we know is that $q \cdot c_T = q \cdot y_T$, and $q \cdot \bar{c} = q \cdot \bar{y}$.

We are now in a position to derive two specific measures of the gain from trade for this economy. The first, which we call the 'steady-state' measure, is simply the difference between the present values of the autarkic and with-trade equilibrium consumption streams. If we denote this by ΔC, then

$$\Delta C = \frac{q \cdot y_T - q \cdot y_A}{i} \tag{9}$$

where i is the rate at which future consumption is discounted. Thus ΔC is simply the 'comparison gain' discussed above, divided by the rate of discount.

The second measure of gain, which we shall call the 'inclusive' measure, is equal to this steady-state measure plus an allowance for the change in consumption during the transitional period. Let V_A be the present value of the autarky consumption stream. Then

$$V_A = q \cdot y_A + \frac{q \cdot y_A}{1+i} + \ldots + \frac{q \cdot y_A}{(1+i)^n} + \ldots$$

Similarly, let V_T be the value of the complete consumption stream associated with the switch to trade, i.e., inclusive of the transitional consumption component, so that,

$$V_T = q \cdot \bar{y} + \frac{q \cdot y_T}{1+i} + \ldots + \frac{q \cdot y_T}{(1+i)^n} + \ldots$$

A Note on the Gain from Trade

The inclusive gain from trade is then measured by

$$\Delta V = V_T - V_A = q \cdot (\bar{y} - y_A) + \frac{q \cdot (y_T - y_A)}{i}$$

$$= q \cdot (\bar{y} - y_A) + \Delta C \qquad (10)$$

Equation (10) indicates that the inclusive gain from trade is equal to the steady-state gain, ΔC, plus the present value of the change in consumption during the transitional period relative to the value of autarky consumption. Since we know that ΔC may be positive, zero or negative, the question arises whether we can be more certain about the sign of ΔV. To clarify this we may simplify equation (10) as follows. Let Z denote total primary income, wages plus rents, measured in terms of commodity 2. Then, from the definition of national income,[17] we have

$$q \cdot y_A = Z_A + rq \cdot k_A$$
and
$$q \cdot y_T = Z_T + rq \cdot k_T,$$

where r is the equilibrium rate of interest, equal to the rate of time preference.

Making use of the above definitions of national income, we obtain, from (9)

$$\Delta C = \frac{Z_T - Z_A}{i} + \frac{r}{i} q \cdot (k_T - k_A),$$

and from equation (8),

$$q \cdot (\bar{y} - y_A) = q(k_A - k_T).$$

Substitution of these two relationships into equation (10) will yield

$$\Delta V = \frac{Z_T - Z_A}{i} + q \cdot (k_T - k_A) \left[\frac{r}{i} - 1 \right] \qquad (11)$$

as the general expression for the inclusive gain from trade. We should note that equation (11) has been derived solely from definitions and national accounting identities and is thus quite independent of any relation between relative commodity prices and marginal rates of transformation in production. If we now make the further assumption that future consumption is discounted at a rate equal to the rate of time preference, equation (11) is further simplified and reduces to

$$\Delta V = \frac{Z_T - Z_A}{r}. \qquad (12)$$

The inclusive gain from trade is thus equal to the additional (discounted) primary income yielded by the with-trade technique of production, relative to that yielded by the autarkic technique of production, when each is notionally operated at international prices. We must stress that this result depends crucially upon our assumptions of an unexpected opening of trade and the discounting of consumption streams at a rate equal to the equilibrium rate of interest. If either of these conditions is abandoned, such clear-cut results are not attainable.

We may now consider how the gain from trade is affected by notional variations in the terms of trade. As far as the steady-state measure is concerned, the analysis is straightforward. For terms of trade such that $p^* \leq \pi < k$, ΔC is negative so that there is a steady-state loss from trade, for exactly the same reasons as when we compared different economies above. Similarly, when $\pi = k$, ΔC is zero, so that the steady-state gain from trade is zero. Finally, for $\pi > k$, ΔC is positive, so that the gain from trade in this steady-state sense is positive.

The problem now is to compare this steady-state measure with the more complete assessment of the gain from trade given by the inclusive measure. Here we need only remember that, in the absence of factor market distortions and at the ruling rate of interest and commodity price ratio, the technique of production which will be chosen in competitive equilibrium is the one that happens to maximise the value of primary income. Consider first the case $\pi = p^*$, so that, at the ruling international terms of trade, the techniques a and b are equally profitable. It follows that they must also generate the same total value of primary income, $Z_T = Z_A$, and so, from equation (12), the inclusive gain from trade is exactly zero even though there is a steady-state loss. In all other relevant cases, $\pi > p^*$; the technique operated in the trade situation necessarily generates more primary income than would the autarkic technique if the latter were operated at international prices. Hence $Z_T > Z_A$, and so $\Delta V > 0$; for all $\pi > p^*$, the inclusive gain from trade is positive, irrespective of the sign and magnitude of the steady-state gain. In particular, for $p^* < \pi < k$, ΔC is negative while ΔV is positive.

The various possible outcomes are set out in Table 4.1, where $p^* < k$ throughout.

The economic rationale behind these results may be brought out by emphasising two particular cases. Consider first the situation when $\pi = p^*$. Then we know that steady-state primary income is the same in both trade and autarky and that steady-state national income is smaller in the trade situation. It follows that the value of total interest payments is greater in the autarkic situation and hence, since the rate of interest is the same in each steady state, the value of the equilibrium stocks of means of production is greater in autarky. Thus the switch from autarky to trade involves a switch to a lower equilibrium value of means of production and so, over the transition, as disinvestment occurs, the economy enjoys a temporary, one-period boost in the value of consumption, the present value of which exactly offsets the present value of the permanent steady-state loss from trade. As a second example, consider the case $\pi = k$, with identical values of steady-state national income under trade and autarky but a lower value of primary income associated with the use of the autarkic technique of production. As in the previous case, the value of the equilibrium stocks of intermediate goods is lower in the trade situation, so once again the switch to trade yields a temporary boost to consumption. Since, in this case, the steady-state gain is zero, this leaves a positive inclusive gain on the switch from autarky to trade.

TABLE 4.1 Possible outcomes

	ΔC	ΔV
$p^* = \pi$	negative	zero
$p^* < \pi < k$	negative	positive
$k = \pi$	zero	positive
$k < \pi < \bar{p}^b$	positive	positive

FINAL REMARKS

We have shown that when we compare two stationary, capitalist economies, one autarkic and the other trading, but both with the same positive rate of interest, the value, at international prices, of consumption in the open economy may be greater than, equal to, or less than the value of consumption in the closed economy. In a comparison sense, the gain from trade may be positive, zero, or negative.

Then, by contrast, we showed that the inclusive measure of the gain from trade, i.e., a discounted measure that takes account of the transition between autarkic and with-trade equilibria, is necessarily positive for our capitalist economy, provided that the opening of trade is unexpected and the rate of interest (discount) is equal to the rate of time preference.

In both cases, it is essential to our results that production involves inputs of produced commodities and that a rate of interest is charged on the value of these means of production. By contrast, in the traditional textbook analysis of the gain from trade, production is instantaneous and is by means of primary inputs alone. No transitional problems therefore arise and so our distinction between the various measures of the gain from trade cannot be employed.

Needless to say, our results are based on fairly severe assumptions, in particular we have not taken account of the possibility of 'perverse' switching of techniques or the foundation of more complex expectational responses.

NOTES

* This is a slightly revised version of an essay first published in the *Economic Record*, 1974. We wish to thank Professor M. C. Kemp for helpful comments on an earlier version.
1. In the sense of Robbins [3].
2. See Batra [1], chapters 7 and 8.
3. One may consider the community utility function to be of the form

$$U = \sum_{t=0}^{\infty} \frac{f[C_1(t), C_2(t)]}{(1+d)^t}$$

where $f[\ ]$ is a homothetic preference function for commodities, $C_1(t)$ and $C_2(t)$ are the consumption levels for commodities 1 and 2 at time t, and d is the universal rate of time preference.
4. No loss of substance is involved by this simplification, nor by the restriction of the argument to two primary inputs and two produced commodities.
5. For each commodity, own use is set equal to zero.
6. Although the positions of points a and b depend on the primary input endowment, the magnitude of k is independent of the input endowment and depends only upon the production coefficients of the two techniques. This is, of course, a direct implication of the Rybczynski theorem.
7. Neither the fact that we assume a circulating, rather than a fixed, capital model nor the fact that wages and rents are paid at the end of the production cycle, rather than at the beginning, materially affects our analysis.
8. For details, see Essay 2 above, where the case without a factor market distortion is discussed. On distortions, see Batra [1], chapter 10.
9. Actually $\alpha > 1$, while a sufficient condition for the stated result, is not necessary. It can be shown that sign $[\partial p/\partial (W/w)] = $ sign $[(A_1/a_1) - (A_2/\alpha a_2)]$ for a; similarly for b. We therefore assume that $\alpha > (A_2 a_1/A_1 a_2) > (B_2 a_1/A_1 b_2)$; see Batra [1], pp. 243–7.
10. Since $\underline{p}^a$ holds when $(W/w) = 0$, and $\bar{p}^a$ holds when $(W/w) = \infty$, it follows from (2) and (3) that

$$\underline{p}^a = \frac{a_1 + a_{21} a_2 \alpha \beta}{a_{12} a_1 \beta + \alpha a_2}, \quad \bar{p}^a = \frac{A_1 + a_{21} A_2 \beta}{a_{12} A_1 \beta + A_2}.$$

A Note on the Gain from Trade 63

11. For $\beta > 1$, $p < p^*$ does not necessarily imply that technique a will be chosen instead of technique b; see Essay 2 above. Note that we ignore any effects of a distortion and a positive rate of interest upon the set of techniques defining the production possibility frontier. Nothing is lost from the present discussion by ignoring this.
12. Since the sign of ($\partial p^*/\partial \beta$) is not known *a priori*, it follows that $(d\alpha/d\beta)$, for $p = p^*$, may be positive or negative (($\partial p^*/\partial \alpha$), will, of course, be negative).
13. See Batra [1], p. 87, and Kemp [2], p. 259. We ignore any effect of trade on primary input supplies.
14. Note that because we work in terms of a limited number of techniques, our use of the term 'marginal rate of transformation' is not strictly equivalent to that of the literature, where an infinite number of techniques is normally assumed. However, nothing of substance is involved: we merely replace strict equalities by weak inequalities, when appropriate.
15. The possibility thus arises that the specialisation 'loss' may outweigh the exchange 'gain' giving an overall loss from trade. This, however, is secondary to the main point about a distortion, which is that in its presence the profit–maximising choice of technique can yield a specialisation 'loss'.
16. See Spaventa [4], pp. 170–5.
17. Note carefully that Z_A is the value of primary income that would result if, at international prices, the autarkic technique of production were to be utilised.

REFERENCES

[1] Batra, R. N. *Studies in the Pure Theory of International Trade*. Macmillan, London, 1973.
[2] Kemp, M. C. *The Pure Theory of International Trade and Investment*. Prentice–Hall, Englewood Cliffs, N. J., 1969.
[3] Robbins, L. 'On a certain ambiguity in the conception of stationary equilibrium'. *Economic Journal*, 1930, pp. 194–214.
[4] Spaventa, L. 'Notes on problems of transition between techniques'. In J. A. Mirrlees and N. H. Stern (eds.), *Models of Economic Growth*, Macmillan, London, 1973.

5 Heterogeneous Capital and the Heckscher–Ohlin–Samuelson Theory of Trade*

J. S. METCALFE and IAN STEEDMAN

While many objections have been raised as to the validity of the assumptions underlying the Heckscher–Ohlin–Samuelson theory of trade, that theory is widely regarded as immune from criticism of its internal logic, once the assumptions are granted. If the theory is to be useful in the understanding of real world trade, however, the assumption that each country has a given endowment of capital must be interpreted in such a way that the heterogeneity of capital goods can be allowed for. Such an interpretation is indeed possible but it immediately raises doubts as to whether recent results from the controversy over capital theory might not show the internal logic of the HOS analysis to be open to criticism. The object of the essay is to suggest that the existence of heterogeneous capital goods does lead to a breakdown of the logic of the HOS theory and hence to that of its major conclusions.

THE ASSUMPTIONS

In order to focus attention explicitly on the role of capital in HOS trade theory we shall make the normal assumptions of the *two* consumption commodity, *two* factor, *two* country model of trade. Thus we assume that:

(a) two countries, A and B, produce the same two consumption commodities, 1 and 2,

(b) each country has a given endowment of factors, identical with respect to the quality of the factors but different with respect to relative quantities,

(c) productive techniques are identical between countries and are of the constant returns to scale type everywhere,

(d) the two consumption commodities are produced with different and uniquely ordered factor intensities. There are thus no 'factor intensity reversals',

(e) all consumers in the two country world have identical homothetic preference maps,

(f) perfect competition rules in all markets, transport costs are absent and there is free trade in consumption commodities (unless otherwise stated).

It is to be stressed that we make all the above assumptions and that our analysis is in no way concerned with the usual objections to HOS theory based on the rejection of one or more of the above assumptions. We are thus solely concerned with the internal logic of the argument.

Assumption (b) requires further consideration. It is assumed that a country's factor endowment consists of given supplies of two homogeneous resources, one of which is taken to be labour. If the other were taken to be an endowment of a single homogeneous capital good, then the HOS analysis would be logically unassailable[1] but would be of limited interest until it were known that the results could be extended to systems in which there are many different capital goods. The object of this essay is to question the possibility of such an extension.

It might be thought that one way of allowing for the heterogeneity of capital goods would be to relax the assumption that there are only two factors and to interpret a country's 'endowment of capital' as a given *set* of physically specified capital goods.[2] (The simple analysis with two factors and two commodities could then be presented as a useful first step toward the full analysis.) Such an interpretation of capital endowment would, however, be out of place in a theory of comparative advantage, since the latter 'would seem properly to be a long-run theory'[3] and, by definition, in a long-run equilibrium analysis, the stocks of physical capital goods are not given but have been so chosen (by profit-maximising capitalists) as to yield a uniform rate of return. The normal concern of HOS trade theory has always been the comparison of long-run equilibria and in such analyses the assumption of given sets of capital goods can have no place.[4]

Assumption (b) can, however, be given an alternative interpretation which is quite consistent with the existence of many different capital goods, namely, that the capital endowment consists of a given equilibrium value of capital in terms of some standard of value.[5] The physical composition of the capital stock is then free to vary in accordance with the variations in the pattern of consumption commodity output, provided only that the value of the stock is constant and equal to the given capital endowment. Since a central feature of HOS trade theory is that no-trade factor prices are related to factor endowments we can, indeed, say that, with heterogeneous capital goods, we *have* to interpret the capital endowment as a value of capital. If there are many different capital goods then the 'price of capital' can only mean the rate of interest and the only 'factor quantity' to which a rate of interest can be related is, ultimately, a value of capital.[6]

That the 'capital endowment' has been taken to be a value aggregate is strikingly confirmed by the discussion of the Leontief paradox.[7] In both his papers, Leontief measured 'capital' in value units and while the ensuing discussion of his tests of HOS theory has been both long and highly critical, no one has ever questioned, so far as we know, the appropriateness of using a value measure of capital when testing the HOS theory. (Indeed those who have sought to remove the paradox by taking account of 'human capital' have done so precisely by summing human and non-human capital in value terms.) We would suggest that anyone wishing to argue that the capital endowment has *not* been taken to be a value aggregate is obliged to explain why, in that case, Leontief's work has been thought to constitute a test of HOS theory.

In this paper we shall therefore assume that each country has a given endowment of 'capital value' measured, let us say, in terms of the first consumption commodity.[8] We not only ignore the possibility of international transfers of 'free' capital but also rule out the possibility of trade in produced means of production; the latter assumption is made simply in order to confine our attention to the normal static HOS analysis, in which only consumption commodities are traded.

TWO CRUCIAL RELATIONSHIPS

The HOS analysis depends crucially on the properties of two relationships;

1. The consumption commodity price ratio is monotonically related to the rate of interest;
2. The rate of interest is monotonically related to the capital–labour ratio in the production of each commodity.

These relations are displayed in Figure 5.1.

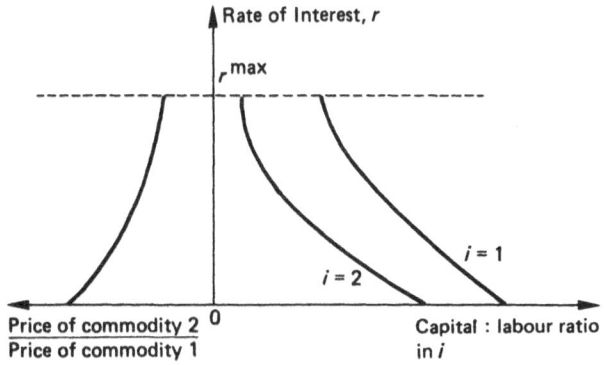

FIGURE 5.1

The righthand side of Figure 5.1 illustrates the relationship between the rate of interest and the capital : labour ratios in the two consumption commodity industries, industry one being the more capital intensive at each rate of interest. Notionally higher rates of interest are associated with more labour intensive processes of production in each industry and with a lower relative price of commodity two, as shown in the lefthand side of Figure 5.1. That there is no objection to using the rate of interest on the vertical axis, rather than a rent/wage ratio, has been shown by Samuelson.[9] It will be clear that this formulation with the rate of interest has to be used in a discussion of the multi-capital good world, since in such a world, in long-run equilibrium, the rate of interest must be uniform on the value of all capital goods while the rentals on different capital goods will, in general, differ.

Now if assumption (b) is interpreted to mean that the non-labour resource is a single homogeneous capital good, then the relationships 1 and 2 do indeed follow from assumptions (b) to (d). However, if assumption (b) is interpreted in terms of homogeneous labour and a given *value* of capital, then these two crucial relationships are *not* entailed by assumptions (b) to (d). The next section of this paper will be devoted to a proof of this assertion by means of a numerical example. In the subsequent sections we shall discuss the implications of this assertion for the fundamental theorems in HOS trade theory.

A NUMERICAL EXAMPLE

In this section we present a numerical example of an economy in which net output consists of quantities of two consumption commodities. Each consumption commodity is produced in its own integrated sector, a sector, that is, which produces the consumption commodity in question by means of labour and a machine and also produces that machine by means of labour and further machines of the same type. The *kind* of machine used will vary as the rate of interest varies but at any given interest rate the same kind of machine is used in the production of machines and of the consumption commodity.[10] We are able to refer to the use of machines, rather than machine services, in production since all machines in our example are fully used up (worn out) within one year. In both sectors there is an infinite number of alternative constant-returns-to-scale methods of producing the consumption commodity; thus we make the normal assumptions about the available methods of production.

Since production is by means of labour and *heterogeneous* capital goods, we mean the *value* of capital per worker when we refer to the capital intensity in either sector and if we are to compare the capital intensities in the two sectors, as we need to, we must value the capital in the two sectors in terms of a common standard. We use as our common standard of value the first consumption commodity. Our example has been so constructed that, in the sense just explained, production of the first consumption commodity is more capital-intensive than that of the second at every interest rate. There is, in other words, *no* 'factor-intensity-reversal' in our example and we may unambiguously refer to the first consumption commodity as the more capital-intensive commodity.

We take as our first integrated sector, the sector producing the first consumption commodity, the sector for which the relevant data are set out in Table II of the Appendix to Garegnani's paper [6], p. 429. This table gives, for thirteen alternative values of the interest rate, r, the value of the wage in terms of the first consumption commodity, w_1 say, and the value of capital per worker, in the integrated sector, in the same standard, k_1 say. We take as our second integrated sector, producing the second consumption commodity, a sector which belongs to the family of sectors discussed by Garegnani [6], pp. 431–2. In this second sector, the wage in terms of the *second* consumption commodity, w_2, is given by

$$w_2 = 1 - r - 20r^2$$

Heterogeneous Capital and H–O–S Theory

and the value of capital per worker, in terms of the *second* consumption commodity, k_2' is given by

$$k_2' = 1 - 10r + 50r^2$$

For each of the interest rates appearing in Garegnani's Table II we can calculate w_2 and k_2'; the price ratio of the two consumption commodities, (p_2/p_1), is then calculated[11] from $(p_2/p_1) = (w_1/w_2)$ and the capital-intensity in sector two, in terms of the *first* consumption commodity, k_2, is calculated from $k_2 = (p_2/p_1)k_2'$. We thus obtain our Table 5.1.

TABLE 5.1

$r\%$	(p_2/p_1)	k_1	k_2
0	0.200	1.080	0.200
2.6	0.182	0.635	0.141
4.1	0.183	0.393	0.123
6.1	0.184	0.257	0.106
8.3	0.194	0.184	0.100
10.5	0.213	0.148	0.107
12.9	0.240	0.179	0.130
14.4	0.238	0.379	0.142
15.1	0.211	0.552	0.133
15.9	0.182	0.715	0.123
16.9	0.158	0.850	0.117
17.5	0.122	0.947	0.095
20.0	0.103	1.000	0.103

On plotting the price ratio and the two capital-intensities as functions of the interest rate, in the usual way, we obtain Figure 5.2.

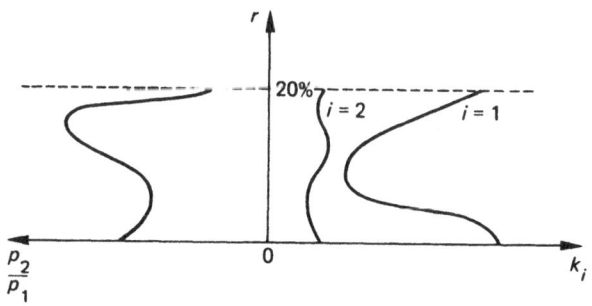

FIGURE 5.2

70 Fundamental Issues in Trade Theory

It will be seen at once that Figure 5.2 is strikingly different from Figure 5.1. On the righthand side we find that in neither sector is there an inverse, monotonic relation between the interest rate and the capital-intensity of the technique used. On the lefthand side we find that, despite the complete absence of 'factor-reversal' on the righthand side, there is not a monotonic relation between the consumption commodity price ratio and the rate of interest. Thus both the crucial relations on which HOS trade theory rests are, in general, invalid when there are heterogeneous capital goods, even when all the normal linear process assumptions are made about the available methods of production.[12]

THE BASIC THEOREM

We now use the results of the last section to discuss the fundamental propositions of the Heckscher–Ohlin–Samuelson analysis; we naturally start with the basic theorem relating the pattern of trade to the relative 'factor endowments' of the two countries. This basic theorem may be stated in two alternative forms, corresponding to 'price' and to 'quantity' interpretations of relative factor endowment. When the two factors are 'capital' and labour and their relative 'prices' are expressed by the rate of interest, these two forms of the theorem become:

1. The country with the lower *no-trade* rate of interest will export the capital-intensive consumption commodity;
2. The country with the higher ratio of capital to labour will export the capital-intensive consumption commodity.

We have shown in our example that, when capital goods are heterogeneous, the usual assumptions (*a*) to (*f*) do not entail the existence of a monotonic relation between the rate of interest and the consumption commodity price ratio. It follows immediately that the basic theorem in form 1, the 'price' form, is not of general validity when capital goods are heterogeneous. (This is easily seen from the lefthand side of Figure 5.2.)

The failure of the basic theorem in its 'price' form leads, in turn, to the conclusion that it is not of general validity in its 'quantity' form, form 2 above, even if the country with the higher ratio of capital to labour has the lower no-trade interest rate.[13] All that would be guaranteed by an inverse relation between relative capital–labour ratios and relative no-trade interest rates would be that the theorem either gave a correct prediction in both forms or gave a false prediction in both forms. If there is not such an inverse relation then the basic theorem could give a correct prediction in one form and a false prediction in the other form. More important, however, is the simple result that, with heterogeneous capital goods and endowments of 'value capital', neither form of the basic theorem is of general validity; the assumptions (a) to (f) do not lead to any predictions about the pattern of trade.

THE STOLPER–SAMUELSON THEOREM

The Stolper–Samuelson theorem states, essentially, that an increase in the domestic relative price of a consumption commodity will raise the real return to the factor used relatively intensively in the production of that commodity. Since this result depends on there being a monotonic relationship between the consumption commodity price ratio and the interest rate, our example shows that it is not of general validity in a world with heterogeneous capital goods.

Consider country B and suppose that it is importing consumption commodity two, the labour intensive commodity, at international terms of trade p. In Figure 5.3 these terms of trade are consistent with interest rates of r_1, r_2 and r_3 in B.

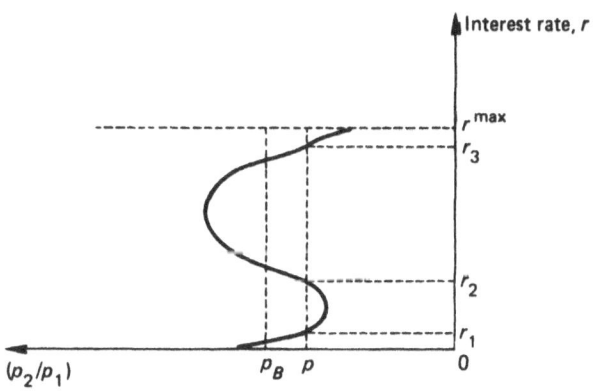

FIGURE 5.3

Suppose now that a tariff is imposed on B's imports and that, as in the original Stolper–Samuelson analysis [16], the imposition of the tariff leaves the international price ratio, p, unaltered. The domestic consumption commodity price ratio will increase to, say, p_B but whether the interest rate will rise or fall it is impossible to say. If, for example, the no-tariff interest rate were r_2 then, even if the tariff led to the smallest of the three possible interest rate changes in Figure 5.3, the with-tariff interest rate would be higher than r_2.[14] Now in any system of production involving no joint products, the interest rate is inversely related to the real wage rate, no matter what (single or composite) commodity the latter is measured in terms of:[15] a rise in the interest rate would then imply a fall in the real wage. Since, as we have seen, a tariff on the labour-intensive import can *raise* the interest rate, it follows that such a tariff can *lower* the real wage. With heterogeneous capital goods, there is no *a priori* relation between the consumption commodity price ratio and the real wage, even in the absence of 'factor reversal', and hence the HOS analysis tells us nothing about the effect of a tariff on income distribution, even when the terms of trade are unaffected by the tariff.

EQUALISATION OF THE INTEREST RATE AND REAL WAGE

As we have shown by means of our numerical example, in a world with heterogeneous capital goods there need not be a one-to-one relation between the consumption commodity price ratio and the rate of interest. It follows immediately that free trade in the two consumption commodities does *not* guarantee that both countries have the same interest rate and real wage when they trade with one another, even if specialisation is incomplete in both countries.[16, 17]

THE LEONTIEF PARADOX

We consider, finally, Leontief's statistical findings [10, 11] that the ratio of value capital to labour in the production of US exports was less than the corresponding ratio for competitive US imports. Since the USA is generally considered to be abundantly endowed with capital per worker relative to its major trading partners, these findings appeared to contradict the basic HOS theorem in its 'quantity' form.[18] A common response to this 'paradox' was to modify the assumptions (*a*) to (*f*) so as to obtain predictions consistent with Leontief's findings.[19] We have shown above, however, that, in the presence of heterogeneous capital goods, there is no need to modify any of the assumptions in order to remove the 'paradox'; it is sufficient to recognise that when the endowment of capital means the value of capital, the HOS analysis gives no prediction whatever concerning the pattern of trade and thus neither Leontief's findings nor any other empirical findings relating to the pattern of trade can be regarded as 'paradoxical'.

CONCLUSION

The Heckscher–Ohlin–Samuelson analysis of trade has always been concerned with the comparison of static long-run equilibria. In such a comparison, in a world of heterogeneous capital goods, the assumption that each country has a given endowment of capital must be interpreted to mean that it has a given value of capital. It then follows, from recent work in the theory of capital, that there is no rational basis for the existence of the two crucial relations on which HOS analysis turns. It follows that the basic HOS theorem (in either form), the Stolper–Samuelson theorem and the interest-rate equalisation theorem all cease to hold. For an analysis of real-world trade the HOS analysis is therefore of somewhat limited use.

Recent arguments in the theory of capital, value and distribution have not only undermined the theoretical foundations of the HOS analysis, i.e. the neoclassical analysis of value and distribution: they have also suggested that the work of the classical economists, such as Ricardo, may prove to be a valuable starting point for the analysis of capital, value and distribution.[20] This suggests that it may be fruitful for trade theorists to return to Ricardo's approach to the analysis of trade. In saying this, we do not suggest that no-trade price ratios should be assumed to be equal to embodied labour ratios, for the essential features of Ricardo's approach can be retained without that assumption. Nor do we suggest that the role of capital and interest should be glossed over, as it is in much analysis described as 'Ricardian'; on the contrary, we suggest first that trade theorists might follow Ricardo in regarding the theory of distribution as a major concern of economic theory and second that the production of and trade in produced means of production should be placed at the centre of trade theory.

NOTES

*This paper was presented to the conference of the Association of University Teachers of Economics, Aberystwyth, 1972, and then published in the conference proceedings: J. M. Parkin (ed.), *Essays in Modern Economics*, Longman, London, 1973. We should like to thank C. J. Bliss and J. M. Parkin for helpful comments. (See also note 17, below.)

1. The HOS theory is also logically unassailable if the second resource is taken to be homogeneous land.
2. Since our objection to such a procedure does not turn on the well-known problems which arise when the number of factors is different from the number of commodities, the reader may assume that the number of commodities is assumed to increase *pari passu*.
3. Robinson [13], p. 23. Cf. Kenen's statement: 'Because trade theory is concerned with long-run phenomena, it must treat capital as a stock of "waiting", not as a collection of tangible assets' [9], p. 438. It may also be noted that with given *sets* of capital goods a distinctive feature of HOS theory, the comparison of the countries' relative capital endowments, would be lost.
4. To avoid a possible ambiguity, it should be noted that the usual HOS analysis is, in the sense given by Robbins [12], a static and not a stationary analysis.
5. Cf. Caves [4], pp. 94–6 and the references there given to Ohlin and Haberler. This interpretation of the capital endowment appears, often *implicitly*, in much of the HOS literature. It has been given quite explicitly by Acheson [1], pp. 565–6, who also discusses its frequent implicit use.
6. We say 'ultimately' because, of course, theories have been constructed in which the rate of interest is related to the value of capital only indirectly, there being one or more intervening variables, such as an average period of production or a number of absolute periods of production. Note that in his discussion of trade theory Wicksell assumed explicitly that the available quantity of capital in a country is a sum of value in terms of some standard [18], p. 198.
7. For references, see the section on The Leontief Paradox, below.
8. Since the no-trade commodity price ratio will differ between the two countries, it follows that the country ranking by 'capital–labour' ratio may depend on the choice of value standard. While this would appear to be rather awkward for HOS trade theory, it is not important for our argument.
9. See [14], p. 43, Figure 2. Note that this presupposes the reproducibility of the capital good(s); cf. Kemp [8], pp. 82–3.
10. There is no relation between the kinds of machine used in the two, different, integrated sectors at a given interest rate.
11. At $r = 20$ per cent, $w_1 = w_2 = 0$ and in calculating (p_2/p_1) we therefore replaced (w_1/w_2) by the limit of (w_1/w_2) as r tends to 20 per cent.
12. We have not asserted, it may be noted, that in the presence of heterogeneous capital goods both the crucial relations *inevitably* break down. One can, at will, construct numerical examples in which both relations hold, in which neither holds or in which one holds but the other does not; all that is necessary for our argument is that the two relations do not *necessarily* hold good. While most of our argument will turn on the non-monotonicity of the interest-rate/price ratio relation, it must be remembered that the conditions for the possibility of incomplete specialisation are generally discussed in terms of the right-hand side of the standard diagram.

Heterogeneous Capital and H–O–S Theory 75

13. It should not be taken for granted that there would be an inverse relation between relative capital–labour ratios and no-trade interest rates.
14. Of the two with-tariff interest rates involving 'larger' interest rate changes in Figure 5.3, one would be above r_2 and the other below it.
15. With joint production, the interest rate may be positively related to the real wage in terms of certain commodities (see Sraffa [15], pp. 61–2) but such a relation would not, of course, serve to restore the validity of the Stolper–Samuelson theorem.
16. This result might appear to conflict with Samuelson's conclusion [14], p. 49, but in fact, as Bliss has pointed out [3], pp. 342–3, Samuelson's 'conclusion' is quite empty, in effect stating that equalisation will occur when conditions are such as to make it occur.
17. As was stated in the note* above, this paper was first presented at a conference and then published in the proceedings. In his interesting discussion of the paper (both at the conference and in the proceedings) Christopher Bliss suggested that the 'interest rate equalisation theorem' breaks down here because the capital goods are *untraded*, rather than because of the mere fact of capital good heterogeneity. For further discussion of this important question, see Essay 6 in this volume.
18. See Bhagwati [2], pp. 24–5, for a discussion of similar studies relating to Canada, East Germany, India and Japan.
19. E.g., Clemhout [5], Jones [7], Valavanis-Vail [17].
20. We have in mind particularly, of course, the work of Sraffa [15].

REFERENCES

[1] Acheson, K. 'The aggregation of heterogeneous capital goods and various trade theorems'. *Journal of Political Economy*, 1970, pp. 565–71.
[2] Bhagwati, J. 'The pure theory of international trade: a survey'. *Economic Journal*, 1964, pp. 1–84.
[3] Bliss, C. J. 'Collected scientific papers of Paul Samuelson'. *Economic Journal*, 1967, pp. 338–45.
[4] Caves, R. E. *Trade and Economic Structure*. Harvard University Press, 1960.
[5] Clemhout, S. 'Production function analysis applied to the Leontief scarce-factor paradox of international trade'. *Manchester School*, 1963, pp. 103–14.
[6] Garegnani, P. 'Heterogeneous capital, the production function and the theory of distribution'. *Review of Economic Studies*, 1970, pp. 407–36.
[7] Jones, R. 'Factor proportions and the Heckscher–Ohlin theorem'. *Review of Economic Studies*, 1956–7, pp. 1–10.
[8] Kemp, M. C. *The Pure Theory of International Trade and Investment*. Prentice-Hall, 1969.
[9] Kenen, P. B. 'Nature, capital and trade'. *Journal of Political Economy*, 1965, pp. 437–60.
[10] Leontief, W. 'Domestic production and foreign trade: the American capital position re-examined'. *Proceedings of the American Philosophical Society*, 1953, pp. 332–49.
[11] Leontief, W. 'Factor proportions and the structure of American trade:

further theoretical analysis'. *Review of Economics and Statistics*, 1956, pp. 386–407.
[12] Robbins, L. 'On a certain ambiguity in the conception of stationary equilibrium'. *Economic Journal*, 1930, pp. 194–214.
[13] Robinson, R. 'Factor proportions and comparative advantage: Part I'. *Quarterly Journal of Economics*, 1956, pp. 169–92.
[14] Samuelson, P. A. 'Equalization by trade of the interest rate along with the real wage'. In R. E. Baldwin, *et al.* (eds.), *Trade, Growth and the Balance of Payments (Essays in Honor of Gottfried Haberler)*, North-Holland, 1965.
[15] Sraffa, P. *Production of Commodities by Means of Commodities*. Cambridge University Press, 1960.
[16] Stolper, W. F. and Samuelson, P. A. 'Protection and real wages'. *Review of Economic Studies*, 1941, pp. 58–73.
[17] Valavanis–Vail, S. 'Leontief's scarce factor paradox'. *Journal of Political Economy*, 1954, pp. 523–8.
[18] Wicksell, K. *Lectures on Political Economy*, Vol. 1. Routledge & Kegan Paul, 1934.

6 Relative Prices and 'Factor Price' Equalisation in a Heterogeneous Capital Goods Model*

L. MAINWARING

In recent years there has been some debate on the consequences for some well-known international trade theorems of the inclusion of heterogeneous capital goods in the process of production.[1] In one contribution Steedman and Metcalfe [12] have shown by means of a simple numerical example that the equalisation by trade of so-called 'factor prices', the wage and rate of profits, may not occur in these circumstances. Such a result requires a non-monotonic relationship between relative commodity prices and 'factor prices'. The purpose of this paper is to examine this relationship in the context of a multi-commodity, multi-technique circulating capital model of the type familiarised by Sraffa [11]. We shall attempt to show that circumstances exist in which 'factor price' equalisation (f.p.e. for short) may not be realised, and that such circumstances are not dependent on there being complete international specialisation, nor on reversals of 'factor' intensity.

We begin by considering price behaviour with a single technique, and then generalise to the case of many techniques.

A SINGLE TECHNIQUE

Consider an economy in which m commodities are produced by means of labour and the same m commodities. Production takes place in annual cycles with the wage paid at the end of each cycle. The technique is summarised by the matrix $||a_{ij}||$, where a_{ij} $(i, j = 1, 2, \ldots, m)$ is the input of commodity i required in the production of one unit of commodity j; and the vector $(a_1, a_2, \ldots, a_m)$, where a_j is the input of labour required in the production of a unit of j. Each commodity is 'basic' in the sense of Sraffa [11], p. 8.

Taking good 1 (arbitrarily) as the standard of value, the price equations for each activity may be written[2]

$$p_j = (1+r)\Sigma_{i=1}^m p_i a_{ij} + w a_j \quad (j = 1, 2, \ldots, m) \qquad (1)$$

where w is the wage in terms of good 1; p_j the price of good j relative to that of good 1 ($p_1 = 1$); and r the rate of profits. Competition ensures that w, r and relative prices are the same for each activity. From these equations may be derived the 'wage curve', a trade-off relationship between the wage and the rate of profit.[3] This is downward sloping but may have inflexions.[4] Associated with each level of r ($0 \leqslant r \leqslant r_{max}$) there is one, and only one, vector of relative prices which is positive and finite [10]. We cannot say that this price vector (P) varies with r in a definite way[5] but, as we demonstrate below, we can say that a given price vector will not occur at more than one rate of profits, unless at *all* rates of profits.[6]

If we take each activity on its own, then for a *given* set of relative prices we can write out individual $w-r$ trade-off relationships; for activity j:

$$w = (p_j - \Sigma_i p_i a_{ij} - r\Sigma_i p_i a_{ij})/a_j \qquad (2)$$

Each activity trade-off is a straight line at a given set of prices. It is in the nature of a competitive solution to (1) that for any rate of profits, w and P are the same for each activity. Let w^*, r^* and P^* represent a competitive equilibrium. Then the individual trade-off lines for the set of relative prices P^* must all pass through the point w^*, r^* (Figure 6.1).

Inspection of equation (2) shows that if the vector of prices (*i.e.*, the p_i) is given ($p_i = p_i^*$) the slopes and intercepts of the trade-offs are fixed. Now two possibilities arise: either (i) the trade-offs for *all* activities have the same slopes and (since they must all pass through the same point, w^*, r^*) the same intercepts; or (ii) at least two trade-offs have different slopes and hence different intercepts.

Consider the first possibility. The slope of the trade-off for good j is $\Sigma_i p_i a_{ij}/a_j$ which is the ratio of value of direct capital: labour.[7] For the first possibility to arise, then, the value-capital: labour ratios are the same for every activity at the set of prices P^*. Since the trade-offs all pass through the same point w^*, r^* they must coincide; at the set of prices P^*

Relative Prices with Many Capital Goods 79

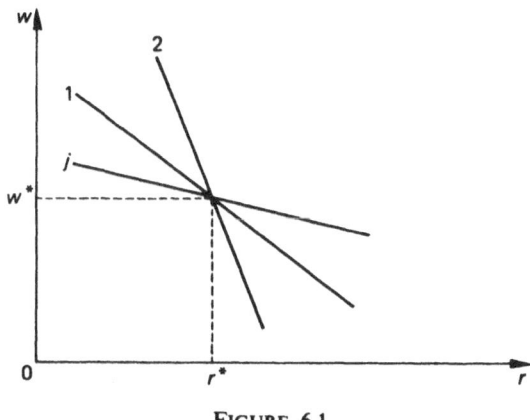

FIGURE 6.1

an infinite number of combinations of w and r is possible: the wage curve is a straight line and relative prices are constant.[8]

With a single technique this is the only case in which a given price vector can, in equilibrium, be associated with more than one value of r, for consider the second possibility. If at least two trade-offs have different slopes and different intercepts then there is only one combination of w and r through which they can pass, at a given set of prices. Hence at prices P^* the solution w^*, r^* is unique.[9]

Our line of argument fits in neatly with Sraffa's distinction between 'deficit' and 'surplus' industries [11], Ch. III. The former are those industries having relatively high value-capital: labour ratios at a given level of the wage, and the latter those industries having a relatively low ratio.[10] In other words, deficit industries are those whose straight line trade-offs have a relatively large (absolute) slope, surplus industries those having a relatively small slope, at the set of prices prevailing at a given wage.

In Figure 6.2 suppose that the trade-offs are drawn for a deficit industry i and a surplus industry j. Let us consider a move in logical time along the wage curve from the initial point $w'r'$ to $w''r''$, and let us suppose, initially, that this move could be completed without any change in relative prices. It follows that the trade-offs for i and j are fixed. With a reduction in the wage from w' to w'' at a constant set of prices, after payment of the wage at the *new* rate, deficit industries do not have sufficient value of net output to make profits payments at the new general rate r''. That is, they have a deficit on their profits payments. Thus industry i is able to pay profit at the rate of only $w''d$ and is in deficit by

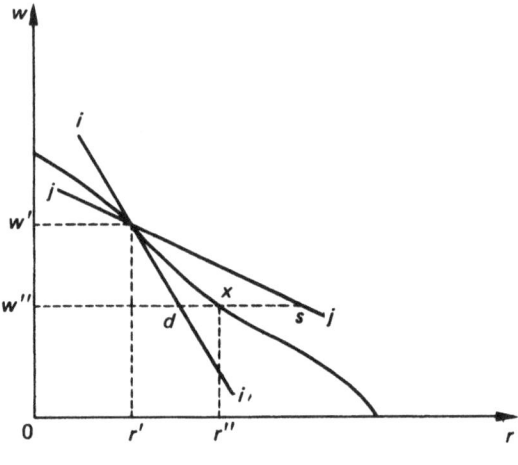

FIGURE 6.2

the amount dx (alternatively, if such industries pay the full rate of profits they have a deficit on wages payment). On the other hand, surplus industries have more than sufficient value of net output to pay both the wage and profits at the new general rate. Thus after payment of the wage at the rate w'' and profits at the rate r'', industry j is left with a surplus sx.

The point which Sraffa makes is that, in order to remove the deficits and surpluses, price changes are called for. There is an initial presumption that this objective could be attained if the prices of all deficit commodities increased and those of all surplus commodities decreased, but this does not necessarily follow:

> The reason for this seeming contradiction is that the means of production of an industry are themselves the product of one or more industries which may in their turn employ a still lower proportion of labour to means of production (and the same may be the case with these latter means of production, and so on); ... The result is that as the wages fall the price of the product of a ... 'deficit' industry may rise or it may fall, or it may even alternate in rising and falling ... [11], p. 14.

Consider the following example in which there are four basic commodities. For simplicity suppose there is only one deficit commodity (commodity 1) which is also the standard of value.[11] The trade-offs for these four industries are shown in Figure 6.3. Imagine a reduction of the

Relative Prices with Many Capital Goods 81

wage from w' to w''. The initial presumption is that the price of commodity 1 should rise relative to its means of production, i.e., relative to the value of some combination of 1, 2, 3 and 4. Since industry 1 is the only deficit industry its means of production *cannot* themselves be the product of one or more industries employing a still lower proportion of labour to means of production. Hence in this case the initial presumption is valid: the price of a unit of 1 rises relative to the value of 1, 2, 3 and 4 used in its production, and hence to the value of 2, 3 and 4 used in its production. Or, since we are taking commodity 1 as the standard of value, we know that, taken together the value of 2, 3 and 4, used in the production of unit of 1, falls.

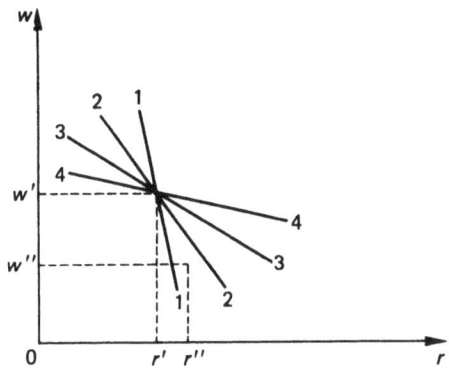

FIGURE 6.3

Now look at commodity 2. The initial presumption is that its price should fall. But commodity 2 has in its means of production some commodities (3 and 4) which are themselves products of industries with a still higher proportion of labour to means of production. Hence its price may fall, rise or alternate. Conceivably, then, its price relative to that of commodity 1 might be the same as it was initially. The same reasoning applies to commodity 3–again its price may remain the same. Commodity 4, however, is not the product of commodities having a still higher proportion of labour to means of production, and the initial presumption must carry through–its price must fall. Thus, starting with a price vector $[1, p_2, p_3, p_4]$ at a wage w', we might possibly have a price vector $[1, p_2, p_3, p_4^*]$ at a wage w'', where $p_4 > p_4^*$.

A similar argument applies if we increase the number of commodities, including deficit commodities. Then corresponding to distinct levels of

82 Fundamental Issues in Trade Theory

the wage we might have price vectors having some common elements but differing in at least one element. Thus, while it is not possible, in general, for the entire price vector to be repeated, it is possible that the relative prices of some sub-set of commodities be repeated, over a range of the rate of profits.[12]

MANY TECHNIQUES

In the last section we effectively derived the proposition that the wage curve in an m-commodity economy is the locus of intersections of the individual activity trade-offs at given (continuous) sets of relative prices. If we assume away the possibility of equal capital : labour ratios, a given price vector cannot be associated with more than one point on the wage curve of a single technique. We now propose to show that a given price vector may repeat itself at different rates of profits when there exists more than one technique.

Consider two alternative techniques, A and B, which can be used for producing three commodities, and suppose that *they have one method in common*–method 1. The trade-off for that method at the set of prices p^* is shown by the straight line 1–1 in Figure 6.4 along with A's wage curve AA. At these prices the rate of profits and wage appropriate to technique A are r' and w'. We have to show that these prices can occur at a different combination of r and w, say r'' and w'', when the alternative technique B is operated. In other words we must find two methods, 2_B and 3_B, which,

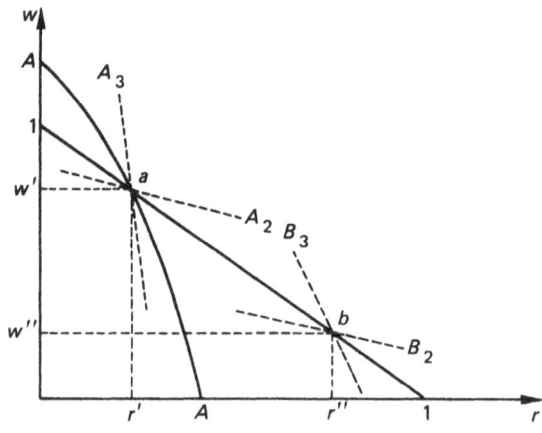

FIGURE 6.4

when allied to method 1, form a technique whose $w-r$ frontier passes through point b.

The price equations of these methods must satisfy

$$p_i^* = (1 + r'')(b_{1i} + p_2^* b_{2i} + p_3^* b_{3i}) + w'' b_i \qquad (i = 2, 3)$$

It is not difficult to find non-negative coefficients which satisfy these equations[13] and which, therefore, may be used to construct the required technique B.

By similar reasoning it is clear that if A and B have *no* methods in common there is no reason why prices P^* should not be associated with one r, w combination on A and another on B. From this it might appear trivial that the price vector can recur when there exists more than one technique. However, we have so far neglected the fact that when there exist two techniques which differ by more than one method then there also exist a number of techniques made up of combinations of these two. For example, given two techniques A and B consisting of the methods $[1, 2_A, 3_A]$ and $[1, 2_B, 3_B]$, there also exist techniques C and D comprising $[1, 2_A, 3_B]$ and $[1, 2_B, 3_A]$. Though it is *necessary* to show that the same prices may occur at two points a and b in Figure 6.4, the possibility of recurrence is only economically meaningful if at $r = r'$ technique A dominates (*i.e.*, is more profitable than) other possible techniques, while at $r = r''$ B is dominant. Although we have been unable to give mathematical expression to this condition, the possibility is demonstrated in Appendix I by a simple numerical example for the three-commodity case.[14]

There are, however, additional restrictions to price vector recurrence. Returning to Figure 6.4, we know that through point a on AA there pass two other trade-offs (for methods 2_A and 3_A) appropriate to prices P^*. If A's wage curve is not a straight line then at least one of these trade-offs has a slope different from that of 1-1. In the first instance suppose that no two trade-offs have the same slope and consider an alternative technique C having *two* methods (1 and 2_A) in common with A. If prices P^* are to occur when technique C is in operation it must be at that rate of profits at which the trade-offs for 1 and 2_A intersect, i.e., it must be at r'. Thus unless techniques C and A switch at point a, prices P^* cannot occur at any rate of profits when C is operated. In either event P^* cannot occur at two distinct rates of profits using only A and C.

We may repeat this argument for any number of commodities and, provided that the trade-offs for all m methods of technique A have different slopes at prices P^*, we can state the following: a necessary condition for the repetition of the price vector at distinct rates of profits is that the most profitable techniques at these rates have *not more than one activity* in common.

The preceding argument assumes away the possibility that at prices P^* more than one of the trade-offs *do* have the same slope; e.g., in the three commodity case, the capital:labour ratios may be the same for methods 1 and 2_A. In this case repetition is possible even when A and C have these two methods in common since their trade-offs would coincide and both therefore pass through a and some other point c. But since it is our intention in the following section to show that f.p.e. may not occur under conditions which do not require such restrictive assumptions, we wish to show that we have no need to appeal to the possibility of several methods having the same capital:labour ratios at a given set of prices. Accordingly, we assume from now on that at no set of prices are there two or more methods having the same capital:labour ratios.

The above condition for repetition can be stated in an alternative form relating to the number of commodities. Any two techniques A and B generate additional techniques $C, D, \ldots$, some of which may not be (potentially) profitable in the sense that their wage curves do not comprise part of the wage envelope. We may define the technological possibilities of the economy as the set of available profitable techniques. The intersections of wage curves on the wage envelope are known as switch points. According to a theorem by Bruno *et al.* [3], '"Adjacent" techniques on two sides of a switching point will usually differ from each

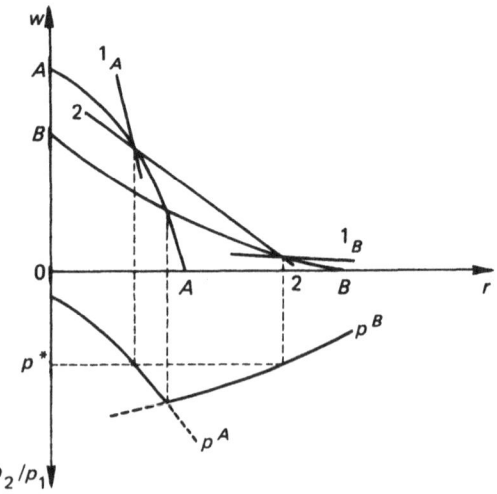

FIGURE 6.5

other only with respect to *one activity*' (their italics).[15] We have seen that if price recurrence is to occur in an m-commodity economy there must exist two profitable techniques having at least $m-1$ different methods. Since only one method changes with each switch of technique this requires that there are at least m profitable techniques in all. Thus price vector repetition may occur in an m-commodity economy in which there are m or more profitable techniques. The special case of a two-commodity economy, a numerical example of which is provided by Steedman and Metcalfe [12], is shown in Figure 6.5.

'FACTOR PRICE' EQUALISATION[16]

We are now in a position to make a general statement concerning the effect of trade[17] on the wages and rates of profits in the participating countries. As is usual in the f.p.e. literature, we assume (i) that countries are able to choose from the same set of available techniques, (ii) that countries are able to produce, with trade, some of all commodities.

Samuelson [9] has argued that with heterogeneous capital, under certain conditions, the rate of profits is equalised by trade in two goods (i and j) alone when there are 'uniform differences in factor intensity', the implication being that this condition is sufficient for p_i/p_j to be a monotonic function of r. Bliss [1] has argued that this is trivial, pointing to the fact that since Samuelson gives no definition of 'uniform differences in factor intensity' his assertion is essentially tautological. In the absence of such a definition it is not possible to establish f.p.e.[18] To see this, suppose that only $k(<m)$ commodities are traded. Then the relative prices of only those k commodities are determined internationally. We know that the relative prices of a sub-set of goods may be repeated over a range of the rate of profits *with only one technique*. Thus the existence of non-traded intermediate goods brings about the possibility of the non-equalisation of r and w. This view is consistent with that of Bliss who also contends, however, that it is the existence of non-traded intermediate goods rather than of heterogeneous capital, as such, that tends to prevent f.p.e.[19] In the remaining part of this section we shall assume that *all* m commodities enter trade.

It has been argued by Steedman and Metcalfe that, when there exists a choice of technique, 'world-wide uniformity of interest rates and real wage rates is . . . not ensured . . . This is because in an economy with a choice of technique more than one interest rate can be associated with a given set of relative commodity prices' [12]. While this is true we cannot infer that recurrence of the price vector may occur whenever there is a choice of technique, for, as we have seen, recurrence requires (i) that there exist at least m techniques (ii) that at those rates of profits where prices are the same for two techniques a third technique is not more profitable.[20]

As long as the number of techniques is less than m, the world price set is associated with a unique point on the wage envelope and the Samuelson theorem holds: each country has the same wage and rate of profits. But when the number of techniques is greater than or equal to the number of commodities there is a possibility that the world price set is associated with more than one point on the wage envelope. It no longer follows that trade will lead to the equalisation of the wages and rates of profits of the participating countries.

CONCLUSION

Our examination of price behaviour in a heterogeneous capital model has shown that when there are many commodities the relative prices of any two commodities need not be a monotonic function of the rate of profits, even if there is only one technique. This in itself contradicts Samuelson's f.p.e. theorem and is consistent with the view that the existence of non-traded intermediate goods may prevent the equalisation of 'factor prices'. But we have also shown that when all goods enter trade, if there is a sufficient number of techniques the price vector may be repeated over a range of the rate of profits. In this event the f.p.e. theorem breaks down solely as a result of the existence of heterogeneous capital goods.

APPENDIX

THE REPETITION OF THE PRICE VECTOR WITH MANY TECHNIQUES.[21]

Suppose there are three commodities. Only one method (1) exists for the production of commodity 1; two methods (2_a and 2_b) can be used for producing commodity 2; and two methods (3_a and 3_b) for producing commodity 3.

Relative Prices with Many Capital Goods

The vectors of commodity and labour inputs are

$$(j) \qquad (1) \qquad (2_a) \qquad (2_b) \qquad (3_a) \qquad (3_b)$$

$$\begin{bmatrix} a_{1j} \\ a_{2j} \\ a_{3j} \\ \text{----} \\ a_j \end{bmatrix} = \begin{bmatrix} 0 \\ 0.2 \\ 0 \\ \text{-----} \\ 0.05 \end{bmatrix}, \begin{bmatrix} 0.2 \\ 0 \\ 0.1 \\ \text{-----} \\ 0.2 \end{bmatrix}, \begin{bmatrix} 0 \\ 0 \\ 0.32 \\ \text{-----} \\ 0.06 \end{bmatrix}, \begin{bmatrix} 0.1 \\ 0.5 \\ 0 \\ \text{-----} \\ 0.45 \end{bmatrix}, \begin{bmatrix} 1.72 \\ 0 \\ 0 \\ \text{-----} \\ 0.19 \end{bmatrix}$$

This allows for the formation of the following techniques
$I = [1, 2_a, 3_a]$, $II = [1, 2_a, 3_b]$, $III = [1, 2_b, 3_a]$, $IV = [1, 2_b, 3_b]$.
The values of w for each of these techniques, at two distinct rates of profits, 0 and 1.0 are

	I	II	III	IV
$r = 0$	9.41	9.87	10.07	12
$r = 1.0$	4	3.89	1.96	0.97

At $r = 0$, the most profitable technique, IV, has $P = [1, 2, 4]$; at $r = 1.0$, the most profitable technique, I, has $P = [1, 2, 4]$. This set of prices therefore occurs at two distinct points on the wage envelope.

NOTES

*This essay was first published in *Australian Economic Papers*, 1976. I should like to thank, without implicating in any way, Ian Steedman, J. S. Metcalfe, J. A. Kregel and a referee of *A.E.P.* for their helpful comments.
1. See, e.g., Kemp [6] which also lists other relevant references.
2. The following definitions are used: *Activity i* refers to the general act of producing commodity i; *Methods*, e.g., (i_A and i_B) are particular (alternative) ways in which i may be produced; *Techniques* are simply combinations of methods of producing m commodities. Clearly, with a single technique there is a direct correspondence between activities and methods.
3. We offer no theory of distribution but merely say that the equilibrium combination of w and r lies somewhere on the wage curve.
4. The general properties of the wage curve have been well explored. See, e.g., Garegnani [4], particularly footnote 20.
5. Except in the two-commodity case, when p_1/p_2 is a monotonic function of r.
6. The following argument is an m-commodity generalisation of the analysis presented in [7], part III.
7. In Sraffa's terminology, the ratio of 'means of production' to labour.
8. This case corresponds to Marx's 'equal organic compositions of capital' case. The discussion, incidentally, demonstrates that in this case $p_j/a_j = p_i/a_i$.

88   Fundamental Issues in Trade Theory

9. We maintain this argument only in the case of a Leontief circulating capital technology.
10. There does, of course, exist a 'critical' ratio separating deficit and surplus industries, to which corresponds a conceptual industry having a 'balancing' proportion of labour to means of production which is invariant with respect to changes in the rate of profit (Sraffa [11], sections 17 and 21).
11. There must always be at least one deficit commodity and at least one surplus commodity (Sraffa [11], section 17).
12. The preceding is by way of explanation rather than proof but a demonstration is given in Essay 7 in this volume.
13. This can easily be verified by the solution

$$b_{ii} = 1/1 + r'', \quad b_i = b_{ji}(i \neq j) = 0.$$

14. It may be noted that in the example given by Steedman and Metcalfe [12] the two techniques considered differ in only one method so that additional techniques cannot be generated and the problem of domination by such techniques does not arise.
15. For the exception to this rule see Bruno et al. [3]. Note that on our definitions, 'activity' would be replaced by 'method'.
16. 'The so-called factor "price" equalisation theorem is concerned not with factor *prices*, that is, with the prices of more or less durable *capital assets*, but with factor rentals, that is, with the prices of factor services ... In fact the equalisation of rentals is neither a necessary nor sufficient condition of factor price equalisation. For the relation between a factor's rental and its price is determined by (among other things) the rate of interest ...' (Kemp [6], p. 82). It might be thought, therefore, that equalisation of rentals is independent of the equalisation of rates of profit. But, as Kemp goes on to say, this 'depends essentially on the assumption that capital is not itself produced'. In our analysis, for example, the traded commodities are also means of production. Therefore, the prices of traded capital goods are equalised by the assumption of common world prices. Thus, if good i is traded its rental rp_i must be equalised if the rates of profit are equalised. It follows that, for traded commodities, equalisation of the rates of profit implies equalisation of rentals, and vice versa.
17. 'The effect of trade' should not be considered as the consequence of a movement from no-trade to with-trade equilibrium but merely as a comparison of these equilibria.
18. We might add that even if this condition is given a quite plausible interpretation it is still not possible to establish f.p.e. This is discussed further in Essay 7 below.
19. See the discussion between Bliss and Metcalfe and Steedman [2, 8]. Bliss argues: 'Suppose on the other hand that we assume every produced good to be traded: then it is not difficult to show that any condition sufficient for the factor-price-equalisation theorem without capital goods will suffice with capital goods. Furthermore, it is clear that much weaker conditions would do for the capital good case, although these conditions have not yet been derived.' In what follows we consider this argument in the light of our analysis of the behaviour of relative prices.
20. Both these conditions are automatically fulfilled in the Steedman–Metcalfe

example since there are only two commodities and only two possible techniques. This simplicity is lost when the number of commodities is greater than two.

21. I should like to thank Mrs M. Foot for checking the following results.

REFERENCES

[1] Bliss, C. J. 'Collected scientific papers of Paul Samuelson'. *Economic Journal*, 1967, pp. 338–45.
[2] Bliss, C. J. 'Discussion' of Metcalfe and Steedman [8].
[3] Bruno, M. Burmeister, E. and Sheshinski, E. 'Nature and implications of the reswitching of techniques'. *Quarterly Journal of Economics*, 1969, pp. 526–53.
[4] Garegnani, P. 'Heterogeneous capital, the production function and the theory of distribution'. *Review of Economic Studies*, 1970, pp. 407–36.
[5] Kemp, M. C. *The Pure Theory of International Trade and Investment*, Prentice-Hall, Englewood Cliffs, 1969.
[6] Kemp, M. C. 'Heterogeneous capital goods and long-run Stolper–Samuelson theorems'. *Australian Economic Papers*, 1973, pp. 253–60.
[7] Mainwaring, L. 'A neo–Ricardian analysis of international trade'. *Kyklos*, 1974, pp. 537–53. See Essay 9 in this volume.
[8] Metcalfe, J. S. and Steedman, I. 'Heterogeneous capital and the Heckscher–Ohlin–Samuelson theory of trade'. In Parkin, J. M. (ed.) *Essays in Modern Economics*, Longman, London, 1973. See Essay 5 in this volume.
[9] Samuelson, P. A. 'Equalisation by trade of the interest rate along with the real wage'. In R. E. Baldwin, *et al.* (eds.), *Trade, Growth and the Balance of Payments* (*Essays in Honor of Gottfried Haberler*). Rand McNally, Chicago, 1965.
[10] Schwartz, J. T. *Lectures on the Mathematical Method in Analytical Economics*. Gordon and Breach, New York, 1961.
[11] Sraffa, P. *Production of Commodities by Means of Commodities*. Cambridge University Press, 1960.
[12] Steedman, I. and Metcalfe, J. S. 'The non-substitution theorem and international trade theory'. *Australian Economic Papers*, 1973, pp. 267–9. See Essay 10 in this volume.

7 The Interest Rate Equalisation Theorem with Non-Traded Goods*

L. MAINWARING

In his extensive discussion of Ricardian time-phased systems [4] Paul Samuelson returned to the subject of interest rate equalisation through trade. Because of the problem of Wicksell effects in Sraffa–Leontief systems, Samuelson has shifted the emphasis of his discussion on to the 'local' theorem. The purpose of this essay is to show that some straightforward observations on the possibility of equalisation in a global context can be made. We shall suppose, as does Samuelson, that all trading regions share an identical technology. This is characterised in long-run equilibrium by the following price equations

$$P = (1 + r)PA + wa, \qquad (1)$$

where P is the row vector of prices $[p_j]$ ($j = 1, \ldots, n$), r the rate of interest and w the wage. (Any commodity may be chosen as a standard for P and w). A is the matrix of the unit input coefficients $[a_{ij}]$ and a the row vector of unit labour coefficients $[a_{0j}]$. If A is indecomposable and non-negative then for any r ($0 < r < r_{max}$) P and w have unique positive solutions (Schwartz [5]) while $dw/dr < 0$. Although P is unique with respect to r, it does not follow that r is unique with respect to P. If not, then with trade the common price vector P^* may be associated with two or more rates of interest so that these rates need not be equalised.

In his original formulation of the theorem [3], Samuelson attempted to show that when 'there are uniform differences in factor intensity, so that for some two goods that are simultaneously produced in both countries, say goods 1 and 2, $p_1(r)/p_2(r) = p_{12}(r)$ is a monotone, strictly increasing (or decreasing) function of r. Then, the interest rate will be equalised by positive trade in those goods alone' (his italics). Bliss [1] was the first to point out that without an indication of the conditions under which $p_{12}(r)$ is monotonic this statement is essentially tautological. More recently Steedman and Metcalfe [7] and Mainwaring [2] have shown the possibility of nonmonotonicity in the case of the fixed coefficient type model of eq. (1) in which countries share a number of available techniques.[1] Our present concern is with countries having just one technique.

In the following, two possibilities are considered: one in which all goods are traded, and one in which some goods do not enter trade. As is usual, it is assumed that countries continue to produce all goods in the trading equilibrium.

ALL GOODS TRADED

When all goods enter trade the price vector P^* is common to all countries. Nonequalisation of r would require P^* to be associated with distinct levels of r, say r' and r''. Then

$$P^* = (1+r')P^*A + w'a, \qquad (2)$$

$$P^* = (1+r'')P^*A + w''a, \qquad (3)$$

from which

$$(r''-r')P^*A = (w'-w'')a.$$

We cannot have $w' = w''$, hence

$$a = \lambda P^*A, \qquad (4)$$

where $\lambda = (r''-r')/w'-w'') > 0$. Thus P^* occurs at two levels of r only if, for each activity, the value of direct inputs is the same multiple of the labour inputs, at these prices. We now show that if equality of value capital:labour ratios occurs at any two levels of r, it occurs at all r, and at prices P^*. Substituting (4) into (2),

$$P^* = (1+r')P^*A + w'\lambda P^*A = vP^*A, \qquad (5)$$

where $v = 1 + r' + w'\lambda > 0$. Expanding,

$$P^* = (v-x)P^*A + xP^*A$$

$$= (v-x)P^*A + (x/\lambda)a. \qquad (6)$$

The straight line joining r', w' and r'', w'' has the equation

$$w = w' + (r'/\lambda) - (r/\lambda) = (v-1-r)/\lambda$$

(note that when $w = 0$, $r = v - 1$). Consider any combination of w and r on this line. Taking x such that $0 < x < v - 1$ and setting

$$r = v - 1 - x, \tag{7}$$

then

$$w = x/\lambda. \tag{8}$$

Substituting (7) and (8) into (6) gives

$$P^* = (1 + r)P^*A + wa.$$

It follows that any point on the line $w = w' + (r'/\lambda) - (r/\lambda)$ with $0 < r < v - 1$ is a solution to the system of equations (1) with prices P^*. Since the set of positive prices associated with each r is unique, equilibrium prices (and capital–labour ratios) are the same for all r. If a given vector of prices occurs at more than one rate of interest, it occurs at all rates. It may be noted that equality of all capital–labour ratios for all goods at all interest rates is equivalent to Marx's case of 'equal organic compositions of capital.' Effectively, the n goods may be regarded as a single composite commodity.

So far as interest rate equalisation is concerned, this case is not particularly interesting. Quite apart from the requirement that all processes have the same capital-labour ratios, if two countries share the same technique then, no matter how different their rates of interest without trade, relative prices are the same and there is no scope for trade in the first place.

We may conclude then that if free trade (in all goods) occurs between countries sharing the same (single) technique it will lead to the equalisation of all rates of interest. Notice that this conclusion holds quite independently of *any* restrictions on factor intensity, however defined.

SOME GOODS NOT TRADED

If goods $1, \ldots, k$ are traded while goods $k + 1, \ldots, n$ are not, then only the vector of prices $P^k = [p_1, \ldots, p_k]$ is common to all countries. We now ask whether P^k can occur at distinct rates of interest. Consider a technique having equilibrium prices P^* at r', w' (eq. (2)). Is it possible to find a price vector $P^* + \theta$ at $r'' > r'$, such that $\theta = [0, \ldots, 0, \theta_{k+1}, \ldots, \theta_n]$ and $(p^* + \theta)_i > 0 (i = k + 1, \ldots, n)$?

At r', prices are given by (2); at r'' by

$$P^* + \theta = (1 + r'')(P^* + \theta)A + w''a. \tag{9}$$

Interest Equalisation with Non-Traded Goods 93

Rearranging (2) and (9) to form expressions for a and then equating,

$$[(P^* + \theta)(1 + r'')(1/w'') - P^*(1 + r')(1/w')]A$$
$$= (P^* + \theta)(1/w'') - P^*(1/w'), \qquad (10)$$

which may be written as

$$zA = q. \qquad (11)$$

The $\theta_i (i = k+1, \ldots, n)$ may, in general, be positive or negative. To ensure that z and q are both positive it is sufficient that

$$|\theta_i| < p_i^*(1 - w''/w') \qquad (12)$$

(it follows, of course, that $(p^* + \theta)_i > 0$, for all i).

Writing $A = [A_1, A_2, \ldots, A_n]$, where $A_h (h = 1, \ldots, n)$ is the column vector of inputs into process h, $[a_{ih}]$, (11) may be written

$$[zA_1, zA_2, \ldots, zA_n] = q. \qquad (13)$$

Now suppose that all-positive values are specified for p_i^*, w', w'', r', r''; and values for θ_i satisfying (12). Suppose also that for each A_h there are assigned $n-1$ nonnegative coefficients; then (13) allows the determination of the nth coefficient for each process. By the appropriate choice of the predetermined coefficients the last n can all be made positive. Thus a nonnegative matrix A can be found to satisfy (10) and hence (2) and (9).[2]

From (2) the necessary condition for $a > 0$ is that $P^* > (1 + r')P^*A$, or $(1/1 + r')P^* > P^*A$, which implies (Schwartz [5], p. 23) that the dominant eigenvalue of A, dom (A), is such that

$$\text{dom}(A) < (1/1 + r'). \qquad (14)$$

Since $\text{dom}(A)$ is an increasing function of each element of A, $a > 0$ can be ensured by making the elements of A sufficiently small, as follows: from (10), taking given initial values of all elements other than w',

$$\delta z_i / \delta(1/w') = -p_i^*(1 + r'),$$
$$\delta q_i / \delta(1/w') = -p_i^*,$$

i.e. an increase in w' effects a greater increase in z_i than in q_i. It is possible therefore, to choose some w' large enough for $z_i > q_i$, for all i.[3] Then (11) may be written

$$q = qA + (z - q)A,$$

where $(z - q)A > 0$. Hence

$$qA < q,$$

which implies that $\mathrm{dom}(A) < 1$. Clearly, by making z_i sufficiently larger than q_i, $\mathrm{dom}(A)$ can also be made less than $(1/1 + r')$.[4]

It is, then, possible to construct a technique in which a subvector of prices $P^k (k < n)$ occurs at distinct rates of interest. If only k goods enter trade the set of international prices of those k goods may be consistent with distinct values of r in different countries, with no tendency for these values to be equalised.

FACTOR INTENSITY CONDITIONS[5]

Nothing has yet been said about the factor intensity conditions for the case in which some goods remain untraded. According to Samuelson [3], equalisation will occur if for some two traded goods, 'there are uniform differences in factor intensity.' Unfortunately this condition is subject to several alternative interpretations but we shall attempt to show that our conclusions are applicable to a wide range of interpretations. There are two sources of ambiguity: the first is the concept of relative factor intensity, per se; the second is the meaning to be attached to the phrase 'uniform differences.'

One way of interpreting the condition would be to treat each input as a separate 'factor,' in which case we would require that if

$$a_{gi}/a_{hi} > a_{gj}/a_{hj} \quad \text{(for all } g, h = 0, 1, \ldots, n; \text{ and } i, j = 1, \ldots, k\text{)}$$

at some r, then the inequality holds for all r in the interval $(r' \leq r \leq r'')$. Such a condition must hold in the present case since input proportions do not vary with relative prices, by assumption.

If, on the other hand, we wish to consider all nonlabour inputs together as 'capital' then, as Bliss has made clear, the capital has first to be valued. One (not unreasonable) interpretation of relative factor intensity would then be that if

$$\sum_{h=1} p_h a_{hi}/a_{0i} > \sum_{h=1} p_h a_{hj}/a_{0j} \tag{15}$$

holds for some set of prices, then good i is relatively more 'capital' intensive than good j, at those prices. If we accept (15) then it is necessary to examine further the meaning of 'uniform differences' in this context.

As a preliminary to this consider the following three-commodity system:

$$A = \begin{Bmatrix} 0 & a_{12} & 0 \\ 0 & 0 & a_{23} \\ a_{31} & 0 & 0 \end{Bmatrix}, \quad a = [1, 1, 1].$$

Employing Sraffa's 'standard commodity' as the unit of value ([6], ch. IV), the rate of interest is given by

$$r = \mu\phi, \quad (16)$$

where $(1-\phi)$ is the share of net product which goes to wages $(0 \leq \phi \leq 1)$ and μ is the rate of interest which obtains when $\phi = 1$. The price equations of this system may be written as

$$P = (1+\mu\phi)PA + (1-\phi)a \quad (17)$$

which may be solved for individual prices as functions of $\phi < 1$:

$$\Delta p_i = 1 + (1+\mu\phi)^3 a_{hi} + (1+\mu\phi)^2 a_{hi} a_{jh}, \quad (18)$$

where $h > j$ for $i = 1, 3$ and $h < j$ for $i = 2$; and

$$\Delta = [1 - (1+\mu\phi)^3 a_{12} a_{23} a_{31}]/(1-\phi).$$

Note that $\Delta > 0$, for $0 \leq \phi < 1$, for a productive system.

From (18) we may obtain expressions for relative capital intensity and relative prices. The difference in capital intensity of processes 3 and 2 is given by

$$\Delta(p_2 a_{23} - p_1 a_{12}) = (a_{23} - a_{12}) + (1+\mu\phi)a_{12}(a_{23} - a_{31}). \quad (19)$$

The behaviour of relative prices can be seen by differentiating p_2/p_3 with respect to ϕ:

$$(p_3\Delta)^2 dp_{23}/d\phi = \mu[(a_{12} - a_{23}) + (1+\mu\phi)^2 a_{23} u_{12}(a_{31} - a_{12}) + 2(1+\mu\phi)a_{12}(a_{31} - a_{23})]. \quad (20)$$

Now, since $p_3 > 0$, the behaviour of p_{23} can be inferred by evaluating the sign of (20) at different values of ϕ: any change in sign implying nonmonotonic behaviour. The question then arises whether such behaviour is consistent with the nonreversal of the sign of (19). That it is can easily be checked by a simple numerical example: for $a_{12} = 1.0$, $a_{23} = 0.4$ and $a_{31} = 0.38$ (implying $\mu \simeq 0.874$) (20) is positive for $\phi = 0$, becoming negative as $\phi \to 1$, while (19) is always negative for $0 \leq \phi < 1$.

In fact, the intensity ranking may be seen to be constant over all three processes.

With this example in mind, return now to the meaning of 'uniform differences.' We consider four possible interpretations:

(i) If (15) holds for *any* two traded goods (any $i, j = 1, \ldots, k$) at some r in the range ($r' \leq r \leq r''$) then it holds for all r in that range.

In the example suppose that goods 2 and 3 are traded, but not good 1. We have seen that nonmonotonic changes in p_{23} need not imply factor intensity reversal for these processes. One would intuitively expect that results obtained for a three-commodity system would hold *a fortiori* for more general systems. For example, where $k > 2$, partition the traded commodities into groups $1, \ldots, f$ and $f+1, \ldots, k (f < k)$. It may then be conjectured that if goods in the first group have *sufficiently similar* input coefficients, and likewise for goods in the second group, what is true for $k = 2$ is also true for this case.

(ii) If (15) holds for *all* $i = 1, \ldots, f$ and all $j = f+1, \ldots, k$ at some r in the relevant range, it holds for all r in that range.

This extends the pair-wise intensity restrictions over a much wider range. Even so, it follows from our preceding remarks that if goods within the same group have sufficiently similar technical coefficients the recurrence of P^k still need not imply violation of (15).

Our third and fourth interpretations place restrictions on all n rather than just the k traded commodities:

(iii) That (15) holds for any $i = 1, \ldots, m$ and $j = m+1, \ldots, n (m < n)$ over the relevant range of r.

In the example suppose that commodities are partitioned as follows: $\{1, 3|2\}$ (where 3 and 2 are traded). The present condition requires that processes 1 and 3 are always less (more) capital intensive than process 2. This, in fact, is true of the numerical example suggested. Nevertheless, condition (iii) does help us to recognise a particular case in which interest rates *will* be equalised. If commodities within the same group have sufficiently similar coefficients the system reduces to the two-commodity case in which the price ratio is known to be monotonic. Then if the traded goods include at least one from each group, interest rates must be equalised.

(iv) That (15) holds for *all* $i = 1, \ldots, m$ and $j = m+1, \ldots, n$.

This condition requires that the factor intensity ranking is constant over all commodities at all rates of interest. Again this is satisfied by our chosen example.

CONCLUDING REMARKS

Our findings may be summarised as follows. When trade in all commodities occurs then the common price vector in the trading equilibrium must be associated with a unique rate of interest. Thus the assumptions of incomplete specialisation and a common technique of production imply that interest rates must be equalised through trade.

However, it has been shown that it is possible to construct a technique in which a *part* of the price vector exists at distinct rates of interest. This implies that if some commodities do not enter trade the common vector of prices of traded goods may be associated with more than one interest rate. Whether or not this is inconsistent with Samuelson's original conjecture depends on the interpretation which is given to his factor intensity conditions. Although we have not been able to say anything of a general nature here, it appears from a simple numerical example that even if certain (seemingly plausible) conditions are satisfied, the common price vector may still recur, though it is also possible to recognise conditions in which recurrence is ruled out.[6]

In his recent article [1975], Samuelson does derive conditions (involving tastes and endowments) from which reasonably strong 'local' theorems can be deduced, provided the number of traded goods exceeds the number of primary factors. Such local theorems are not ruled out in the present analysis, though their usefulness depends on the number of distinct localities involved which, in turn, depends on the number of recurrences of P^k. The maximum number of recurrences is determined by the number of commodities entering trade. At one extreme, when $k = n$, there is just a single locality and so the theorem holds globally. At the other extreme, when $k = 2 (< n)$, $p_{12}(r)$ is a ratio of polynomials of degree $(n-1)$ and may admit *up to* $n^2 - 3n + 2$ recurrences of p_1/p_2 (though we cannot be sure that they will all occur for $r \geq 0$).[7]

NOTES

* This essay was first published in the *Journal of International Economics*, 1978. I should like to thank G. Harbour, D. J. White and referees of the *J.I.E.* for helping me to clarify certain points in the argument. Remaining confusions are my own responsibility.
1. The latter paper contains some nonrigorous comments on the present case, together with a simple numerical example.

2. Since all the elements of A can be made positive, it is assumed in what follows that A is indecomposable.
3. If in the construction of the technique r' is specified as zero, then from (10), any value of w' will suffice for $z_i > q_i$.
4. If, as in the previous note, $r' = 0$, condition (14) is automatically satisfied.
5. It is proper to note here that this section was considerably influenced by the suggestions of a referee who is in no way responsible for any errors in the conclusions reached.
6. This conclusion could be extended to cover fixed capital systems by, for example, allowing a particular case of joint-production in which partly-used machines appear as outputs.
7. Since a turning point of the function $p_{12}(r)$ is necessary (but not sufficient) for each recurrence, this assertion can be verified by differentiating the function with respect to r and calculating the maximum number of turning points.

REFERENCES

[1] Bliss, C. J. 'Collected scientific papers of Paul Samuelson'. *Economic Journal*, 1967, pp. 338–45.
[2] Mainwaring, L. 'Relative prices and "factor price" equalisation in a heterogeneous capital goods model'. *Australian Economic Papers*, 1976, pp. 109–18. See Essay 6 in this volume.
[3] Samuelson, P. A. 'Equalisation by trade of the interest rate along with the real wage'. In R. E. Baldwin *et al.* (eds.), *Trade, Growth and the Balance of Payments (Essays in Honor of Gottfried Haberler)*. Rand McNally, Chicago, 1965.
[4] Samuelson, P. A. 'Trade pattern reversals in time-phased Ricardian systems and inter-temporal efficiency'. *Journal of International Economics*, 1975, pp. 309–63.
[5] Schwartz, J. T. *Lectures on the Mathematical Method in Analytical Economics*. Gordon and Breach, New York, 1961.
[6] Sraffa, P. *Production of Commodities by Means of Commodities*. Cambridge University Press, 1960.
[7] Steedman, I. and Metcalfe. J. S. 'The non-substitution theorem and international trade theory'. *Australian Economic Papers*, 1973, pp. 267–9. See Essay 10 in this volume.

8 'On Foreign Trade'*

IAN STEEDMAN and J. S. METCALFE

In the first chapter of his *Principles*[1], Ricardo stated clearly that, in general, the relative value of any two commodities is not determined exclusively by the quantities of labour embodied in those two commodities. Relative value would be so determined, he said, only for commodities in the production of which fixed and circulating capital were used in the same proportions, the fixed capital being of equal durability for both commodities and both commodities requiring the same time to be brought to market.[2] Having recognised clearly that price ratios would normally diverge from the corresponding ratios of quantities of embodied labour, Ricardo maintained that the magnitude of these divergences would be small.[3] It was perhaps on this ground that in the seventh chapter of the *Principles*, 'On Foreign Trade', Ricardo assumed that no-trade price ratios would equal the corresponding ratios of quantities of embodied labour.[4] This assumption is implicitly made throughout the chapter and is made explicitly in the statement that 'The quantity of wine which [Portugal] shall give in exchange for the cloth of England, is not determined by the respective quantities of labour devoted to the production of each, as it would be, if both commodities were manufactured in England, or both in Portugal.'[5] Basing his analysis on the assumption that no-trade price ratios will equal the corresponding ratios of quantities of embodied labour, Ricardo obtained, amongst others, the following three important conclusions concerning foreign trade. First, trade will increase the rate of profits in a country, if and only if the imported commodities enter the real wage in that country. Secondly, the pattern of trade will be determined entirely by the methods of production available in the several trading countries. Thirdly, trade will 'increase the mass of commodities, and therefore the sum of enjoyments' in each of the trading countries.[6] Since Ricardo could, at best, only have defended his basic assumption, concerning no-trade price ratios and embodied labour ratios, as an approximation and, at worst, would have had to admit that it could be a poor approximation, it may be of interest to ask whether his three conclusions stand when no-trade price ratios are not identified with embodied labour ratios. The purpose of this essay is to show that only the first of the three conclusions mentioned above is independent of the relation between no-trade price ratios and embodied labour ratios; in general, the pattern of trade could not be predicted by Ricardo from a knowledge of production methods alone and nor could Ricardo have shown that trade must increase the 'mass of commodities' available in each trading country.

THE ASSUMPTIONS

In his analysis of trade between England and Portugal,[7] Ricardo considered a no-trade situation in which each of two countries produces two commodities, each commodity being produced by means of unassisted labour paid for at one moment of time. In the trade situation he assumed that each country specialises completely.[8] In order to remain close to Ricardo's analysis, and for ease of exposition, we shall assume two countries, two commodities, production by unassisted labour paid at one moment of time[9] and complete specialisation. We shall assume that each country possesses one, constant returns to scale, method for the production of each commodity. We shall also make Ricardo's assumption that in a given country, at a given time, the real wage, specified as a particular bundle of commodities, is to be taken as a datum for the purpose of economic analysis.[10] This real wage was not, of course, taken by Ricardo to be a 'physical subsistence' wage. He stated that, 'It is not to be understood that the natural price of labour, estimated even in food and necessaries, is absolutely fixed and constant. It varies at different times in the same country, and very materially differs in different countries. It essentially depends on the habits and customs of the people'.[11]

Like Ricardo, we shall also assume that trade is carried out by profit-maximising individuals[12] and that the rate of profits, while uniform throughout a given country, can vary as between countries.[13] We ignore transport costs.

THE EFFECT OF TRADE ON THE RATE OF PROFITS

Consider two countries, A and B, each of which produces, in the no-trade situation, two commodities, 1 and 2. In country i ($i = A, B$) production

'On Foreign Trade' 101

of one unit of commodity j ($j = 1, 2$) requires that e_j^i units of labour be applied and paid for n_j^i years before the unit of commodity is available.[14] In country i, the price of a unit of commodity j, in wage-units, is p_j^i, the annual rate of profits is r^i and the given real wage consists of w_1^i of commodity 1 and w_2^i of commodity 2. Then in the no-trade situation we must have for country i ($i = A, B$) the following three relations;

$$p_1^i = e_1^i(1+r^i)^{n_1^i}, \tag{1}$$

$$p_2^i = e_2^i(1+r^i)^{n_2^i} \tag{2}$$

and

$$p_1^i w_1^i + p_2^i w_2^i = 1. \tag{3}$$

Equations (1) and (2) state that each price equals the associated wage costs together with the profits accumulated thereon; equation (3) states that workers are just able to purchase the given real wage. Equations (1) to (3) together determine unique, positive values of p_1^i, p_2^i and r^i.[15]

Suppose that, in the no-trade situation, commodity 1 is relatively cheaper in country A, so that $(p_1^A/p_2^A) < (p_1^B/p_2^B)$, and consider the effect of opening trade, with A producing only commodity 1, B only commodity 2 and trade taking place at terms of trade lying between the two no-trade price ratios. In country A, let P_1^A and P_2^A be the with-trade prices (in wage-units) of commodities 1 and 2 and let r_T^A be the with-trade annual rate of profits. We have, for country A,

$$P_1^A = e_1^A(1+r_T^A)^{n_1^A} \tag{4}$$

and

$$P_1^A w_1^A + P_2^A w_2^A = 1 \tag{5}$$

From (1) and (3) we have

$$e_1^A(1+r^A)^{n_1^A}[w_1^A + (p_2^A/p_1^A)w_2^A] = 1, \tag{6}$$

while from (4) and (5) we have

$$e_1^A(1+r_T^A)^{n_1^A}[w_1^A + (P_2^A/P_1^A)w_2^A] = 1. \tag{7}$$

Equations (6) and (7) imply that

$$(1+r_T^A)^{n_1^A}[w_1^A + (P_2^A/P_1^A)w_2^A] =$$
$$= (1+r^A)^{n_1^A}[w_1^A + (p_2^A/p_1^A)w_2^A]. \tag{8}$$

Since $(p_1^A/p_2^A) < (P_1^A/P_2^A)$, we see immediately from (8) that trade will raise the rate of profits in A ($r_T^A > r^A$) if, and only if, the imported commodity (commodity 2) enters the given real wage in A ($w_2^A > 0$).

Parallel reasoning will show that trade will raise the rate of profits in B if, and only if, commodity 1 enters the real wage in B ($w_1^B > 0$). Thus Ricardo's conclusion that trade will raise the rate of profits in a country if, and only if, the imported commodities enter the real wage in that country[16] does not, in the two-country, two-commodity case, depend on his identification of no-trade price ratios with embodied labour ratios. Nor would it do so in the many-country, many-commodity case.

METHODS OF PRODUCTION, COMPARATIVE ADVANTAGE AND THE DIRECTION OF TRADE

Suppose that commodity 2 enters the real wage in A ($w_2^A > 0$), that commodity 1 enters the real wage in B ($w_1^B > 0$) and that, in the no-trade situation, commodity 1 is relatively cheaper in country A. The analysis of the preceding section, together with the assumption that trade is carried out by profit maximising individuals, then shows that, on the opening of free trade, country A will export 1 and import 2, while B will export 2 and import 1.

The direction of trade then is determined entirely by the relation between the no-trade price ratios, i.e., by the relation between[17]

$$(e_1^A/e_2^A)(1+r^A)^{(n_1^A - n_2^A)} \text{ and } (e_1^B/e_2^B)(1+r^B)^{(n_1^B - n_2^B)} \quad (9)$$

Now, in general, a knowledge of the eight variables in (9) which characterise the methods of production available in A and B, is not sufficient to tell one which of the two expressions in (9) will be the greater, for they depend on the pre-trade rates of profit and thus, more fundamentally, on the real wages (w_1^A, w_2^A) and (w_1^B, w_2^B). Thus a complete knowledge of available methods of production would not have sufficed to permit Ricardo to determine the direction of trade, if he had not identified no-trade price ratios with embodied labour ratios.[18] It follows, *a fortiori*, that Ricardo could not have determined the direction of trade by comparing the embodied labour ratios holding in each country, i.e., by comparing (e_1^A/e_2^A) with (e_1^B/e_2^B) in our above notation. In general, the direction of trade cannot be predicted from a knowledge of comparative advantage alone, where 'comparative advantage' means relative long-run equilibrium embodied labour ratios.

THE MUTUAL GAIN FROM TRADE

Ricardo stated in the *Principles*, in chapter seven and elsewhere, that free trade will make available, to every trading country, a bundle of commodities not available in the no-trade situation.[19] It will be clear that Ricardo could not have asserted this had he not identified no-trade price ratios with embodied labour ratios. For each of two countries to gain, it is necessary that they should specialise according to comparative advantage and then trade at terms of trade lying between their respective embodied labour ratios. The direction of trade, however, is determined by relative no-trade *price* ratios, which are different from the corresponding *embodied labour* ratios: it is possible that commodity 1 is relatively more expensive, in the no-trade situation, in the country possessing the comparative advantage in its production.

Consider the following example, based upon Ricardo's example of trade, in wine and cloth, between England and Portugal.[20] Table 8.1 shows the amount of labour required for the production of one unit of each commodity, in each country. We assume that the labour required for the production of 1 in A, must be applied and paid for five years before the commodity is available. In each of the remaining three cases, the labour must be applied and paid for one year before the commodity is available.

TABLE 8.1

	Commodity 1	Commodity 2
Country A	100	120
Country B	90	80

It will be clear that A has a comparative advantage in the production of $1 \left(\frac{100}{120} = \frac{20}{24} < \frac{27}{24} = \frac{90}{80} \right)$ and that the no-trade price of 1, in terms of 2, will be $\frac{27}{24} \left(= \frac{90}{80} \right)$ in country B, whatever may be the real wage in B. In country A, however, the no-trade price ratio depends on the real wage; suppose that the wage consists of $(1.00/286)$ units of commodity 1 and $(0.9466/286)$ units of commodity 2. Using our earlier notation, equations (1), (2) and (3) become:

$$p_1^A = 100(1 + r^A)^5, \tag{1'}$$

$$p_2^A = 120(1 + r^A) \tag{2'}$$

and

$$\left(\frac{1.00}{286}\right)p_1^A + \left(\frac{0.9466}{286}\right)p_2^A = 1. \qquad (3^1)$$

As the reader may easily check by substitution, the solution to (1^1), (2^1) and (3^1) is given by

$$r^A = 10\%, \; p_1^A = 161.05, \; p_2^A = 132.00;$$

the no-trade price of 1, in terms of 2, is thus given by

$$(p_1^A/p_2^A) = \left(\frac{161.05}{132.00}\right) = \left(\frac{29.282}{24}\right)$$

Thus, in the no-trade situation, commodity 1 is relatively cheaper in country $B\left(\frac{27}{24} < \frac{29.282}{24}\right)$. If we assume that commodity 2 enters the real wage in B, then we know from our previous analysis that profit-maximising competition, under free trade, will lead to A producing only 2 and B only 1. Country A's comparative advantage in 1 is quite irrelevant for the direction of trade: it is by no means irrelevant for the effect of trade on the bundle of commodities available in country A. In Figure 8.1, the full lines $A_1 A_2$ and $B_1 B_2$ show the sets of commodities available, in the no-trade situation, in countries A and B respectively; the absolute slope of $A_1 A_2$ is less than that of $B_1 B_2$, since A has a comparative advantage in the production of 1. Under free trade, production in A will be at point A_2, in B at B_1.[21] The terms of trade must lie between $\left(\frac{27}{24}\right)$ and $\left(\frac{29.282}{24}\right)$, say at $\left(\frac{28}{24}\right)$;[22] in Figure 8.1 both the

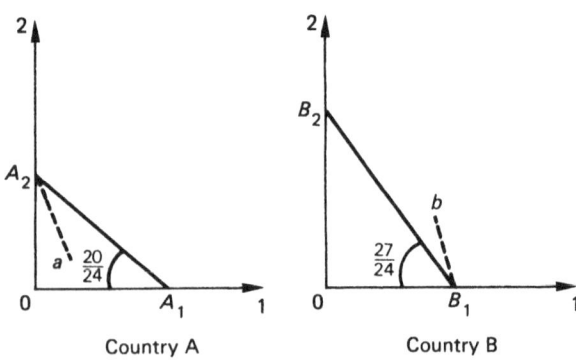

FIGURE 8.1

'On Foreign Trade'   105

dashed lines $A_2 a$ and $B_1 b$ have an absolute slope of $\left(\dfrac{28}{24}\right)$ and they are of the same length. In the with-trade situation, the bundle of commodities available in A is shown at point a and lies *inside* $A_1 A_2$; the bundle available in B is shown at b and lies *outside* $B_1 B_2$.

Thus under free trade and profit maximising competition, the bundle of commodities available in A is unambiguously smaller than some bundles achievable without trade. By assumption, however, the bundle of commodities going to the labourers in A is the same in the trade and no-trade situations[23]; hence it is the capitalists in A who, with trade, have available a bundle of commodities smaller than certain possible no-trade bundles. Why then do the capitalists in A engage in foreign trade? Because they act individually, each seeking to maximise his rate of profits. By trading, each capitalist *does* raise his rate of profits[24] and therefore he trades; that the collective result is a smaller bundle of commodities is not the concern of any decision-taker.

Ricardo could not have shown that profit maximising competition under free trade would result in mutual gain to the trading countries, had he not identified no-trade price ratios with embodied labour ratios. A little experiment with the two-country, two-commodity case will soon show the reader that trade at terms of trade lying between the two no-trade price ratios may, in the usual sense, harm A and benefit B, benefit both A and B, benefit A and harm B or harm *both* A and B.[25]

CONCLUSION

Ricardo's finding that trade would raise the rate of profits in a country if, and only if, the imported commodities entered the real wage in that country, *did not* depend on his identifying no-trade price ratios with embodied labour ratios. His statements that the direction of trade is determined by the available methods of production and that trade will be mutually advantageous, *did* depend on that identification. Since there is no reason to think that no-trade price ratios would equal the corresponding embodied labour ratios, this conclusion may be of some interest.

APPENDIX

In this appendix we make the same assumptions as in the text, except that production in each country requires the simultaneous use of inputs of labour and of the commodities 1 and 2. All production takes place in yearly cycles, all capital being circulating capital; both the commodity inputs and the labour are paid for at the beginning of the year.

Consider country A, in the no-trade situation. Let the inputs of 1, 2 and labour, required for the production of one unit of commodity j, be given by the jth column of $\begin{bmatrix} a_{11} & a_{12} \\ a_{21} & a_{22} \\ a_1 & a_2 \end{bmatrix}$. We assume that $a_{ij} \geq 0, a_j > 0$.

Let p^A be the price of 1 in terms of 2 and w^A the wage in terms of 2; r^A, w_1^A and w_2^A are used as in the text. We then have

$$(1 + r^A)[a_{11}p^A + a_{21} + a_1 w^A] = p^A, \quad \text{(i)}$$

$$(1 + r^A)[a_{12}p^A + a_{22} + a_2 w^A] = 1 \quad \text{(ii)}$$

and

$$p^A w_1^A + w_2^A = w^A \quad \text{(iii)}$$

Using (iii) we can eliminate w^A from (i) and (ii) to obtain

$$(1 + r^A)[(a_{11} + a_1 w_1^A)p^A + (a_{21} + a_1 w_2^A)] = p^A \quad \text{(iv)}$$

and

$$(1 + r^A)[(a_{12} + a_2 w_1^A)p^A + (a_{22} + a_2 w_2^A)] = 1, \quad \text{(v)}$$

which we can rewrite as

$$(1 + r^A)(A_{11}p^A + A_{21}) = p^A \quad \text{(vi)}$$

and

$$(1 + r^A)(A_{12}p^A + A_{22}) = 1, \quad \text{(vii)}$$

on defining A_{ij} by $A_{ij} = (a_{ij} + a_j w_i^A)$. From (vi) and (vii) we have

$$(1 + r^A) = (A_{11} + A_{21}p^{A-1})^{-1} = (A_{12}p^A + A_{22})^{-1} \quad \text{(viii)}$$

By parallel reasoning we obtain, in a self-explanatory notation, the following relation for B;

$$(1 + r^B) = (B_{11} + B_{21}p^{B-1})^{-1} = (B_{12}p^B + B_{22})^{-1} \quad \text{(ix)}$$

Suppose now that $p^A < p^B$ and consider the effect of free trade with A specialising in 1 and B in 2. Let the with-trade price of 1, in terms of 2, i.e. the terms of trade, be p, with $p^A < p < p^B$. It is easy to see that we shall have

$$(1 + r_T^A) = (A_{11} + A_{21}p^{-1})^{-1} \quad \text{(x)}$$

and

$$(1 + r_T^B) = (B_{12}p + B_{22})^{-1} \quad \text{(xi)}$$

'On Foreign Trade' 107

On comparing (x) with (viii) and (xi) with (ix), remembering that $p^A < p < p^B$, we see immediately that

$$r_T^A > r^A, \text{ if and only if } A_{21} > 0,$$
$$r_T^B > r^B, \text{ if and only if } B_{12} > 0.$$

We see, that is, that for trade to raise the rate of profits in, say, country A, it is *not* necessary that the imported commodity (2) should enter *directly* into the real wage in A. If $w_2^A = 0$, trade will still raise the rate of profits in A provided that $a_{21} > 0$, i.e. provided that the imported commodity is used in producing 1 and thus enters *indirectly* into the real wage in A.[26] In the same way, $r_T^B > r^B$ provided that commodity 1 enters, directly *or* indirectly, into the real wage in B. This important point was, of course, lost in the text because of the very simple picture of production adopted there.

The findings of the text, that the direction of trade cannot be predicted from a knowledge of production methods alone and that trade need not be mutually advantageous, in the usual sense, are not affected by our changed characterisation of the methods of production. This change does, however, bring to light certain physical limits to the possibility of complete specialisation; limits which could not appear in the picture of production adopted in the text. Suppose that A is to specialise in 1 and B in 2; let L^A and L^B be the levels of employment in the trade situation. The gross output of 1 in A will be (L^A/a_1) but after allowing for the amount of 1 required in A to replace the production inputs of 1 $(a_{11}L^A/a_1)$ and to replace the quantity of 1 required for the labourers in A $(a_1 w_1^A L^A/a_1)$, the amount remaining will be only $[(1-A_{11})L^A/a_1]$. This must at least equal B's production input and wage requirement of 1, that is $(B_{12}L^B/b_2)$. Thus a necessary condition for complete specialisation is that

$$\left(\frac{1-A_{11}}{a_1}\right)L^A \geqq \left(\frac{B_{12}}{b_2}\right)L^B \tag{xii}$$

In the same way, another necessary condition is that

$$\left(\frac{1-B_{22}}{b_2}\right)L^B \geqq \left(\frac{A_{21}}{a_1}\right)L^A \tag{xiii}$$

(xii) and (xiii) together require that

$$\left(\frac{B_{12}}{1-A_{11}}\right) \leqq \frac{b_2 L^A}{a_1 L^B} \leqq \left(\frac{1-B_{22}}{A_{21}}\right) \tag{xiv}$$

If L^A and L^B do not satisfy (xiv), then it is physically impossible for A to produce only 1 and B only 2, given the methods of production and the fixed real wage in each country. If, say, A is 'too large', then *both* 1 and 2 will have to be produced in A. Thus equations (i) to (iii) will hold, with p in place of p^A, $r_T{}^A$ in place of r^A and $w_T{}^A$, the with-trade wage in terms of 2, in place of w^A; it follows immediately that $p = p^A$, $w_T{}^A = w^A$ and $r_T{}^A = r^A$. One could *not* say, *a priori*, that trade would not be advantageous to A; whether it was, or was not, would depend on the relation between p^A and $(e_1{}^A/e_2{}^A)$.

NOTES

*This essay was first published in *Economia Internazionale*, 1973.
1. All references to the *Principles* will be to the third edition, as printed in *Works and Correspondence of David Ricardo* (Vol. I), edited by P. Sraffa and M. H. Dobb, Cambridge University Press, 1966.
2. *Principles*, pp. 30–43.
3. See *Principles*, pp. 36, 42, 45. In each case Ricardo refers to the small *change* in relative price caused by a *change* in the wage or rate of profits but this implies the assertion made in the text since the price ratio must equal the embodied labour ratio at a zero rate of profits. (Ricardo seldom considers a rate of profits greater than 20%). On the relation between the '*difference* in the relative values of two commodities which are produced by equal quantities of labour' and 'the effect which a rise of wages has in producing a *change* in their relative value', see the Editorial Introduction to the *Principles*, pp. XLVII-XLIX.
4. He had written in the first chapter, '... in the subsequent part of this work ... I shall consider all the great variations which take place in the relative value of commodities to be produced by the greater or less quantity of labour which may be required from time to time to produce them'. (*Principles*, pp. 36–7). While this statement refers to changes through time and not to inter-country differences in no-trade price ratios at one moment of time, it clearly shows that Ricardo intended to emphasise the dependence of prices on methods of production and to relegate to a minor role their dependence on income distribution.
5. *Principles*, pp. 134–5: see also the final paragraph on p. 135.
6. The quotation is taken from the *Principles*, p. 128.
7. *Principles*, pp. 134–41.
8. Ricardo did not only mention two-country, two-commodity situations, of course; see pp. 134, 141, 144. It may also be noted that in his footnote to p. 136, Ricardo considered a case of incomplete specialisation.
9. In the Appendix we consider production by means of labour and commodities.
10. *Principles*, p. 93. We shall assume throughout, as did Ricardo in his seventh chapter, that the 'market price of labour' is always equal to the 'natural price of labour', i.e., to the value of the given real wage.

11. *Principles*, pp. 96–7.
12. *Principles*, pp. 137–9.
13. *Principles*, pp. 134, 136–7.
14. We assume trade in semi-finished commodities to be physically impossible.
15. We assume, of course, that $e_1{}^i w_1{}^i + e_2{}^i w_2{}^i < 1$.
16. *Principles*, pp. 132–3. In the Appendix we show that, if production is by means of labour *and* commodities, rather than by unassisted labour, then trade can raise the rate of profits without the imported commodity entering the real wage *directly;* all that is necessary is that the imported commodity should either be consumed directly by the labourers or be *used in the production of* a commodity consumed directly by the labourers. In this case Ricardo's statement in the first paragraph of p. 133 is not correct.
17. See equations (1) and (2).
18. That Ricardo did determine the direction of trade from a knowledge of production methods alone can be seen from *Principles*, pp. 134–41.
19. See, for example, *Principles*, pp. 133–4, 140, 317, 338, 343. In making such statements, Ricardo assumed that the level of employment in any country will, leaving aside the transitional period, be the same in the no-trade and with-trade situations (see *Principles*, pp. 128–31, 264, 319–20). As P. Garegnani has pointed out to us, this is by no means an innocent assumption. For simplicity, we make this assumption in the text but it is easily dispensed with, by arguing in terms of the bundles of commodities available *per unit of employment*, in the no-trade and with-trade situations.
20. *Principles*, p. 135.
21. We are assuming (see first footnote to this section) that, in each country, employment is the same in the no-trade and with-trade situations.
22. At these terms of trade, the rate of profits in A will be $r_T{}^A = 10.4\%$.
23. Both the real wage and employment are unchanged.
24. In our example, from $r^A = 10.0\%$ to $r_T{}^A = 10.4\%$.
25. All that is required for mutually disadvantageous trade is that trade should take place in the direction contrary to comparative advantage, at terms of trade lying between the two countries' embodied labour ratios. Since the direction of trade is determined by no-trade price ratios which do not equal the corresponding embodied labour ratios, this case is just as likely as the other three.
26. If $w_2{}^A = 0$, then $w_1{}^A$ must be positive, of course.

9 A Neo-Ricardian Analysis of International Trade*

L. MAINWARING

Traditionally, the Ricardian theory of international trade is thought of in terms of a simple Labour Theory of Value, in which prices are proportional to labour inputs. Ricardo himself recognised that the existence of a positive rate of profit could make prices diverge from their direct labour costs but thought the difference was insignificant.[1] Among post-Ricardians, Taussig is one of the few who explicitly recognised that profit on capital could affect the pattern of trade, but he too tended to minimise its importance.[2] More recently, however, differences in the no-trade pattern of income distribution (which when countries use the same techniques implies a difference in their no-trade rates of profit) have been suggested as a basis for international trade.[3]

The purpose of this essay is to develop a general framework for a neo-Ricardian approach to the analysis of trade. Whilst, to some extent, it is pedagogic[4], it does also try to reach some new conclusions in its consideration of trade between countries with different techniques, and between countries having planned economies. But its chief purpose is to emphasise that the analysis of international trade can be viewed essentially as a particular problem of the choice of technique.

The effect of trade is analysed by *comparing* the equilibrium situation in a pair of economies which do not practise trade with a pair that does. The economies *within* a pair may have the same or different technical possibilities, but possibilities are the same as *between* pairs. In other words, although we are talking of trade between two countries A and B, conceptually there are four economies involved: A^0, B^0 and A^T, B^T, the first two being non-trading economies, the second two being their trading counterparts. The 'choice' between, for example, the equilibrium situations A^0 and A^T is made by comparing the obtainable combinations

A Neo-Ricardian Analysis of International Trade

of the real wage and rate of profit. The dual relationship between consumption per worker and the rate of growth is used to assess the gains from trade.

THE WAGE, RATE OF PROFIT AND RELATIVE PRICES IN THE CLOSED ECONOMY

We use a circulating capital model in which production takes place in self-contained periods, the wage being paid at the end of each period. There are two commodities (1 and 2) which are produced by means of labour and the same two commodities: a_j is the input of labour into a unit of j; a_{ij} the input of commodity i into a unit of j. Writing $p(=p_1/p_2)$ as the price ratio, and expressing the wage, w, in terms of good 2, we have the following price equations:

$$p = (1+r)(a_{11}p + a_{21}) + wa_1 \quad (1)$$

$$1 = (1+r)(a_{12}p + a_{22}) + wa_2 \quad (2)$$

Competition ensures the equality of r (the rate of profit), w and p throughout the economy. (1) and (2) are readily solved to obtain a wage-profit $(w-r)$ relationship:

$$w = \frac{\det(I - vA)}{(1 - va_{11})a_2 + a_1 a_{12} v} \quad (3)$$

(where $v = 1 + r$; $A = \|a_{ij}\|$; and I is the identity matrix); and relative prices as a function of r:

$$p = \frac{(1 - a_{22}v)a_1 + a_2 a_{21} v}{(1 - a_{11}v)a_2 + a_1 a_{12} v} \quad (4)$$

Differentiating (4) with respect to v, we find that

$$dp/dv \lessgtr 0 \text{ as } (a_{11}p + a_{21})/a_1 \lessgtr (a_{12}p + a_{22})/a_2 \quad (5)$$

The bracketed terms are the values of commodity inputs into a unit of each process, and the denominators the labour requirements per unit. When these 'capital': direct labour ratios are the same the processes have what Marx called 'equal organic compositions of capital'. In this case relative prices do not vary with r, but generally they are a (monotonic) increasing or decreasing function. By taking the second derivative of w with respect to v in (3), it can be shown that each of these possibilities is associated with a particular shape of the $w-r$ frontier. When $dp/dv > 0$,

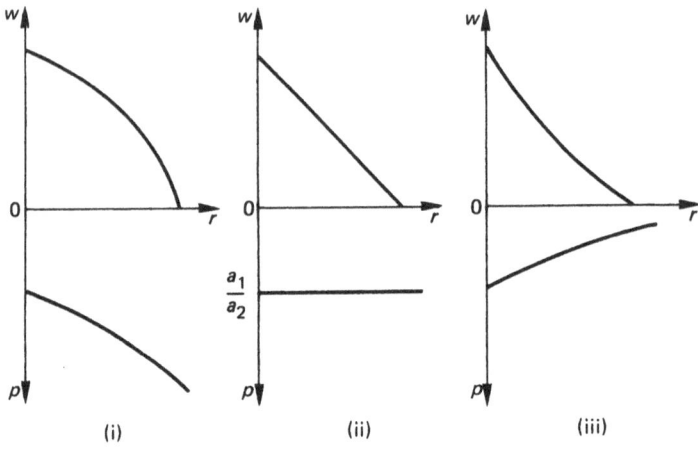

FIGURE 9.1

the $w-r$ frontier is concave to the origin; when $dp/dv = 0$, it is a straight line; and when $dp/dv < 0$ it is convex to the origin (see Figure 9.1).

THE OPEN ECONOMY

The technique represented by the no-trade economy consists, of necessity, of the activities for producing both commodities – of necessity because in the no-trade economy any one activity is not sustainable on its own. But with trade it is possible to have a single activity supported by imported inputs of the other commodity. So the possibility of trade presents two additional techniques, each consisting of a single activity. The problem of technical choice is often presented by superimposing the wage-profit frontiers for each technique to form an outer envelope. Then for any given r, say, the technique that is chosen under competitive conditions is the one which allows the maximum w, i.e., the one on the envelope. In order to approach the analysis in this way it is necessary to derive the wage-profit frontiers for the with-trade techniques. We continue to denote the wage-profit frontier for the no-trade economy by $w-r$; the frontiers for the with-trade techniques will be denoted by $(w-r)_1$ and $(w-r)_2$. For good 1,

$$w = [p - v(a_{11}p + a_{21})]/a_1 \qquad (6)$$

A Neo-Ricardian Analysis of International Trade

a straight line of slope $-(a_{11}p + a_{21})/a_1$. For good 2,

$$w = [1 - v(a_{12}p + a_{22})]/a_2 \quad (7)$$

a straight line of slope $-(a_{12}p + a_{22})/a_2$.

For each good there will be a family of these straight lines, each member corresponding to a different price ratio, and thus having a different slope from every other member. There are two points to note:

(i) From (5) it follows that when $dp/dv > 0$, the slope of $(w-r)_1$ is greater than that of $(w-r)_2$, and vice versa when $dp/dv < 0$.

(ii) The $(w-r)_i$ frontiers bracket the $w-r$ frontier in a particular manner.[5] Differentiating (6) and (7) with respect to v gives

$$\frac{dw}{dv} = \frac{1}{a_1} \cdot (1 - a_{11}v)\frac{dp}{dv} + s_1$$

and

$$\frac{dw}{dv} = s_2 - \frac{a_{12}}{a_2} \cdot \frac{dp}{dv} \cdot v$$

where s_1 and s_2 are the slopes of (6) and (7). It follows that if $dp/dv > 0$, then $s_2 > dw/dv > s_1$, or since all slopes are negative we have

$$dp/dv > 0 \quad \text{when} \quad |s_2| < |dw/dv| < |s_1|$$
$$dp/dv = 0 \quad \text{when} \quad |s_2| = |dw/dv| = |s_1|$$
$$dp/dv < 0 \quad \text{when} \quad |s_2| > |dw/dv| > |s_1|$$

The possible configurations are shown in Figure 9.2.

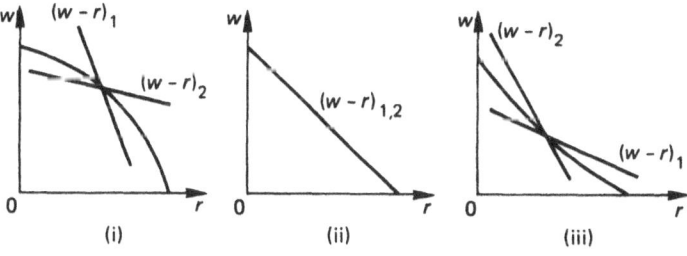

FIGURE 9.2

FOREIGN TRADE

We are now in a position to introduce trading possibilities between two countries, A and B. Our only interest is in the comparison of positions of long-run dynamic equilibrium. We assume that there are no impediments to trade, nor any reasons why specialisation should not be realised in either country.[6] We also assume that, for each country, the rate of profit is the same in no- and with-trade equilibria. (We take this case merely for illustration.) If the 'motive' for trade is the attainment of a superior $w - r$ combination, it is seen that such a combination is attained when each country specialises in the commodity which is relatively cheapest to produce.

To begin, suppose that A and B *have the same techniques*, but different rates of profit. In Figure 9.3(i), A and B have the same $w - r$ and $p - r$ functions. Suppose $r_a < r_b$, and hence $p_a < p_b$. The figure shows $w - r$ trade-offs drawn for goods 1 and 2, separately, at some intermediate set of prices p_I. It can be seen that if A specialises in the production and

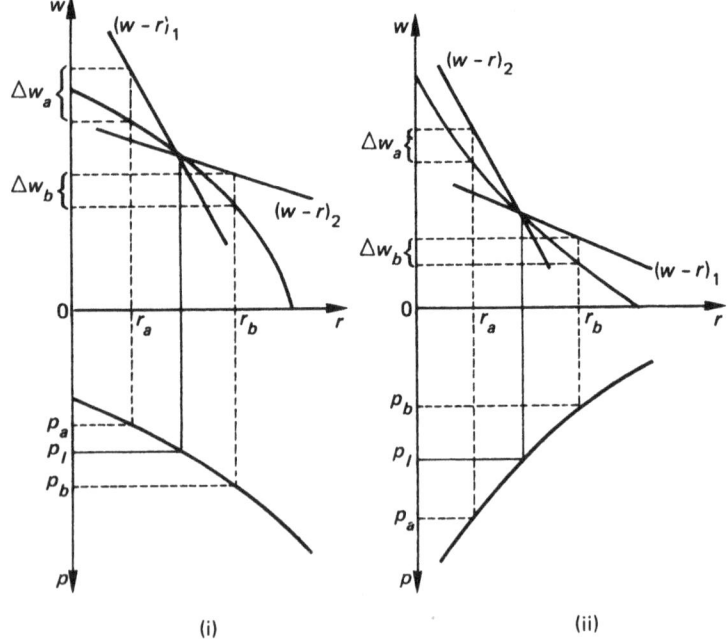

FIGURE 9.3

A Neo-Ricardian Analysis of International Trade   115

export of good 1 it can obtain a higher real wage with trade, at the rate of profit r_a. Similarly, B has a higher wage through specialisation in good 2. Obviously, if the wage were held constant in the comparison each country would obtain a higher rate of profit. Note that if p_I were equal to either of the no-trade price ratios, the country concerned would be indifferent to trade and would not be induced to specialise. Figure 9.3(ii) shows that the pattern of specialisation would be reversed when $dp/dv < 0$. It is evident from Figure 9.2(ii) that when $dp/dv = 0$, then no matter how different the profit rates, trade does not allow the attainment of a superior $w-r$ combination.

THE GAINS FROM TRADE

Writing gross output of good i per worker (p.w.) as x_i, total consumption (wage plus capitalist consumption) p.w. as e_i, and the rate of growth as g, we have, under autarky,

$$x_1 = (1+g)(a_{11}x_1 + a_{12}x_2) + e_1 \qquad (8)$$

$$x_2 = (1+g)(a_{21}x_1 + a_{22}x_2) + e_2 \qquad (9)$$

Assume, for simplicity, that all consumption is in the form of good 2[7]. Then setting $e_1 = 0$ and solving (8) and (9) for e_2 gives

$$e_2 = c = \frac{\det(I - zA)}{(1 - za_{11})a_2 + a_1 a_{12} z} \qquad (10)$$

where c is the consumption p.w. (of good 2) and $z = 1 + g$. Equation (10) describes the consumption-growth frontier which is the exact dual of equation (3). Thus the $w-r$ and $c-g$ frontiers coincide. Letting s be the proportion of profits which is saved (we assume that workers do not save) the rate of growth and rate of profit have the familiar relationship $g = s \cdot r$, in long-run steady growth. We assume that $0 \leq s \leq 1$, so that $0 \leq g \leq r$.

Suppose that, with trade, countries specialise fully in production. We can construct $(c-g)_i$ frontiers for each commodity (analogous to the $(w-r)_i$ frontiers). Consider process 2. In value terms, consumption p.w. is equal to gross output p.w. minus the value of inputs required for next period's production. We have everything in the form of good 2 except $a_{12}x_2$ which must be obtained from imports. It can be converted into an amount of good 2 by exchange at the ruling international price ratio, p_I; then, with balanced trade,

$$c = x_2 - z(pa_{12}x_2 + a_{22}x_2)$$

We thus have an expression relating consumption p.w. as a homogeneous physical quantity, and the rate of growth. This procedure is valid so long as one bundle of goods can be transformed into another bundle by means of exchange at the given price ratio. Clearly it is not valid (in general) in the non-specialised or no-trade economy where net output and consumption combinations are transformed according to a technical relationship. Since, for each process operated on its own, $x_i = 1/a_i$, we can write

$$c = [1 - z(pa_{12} + a_{22})]/a_2 \qquad (11)$$

Similarly, for process 1, we have

$$\begin{aligned}c &= px_1 - z(pa_{11}x_1 + a_{21}x_1) \\ &= [p - z(pa_{11} + a_{21})]/a_1\end{aligned} \qquad (12)$$

Comparison with (6) and (7) shows that the $c - g$ and $w - r$ trade-offs for single processes are identical under balanced trade.

Suppose that, for each country, the rate of profit is the same in no- and with-trade equilibria. In Figure 9.4, the curved lines are the $w - r$ and $c - g$ frontiers, first for the case $dp/dv > 0$, then for $dp/dv < 0$. The straight lines are the $(w - r)_i$ and $(c - g)_i$ frontiers for the set of prices p_I. First look at Figure 9.4(i). With trade both countries have higher real wages (the differences denoted by Δw_a and Δw_b). In A, the difference in consumption p.w. is larger than the difference in wages so that capitalist consumption p.w. must be greater with trade. In B, total consumption p.w. is greater with trade if $g_b > r_I$ (where r_I is that profit rate associated with a price ratio p_I) and less if $g_b < r_I$. But even in the first case $\Delta w_b > \Delta c_b$ so that capitalist consumption p.w. is less.

Now consider Figure 9.4(ii). Again both countries have greater real wages with trade. In A, total consumption p.w. is also greater, but capitalist consumption p.w. may be greater or less, depending on the slope of $(c - g)_2$ relative to that of the $c - g$ frontier. The lower is p_I relative to p_a the more likely it is to be less, since the slope of $(c - g)_2$ is then smaller. In B, total consumption p.w. with trade is greater if $g_b > r_I$ and less if $g_b < r_I$. In the first case, capitalist consumption p.w. may be greater with trade if p_I is large relative to p_b, for then the slope of $(c - g)_1$ is large relative to the slope of the $c - g$ frontier.[8,9]

A Neo-Ricardian Analysis of International Trade

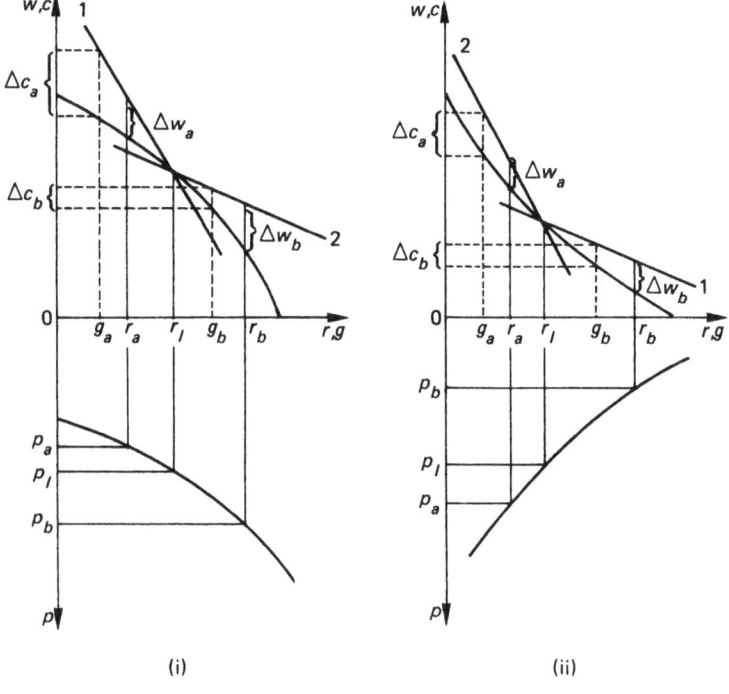

FIGURE 9.4

COUNTRIES HAVING DIFFERENT TECHNIQUES

Trade between countries with different techniques can be represented in the back-to-back digram of Figure 9.5. On the left are the $w-r$, $c-g$ and $p-r$ functions for A; on the right those for B. The textbook approach to Ricardian trade theory assumes either that rates of profit are zero, or that each country's technology is of the 'equal organic composition of capital' type. Thus relative prices are determined purely by technical coefficients of production. Figure 9.5 brings out the possibility that with more general techniques positive rates of profit might offset or even reverse that pattern of relative prices implied by technical differences when rates of profit are zero. They can be neutralised by choosing in each country rates of profit which correspond to the same relative prices (e.g. r_a and r_b); they can be reversed by choosing a rate of profit in A which corresponds to a relative price which is greater than that for r_b (e.g. r_a^*). In the latter event it can easily be seen that *both* countries may lose from trade in the

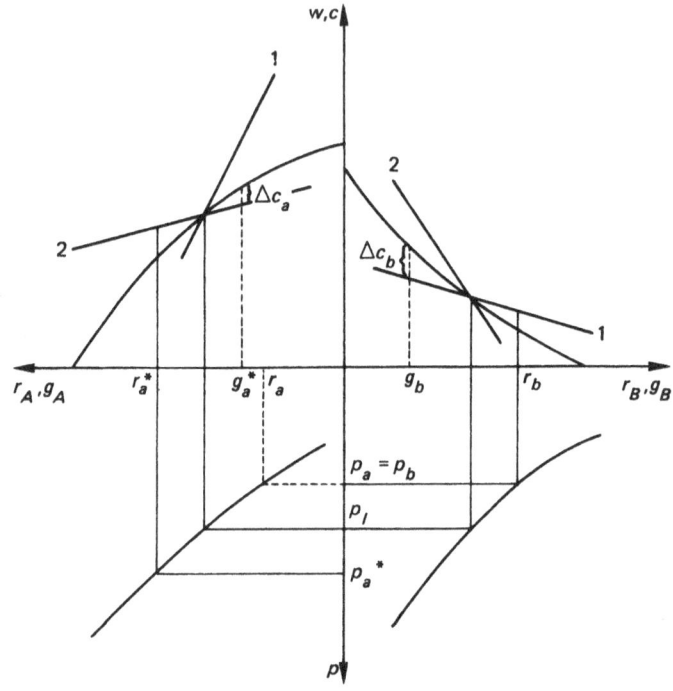

FIGURE 9.5

sense of having lower consumption possibilities at their respective rates of growth ($\Delta c_a, \Delta c_b < 0$).[10]

THE TRADE CRITERION IN A PLANNED ECONOMY

Imagine an economy with a single technique which is planned by a central authority. As before, relationships are defined between the real wage, relative prices and the ratio of the value of net output, less wages, to the value of commodity inputs, which we continue to call the rate of profit. Assume: that all consumption (and hence the wage) is in the form of good 2, that the workforce is growing at a fixed rate n; and that the planner has full knowledge of the technical coefficients of production.

In a *fully* centralised economy the planner 'is a monopsonist in the labour market and fixes the wage rate w, to which labour supply is inelastic.'[11] His functions are twofold: (i) to maintain full employment, and (ii) to maximise p.w. consumption at a given rate of growth. In order to fulfil his first obligation, the planner must ensure that the economy is growing at a rate $g = n$, which is thus a constraint. The level of the real wage must be such that the consequent rate of profit is at least as great as the given growth rate, or the investment required to occupy the workforce in future periods cannot be sustained.

Whether there will be any difference between the trade criterion of planned and free market economies depends on what happens to the surplus product, all of which is appropriated by the state. In the theoretical literature assumptions differ as to how the state disposes of the surplus. According to Pasinetti, 'the state, as such, cannot consume: consumption can be carried out only by individuals. Therefore, if any amount of the national product is not distributed to the members of the community . . . that amount is *ipso facto* saved. This means that the parameter s becomes unity . . .'[12]

In this event, $g = r$ and $c = w$, so that maximising w at given r (the capitalist criterion) also maximises c at given g. On the other hand, Nuti assumes that the planner re-invests some proportion, $s, (0 \leqq s \leqq 1)$ of the surplus product, the rest being distributed by the state either as collective consumption or as a wage subsidy.[13]

If we accept Nuti's assumptions, and take $s < 1$, the trade criterion will be different. Consider the possibility of specialised trade between two planned economies (assuming that their techniques are identical). For each country there is a problem of technical choice, each with-trade technique consisting of a single process, and the desired process is the one giving the highest p.w. consumption at the given rate of growth. In terms of a trade criterion the with-trade situation is superior (inferior) if p.w. consumption, at $g = n$, is greater (smaller) than it is with no trade. It follows that differences in no-trade price ratios are *not* a satisfactory criterion for trade, for maximising w at given r does not imply maximising c at given g. We have already seen that a process chosen according to this criterion might have a p.w. consumption (at given g) inferior to its no-trade level.

But there does exist some trading position which is mutually advantageous, namely, when international prices p_I are such that the associated rate of profit, r_I, has a value such that $n_a < r_I < n_b$ (Figure 9.6). Thus, when two planned economies have the same single technique production possibilities, gainful trade is possible if their given rates of growth are different. It is, therefore, possible for gainful trade to take place when the no-trade price ratios are the same, so long as $s_a \neq s_b$. Conversely, if $r_a \neq r_b$, but $n_a = n_b$, mutually gainful trade is not possible.

120   *Fundamental Issues in Trade Theory*

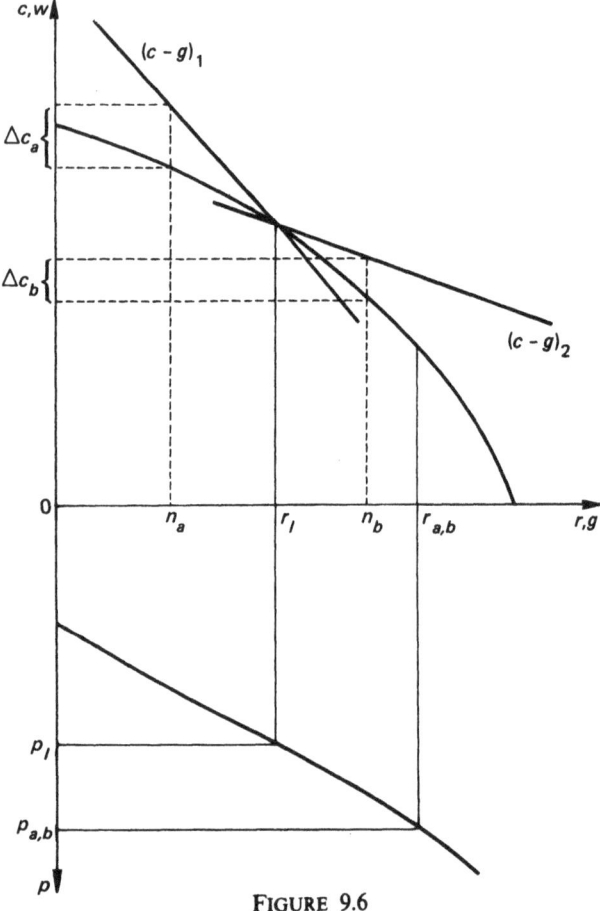

FIGURE 9.6

If the technique in A is different from that in B, the trade situation can be illustrated by means of a back-to-back diagram, gainful trade being possible if those price ratios which would exist if the rates of profit were equal to the respective rates of growth are different.

What happens to the criterion when the economy is not completely centralised?

Under decentralised socialism physical productive assets belong to state firms. Firms have access to a perfectly competitive labour market, and have infinite power of borrowing and lending [capital] from and to the State. . . . They appropriate current output and pay wages and interest out of it. Among the production techniques available, they select the technique maximising the present value of their assets at the ruling rate of interest. The socialist planner will still wish the technique maximising consumption per head to be chosen, but the only way he can affect technical choice is by choosing the rate of interest r, which is the basis of the decisions of State managers.[14]

Firms which are attempting to maximise their assets at a given r, trade according to the capitalist criterion. To ensure that this is consistent with the maximisation of consumption at the given growth rate it is sufficient that the planner sets the rate of profit equal to the rate of growth – Nuti's version of the Golden Rule.

CONCLUSION

Under capitalism and decentralised socialism, firms approach the problem of trade as they would any other problem of technical choice: according to the profit maximising criterion. This is implied by trade according to differences in no-trade relative prices. Under capitalism this approach could well result in one or both of the participants realising a poorer consumption p.w.-rate of growth combination than would be the case under autarky. When both countries practise decentralised socialism the planners' control of the rates of profit can assure that both countries always gain from trade. In fully centrally planned economies the direct purpose of trade is the improvement in $c - g$ possibilities and the trade criterion is not given by differences in relative prices.

The method of analysis presented in this paper can, in principle, be extended in a number of directions, since the consequences for trade of various actions can be deduced from the resulting modifications in the $w - r$ and $c - g$ frontiers.[15]

NOTES

*This essay was first published in *Kyklos*, 1974. I should very much like to thank Ian Steedman for suggesting many improvements. I also wish to thank J. S. Metcalfe and W. Peters for their helpful comments. Of course, errors are entirely my responsibility.
1. Ricardo [3], p. 36.
2. Taussig [4], chapter 7.
3. See Ian Steedman and J. S. Metcalfe, Essay 10 in this volume.

4. In as much as it is an elaboration of the suggestion made by Steedman and Metcalfe (Essay 10).
5. The $w-r$ frontier can be considered as the locus of the $(w-r)_i$ intersections. From (1) and (2) we can obtain expressions for relative prices. These are simply rearrangements of the $(w-r)_i$ expressions; equating and solving for w yields (3).
6. There are technical constraints to specialisation: if one country is very small relative to the other it may not be able to provide all the inputs required in specialised production. In this event the larger country will not be able to specialise. See, in this volume, Essay 8 (Appendix) and Essay 14.
7. This assumption is overly strong. All we require for the following analysis is that the proportions in which the two commodities enter the wage are the same as the proportions in which they enter capitalist consumption. This ensures that the wage and consumption p.w. can be measured in terms of the same commodity bundle. The complete relaxation of this restriction on capitalist consumption would complicate the analysis without substantially changing its conclusions.
8. On the 'gain' from trade, see also, in this volume, Essays 4, 8, 11, 12 and 14.
9. Note that the variation in the capitalist 'gain' from trade with the capitalist savings ratio, in any country, can also be inferred from the diagrams, and will depend on the particular circumstances of that country's equilibrium in trade.
10. It can be seen by inspection, however, that this possibility only arises when the $w-r$ frontier is convex in one country and concave in the other.
11. Nuti [1], p. 35.
12. Pasinetti [2], p. 277.
13. Nuti [1]. (Unlike Nuti, we assume that workers' savings are zero and that the state imposes no taxes on wages.) Presumably, a subsidy would here be defined as that part of workers' consumption which is an addition to that implied by the chosen price ratio.
14. Nuti [1], pp. 35–6.
15. I have in mind the effects of tariffs and domestic taxes. Also, in a multi-commodity analysis the resolution of the $w-r$ frontiers into their component $(w-r)_i$ trade-offs allows for a detailed examination of the behaviour of prices as the rate of profit varies, which proves of use in studying the possibility of 'factor price' equalisation through trade: see Essays 6 and 7 in this volume.

REFERENCES

[1] Nuti, D. M. 'Capitalism, socialism and steady growth.' *Economic Journal*, 1970, pp. 32–57.
[2] Pasinetti, L. L. 'Rate of profit and income distribution in relation to the rate of economic growth.' *Review of Economic Studies*, 1962, pp. 267–79.
[3] Ricardo, D. *On the Principles of Political Economy and Taxation* (Sraffa edition). Cambridge University Press, 1951.
[4] Taussig, F. W. *International Trade*. Macmillan, New York, 1927.

10 The Non-Substitution Theorem and International Trade Theory*

IAN STEEDMAN and J. S. METCALFE

The object of this brief essay is to suggest that recent work in the field of capital theory has an immediate significance for trade theory in a stationary equilibrium setting. Recent capital theory has emphasised the relationships between income distribution and relative commodity prices rather than any particular theory of the determination of distribution and prices. It may therefore provide the basis for studying important aspects of the theory of trade outside a full neo-classical general equilibrium theory and, indeed, outside any other general theory. We are able to see, for example, that even in the absence of specialisation there is no reason to expect *a priori* that free trade in commodities will ensure uniformity of real wage and interest rates.

A CLOSED ECONOMY

Consider a closed economy in which many commodities are produced. The available methods of production all yield constant returns to scale, there are no joint products (and thus no fixed capital goods), technical knowledge is unchanging and there is only one non-produced input, namely labour. If the economy is in a competitive, long-run equilibrium and all relative prices and the interest rate are constant through time, then we know that to any given interest rate there corresponds a unique set of relative prices for commodities available in a given period.[1]

TRADING ECONOMIES

Consider now a number of closed economies, all having identical technical possibilities of the kind described above, and all producing the same commodities. If each economy is in a long-run, constant price and constant interest rate equilibrium but the interest rate differs as between the various economies then, in general, all relative prices will differ as between the economies.[2] It follows that if free trade in all the commodities becomes possible, with zero transport costs, then, under profit-maximising competition, trade will occur. If there is a 'basis of trade' then the *proximate* basis of trade could be said to be the existence of different no-trade interest rates.

The opening of free trade, with zero transport costs, will establish a set of relative commodity prices which is common to all the countries but this does not guarantee world-wide uniformity of with-trade interest rates and real wage rates. This is obvious if not all countries continue, in trading equilibrium, to produce all the commodities. In each country there will be, for each commodity produced in that country, an equation relating the price of that commodity to the country's interest rate and real wage rate and to the prices of the commodities used as inputs in the production of that commodity. However, the set of such equations will not be the same for all countries, even if there is no choice of production methods, and hence the existence of a common set of relative commodity prices clearly does not guarantee world-wide uniformity of interest rates and real wage rates. However, even if all countries do continue, in trading equilibrium, to produce all commodities, world-wide uniformity of interest rates and real wage rates is still not ensured if there is a choice of production methods. This is because in an economy with a choice of technique more than one interest rate can be associated with a given set of relative commodity prices.[3] It should be noted carefully that we are not here contradicting our earlier assertion that to any given interest rate there corresponds a unique set of relative commodity prices; we are merely pointing out that the converse does not hold.

In a well-known paper [3], Samuelson appears to argue that free trade in any two commodities, both of which are produced in each of two countries, will ensure equalisation of interest rates and real wage rates as between those two countries. The apparent conflict between Samuelson's conclusion and the conclusion of our last paragraph does not result from the fact that, unlike us, Samuelson arbitrarily excludes produced means of production from trade. In fact there really is no conflict at all because, as Bliss has pointed out ([1], pp. 342–3), Samuelson does not actually reach a conclusion but simply states that if conditions are such that the relative price of the traded commodities in question is a monotonic function of the interest rate, then free trade in those commodities will equalise interest rates and real wage rates as between countries. Since Samuelson gives no significant account of what these conditions are, this statement is trivial and perfectly consistent with our result.[4]

THE BASIS OF TRADE

While the proximate basis of trade is the inter-economy difference in no-trade interest rates, a more fundamental basis of trade will be found if those interest rates are explained and, indeed, any stationary equilibrium theory of trade based on no-trade commodity price differences must involve a theory of no-trade interest rates. A writer in the classical tradition might argue that the no-trade interest rate in a country is determined by an exogenously given real wage, itself determined by cultural processes not examined within trade theory. A neo-Keynesian writer might relate the no-trade interest rate in an economy to the capitalists' savings ratio and the no-trade growth rate in that economy. Thus according to the theory of distribution adopted,[5] the basis of trade may be found in, e.g., different real wages, different savings behaviour or different growth rates. No matter what the basis of trade may be, however, it must exert its influence by causing inter-economy differences in no-trade interest rates.

NOTES

* This (very short!) essay was first published in *Australian Economic Papers*, 1973. It had benefited from the comments and criticisms of many people, including C. J. Bliss, J. L. Eatwell, G. C. Harcourt, L. Mainwaring, S. Parrinello and a referee of *A.E.P.*
1. See, e.g., Mirrlees [2]. Note that, as Mirrlees shows, the assumptions of 'no jointness' and no technical change can be relaxed somewhat.
2. See, e.g., Sraffa [4], chapter III.
3. We may prove this assertion by presenting a simple numerical example. Consider a two-commodity economy with the following available 'Leontief' techniques, where A, B are the matrices of input-output coefficients and $\underline{a}$, $\underline{b}$

the row vectors of labour input coefficients.

$$A = \begin{bmatrix} 0 & 1 \\ 1/2 & 0 \end{bmatrix}, \quad B = \begin{bmatrix} 0 & 1 \\ 1/4 & 0 \end{bmatrix}$$

$$\underline{a} = [1/9 \quad 1], \quad \underline{b} = [1 \quad 1]$$

If p is the price of the first commodity in terms of the second and r is the annual rate of interest then it is easy to show that $p = (11 + 9r)/(20 + 2r)$ for technique A, that $p = (5 + r)/(8 + 4r)$ for technique B and hence that p is an increasing function of r for A but a decreasing function of r for B. It is also easy to show that technique A will be in use for $0 \leq r < 13.23\%$, while B will be used for $13.23\% < r$. It follows that as r rises from zero to 100% (the maximum possible r with technique B), p first rises and then falls. Thus infinitely many pairs of r values, say r_1 and r_2, yield the *same* p. In fact p is the same for *all* r_1 and r_2 such that $0 \leq r_1 \leq 13.23\%$ and $r_2 = (6 - 31r_1)/(12 + 17r_1)$. [It may be noted that, as L. Mainwaring has pointed out to us, the vector of relative commodity prices cannot recur if there is only one technique available (except in the trivial case in which relative prices are independent of the interest rate): see Essays 6 and 7 in this volume.]

4. See Essay 7 in this volume.
5. One is not, of course, compelled to use the same explanation of the no-trade interest rate for all the various countries.

REFERENCES

[1] Bliss, C. J. 'Collected scientific papers of Paul Samuelson'. *Economic Journal*, 1967, pp. 338–45.
[2] Mirrlees, J. A. 'The dynamic non-substitution theorem', *Review of Economic Studies*, 1969, pp. 67–76.
[3] Samuelson, P. A. 'Equalisation by trade of the interest rate along with the real wage'. In Baldwin, R. E. *et al.*, (eds.), *Trade, Growth and the Balance of Payments* (*Essays in Honor of Gottfried Haberler*), Rand McNally, Chicago, 1965.
[4] Sraffa, P. *Production of Commodities by Means of Commodities*. Cambridge University Press, 1960.

11 The Golden Rule and the Gain from Trade*

IAN STEEDMAN and J. S. METCALFE

The object of this essay is to compare the per worker consumption possibility set in a closed economy with that in an open economy, when both economies are growing at a steady rate, g, and have a uniform and constant rate of profit, r. We shall assume that the same constant returns to scale methods of production are available in each country and that there is only one primary input, homogeneous labour.[1] (Capital is thus not regarded as a primary input.) We shall assume, further, that only consumption commodities are traded, that the open economy can trade at given terms of trade and that there is no government.[2] Our analysis will be a *comparative dynamic* one and we shall not consider the *transition* between no-trade and with-trade steady growth paths.[3]

Consider a closed economy in which a single consumption commodity is produced. We know from the Golden Rule discussion that, if $r > g$, then, in general, the technique chosen under competitive conditions will not yield the consumption per worker which is the greatest technically possible at the growth rate g. It follows immediately that if two economies are alike in every respect, except that one has an extra available method of production which will in fact be chosen at the profit rate r, then the economy with the greater technical choice may have the higher or the lower consumption per worker.

Consider now a closed, or autarkic economy A, in which two consumption commodities, 1 and 2, are produced. Each one is produced in its own integrated sector which produces, in addition to the consumption commodity, all the produced inputs necessary for the production of that consumption commodity. If, with the techniques chosen at the profit rate r, the maximum possible consumption per worker, at growth rate g, is c_1 for the first consumption commodity and c_2 for the second, then the per worker consumption bundle will be constrained to lie on c_1c_2 in Figure 11.1(a). We shall call $0c_1c_2$ the per worker consumption possibility set, or PWCPS. Let B be an economy like A in every respect, except that it has an extra production method available, in sector 2 say, which will in fact be chosen at the profit rate r. It follows from the argument of the last paragraph that the PWCPS in B may be either $0c_1c_2'$ or $0c_1c_2''$ in Figure 11.1(b). The PWCPS may be larger or smaller in B, the economy with the greater choice of production methods.

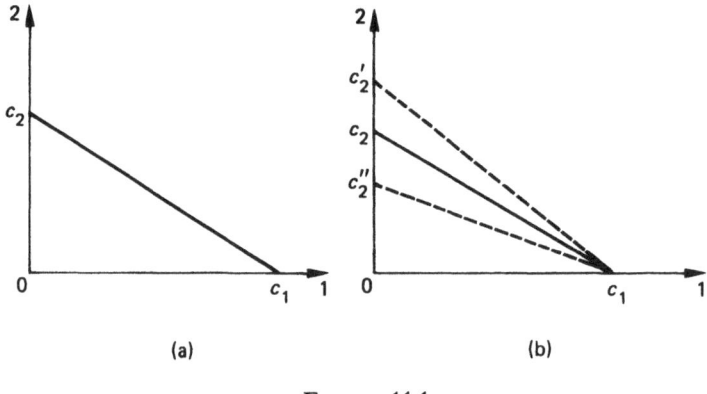

FIGURE 11.1

Now consider an economy T which is like A in every respect, except that it is open to free trade in consumption commodities, at fixed terms of trade which differ from the consumption commodity price ratio in A. Relative to economy A, the position of T is similar to that of economy B. Economy T has, in effect, an extra available method of production of one commodity, namely that of producing the other commodity and then transforming it into the first by trade. Furthermore, this extra production method will certainly be used at the common profit rate r, for specialising and trading will give a higher (equal) real wage in terms of the imported (exported) commodity, by comparison with the real wage in A. We might expect then, that the PWCPS in T, like that in B, may be larger or smaller than that in A.

Taking the second consumption commodity as the standard of value, let the price of the first be p^A in A and p on the world market; let the absolute slope of c_1c_2 in Figure 11.1 be s. It is clear that economy T will be specialised in the production of 1 or 2 according as $p > p^A$ or $p^A > p$, since the real wage would otherwise not be maximised at the given profit rate r. The PWCPS in T will depend on the pattern of specialisation and on p. Let the consumption commodities be so numbered that $p^A > s$; we have to consider three cases.

Case (i); $p > p^A > s$. Economy T will be specialised in 1 and will have a larger PWCPS than A, $0c_1c_2'$ in Figure 11.2(a).

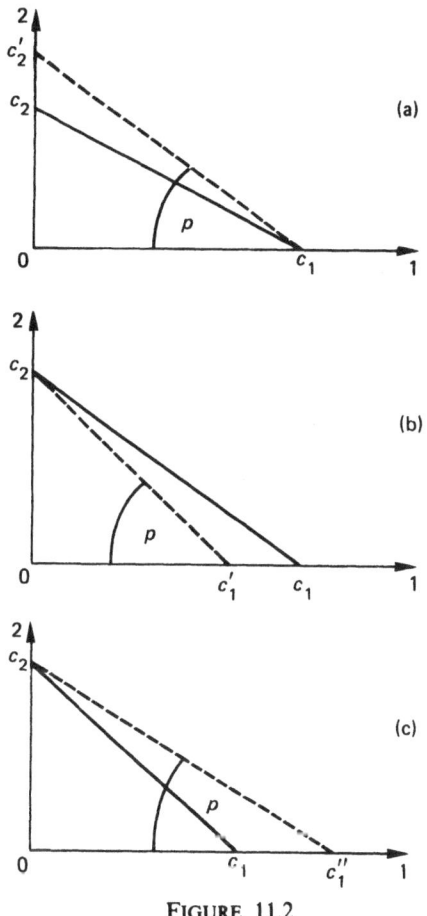

FIGURE 11.2

Case (ii); $p^A > p > s$. Economy T will be specialised in 2 and will have a *smaller* PWCPS than A, $0c_1'c_2$ in Figure 11.2(b).

Case (iii); $p^A > s > p$. Economy T will be specialised in 2 and will have a larger PWCPS than A, $0c_1''c_2$ in Figure 11.2(c).

When we compare two economies, with identical domestic production methods, profit rates and growth rates, one being autarkic and the other open to free trade in consumption commodities, we can, in general,[4] make no *a priori* statement as to which economy will have the larger per worker consumption possibility set. In this comparative dynamics sense, the gain from trade may be negative or positive.[5]

NOTES

*This essay was first published (in French) in C. Berthomieu and J. and L. Cartelier (eds.), *Ricardiens, Keynésiens et Marxistes*, Presses Universitaires de Grenoble, 1974.
1. We shall not assume full employment of labour and, throughout, 'worker' will mean 'employed worker'.
2. These last three assumptions are, of course, common in trade theory.
3. That the distinction between comparisons and transitions is not always sharply made in the gain from trade literature is perhaps due, at least in part, to the fact that production is generally assumed to be timeless (see, e.g., Kemp [2], Samuelson [3]).
4. Of course, if $r = g$ (the Golden Rule case), then $p^A = s$ and a negative 'gain' from trade is impossible. (Note that much discussion of the gain from trade relates to the special case $r = g = 0$).
5. This statement is without prejudice as to the possible results of an analysis of the *transition* from autarky to free trade, perhaps along the lines suggested by Hicks [1] or Spaventa [4]. Stiglitz has analysed the transition in a one consumption commodity, one capital good model, see [5], especially the Appendix. Further on the transition from autarky to free trade, and the importance of capital malleability in such a transition, see Essay 12 in this volume.

REFERENCES

[1] Hicks, J. R. 'A neo-Austrian growth theory'. *Economic Journal*, 1970, pp. 257–81.
[2] Kemp, M. C. 'The gain from international trade'. *Economic Journal*, 1962, pp. 803–19.
[3] Samuelson, P. A. 'The gains from international trade once again'. *Economic Journal*, 1962, pp. 820–9.
[4] Spaventa, L. 'Notes on problems of transition between techniques'. In Mirrlees J. A. and Stern N. H. (eds.), *Models of Economic Growth*, Macmillan, London, 1973.
[5] Stiglitz, J. E. 'Factor price equalisation in a dynamic economy'. *Journal of Political Economy*, 1970, pp. 456–88.

12 On the Transition from Autarky to Trade*

L. MAINWARING

One of the more striking conclusions to emerge from the alternative trade theory presented in this volume is that the free trade level of consumption per worker may be less than the autarkic level. This appears to conflict with the well-known result, dating back at least as far as Ricardo, which states that free trade is not worse and, in general, is better (in some well-defined sense) than autarky. These apparently contradictory results are both reached on the basis of comparing the autarkic and free-trade equilibria. A number of economists have, however, suggested that no real contradiction is involved once the *transition* from autarky to trade is taken into account. Indeed, in Essay 4 of this volume it is shown that *on certain particular assumptions* the 'inclusive' measure of the gain from trade will always be positive irrespective of the sign of the steady-state measure. In the conclusion to that Essay attention was drawn to the severity of the assumptions underlying the result.

The same result has been obtained independently by Stiglitz [4] and Samuelson [2] and more fully developed by Smith [3], and it is clear that these economists see in this transitions argument a means by which the contradiction between steady state losses and the orthodox theory of the gain from trade may be completely resolved.[1] This being so, it seems worthwhile to consider in a little more depth some of the assumptions on which the result of an ever-positive inclusive gain is based. To put our discussion in proper perspective we begin with a brief sketch of the transitional argument.

Where, on the basis of a comparison of the equilibria, there is a loss from trade, it can be shown that the value of capital per worker is lower, and the wage rate higher, in free-trade equilibrium than in autarky. In a transition from autarky to trade the unwanted capital is transformed into consumption goods[2] thus giving a transitional consumption boost. The value of this additional consumption is just equal to the discounted present value (d.p.v.) of the difference between autarkic and free-trade streams of capitalist consumption, if the rate of profits is used as the discount rate. Thus, so far as capitalists are concerned, there is nothing to choose between the autarkic and the trade-plus-transition consumption streams. There is, in consequence, always a gain from trade equal to the difference between free-trade and autarkic wages.[3]

One of the more important assumptions of this argument is the identification of the rate of profits with the rate of time preference, an assumption which is clearly not in the spirit of the classical and neo-Keynesian approach of the essays in this volume. Nevertheless, in welfare considerations of this sort it does seem reasonable to adopt some positive rate of discount and to that extent the inclusive measures will show a smaller loss or greater gain.

We therefore devote our attention to the equally crucial, though largely implicit, assumption that the move to a new steady state can be achieved smoothly without wastage of resources, be they machines or labour. Such wastage may occur if in the switch to specialised production it is not possible to transfer the capital and labour no longer required by the declining sector to the expanding sector, or to transform such capital into consumption goods. The implications of 'non-transferable' (or what we now call 'non-malleable') capital were clearly posed, as early as 1850, by William Whewell in a careful qualification of Ricardo's theory. It is worth quoting at length:

> Upon the principles here laid down, a country cannot lose by foreign trade.
>
> But among the principles here laid down is the principle of *transferable capital*; that is the principle that capital and labour can be transferred, without loss, from the production of one commodity to another, when the state of trade produces, or threatens, a diminution of profits in any branch of production.
>
> This can never be exactly the case. In almost all transfer of capital there is loss. But the loss may be temporary: the gain, or saving of further loss is supposed to be enduring; therefore, on the assumption here made, there may still be a general saving in all foreign trade.
>
> But if it be not true that capital and labour are transferable without enduring loss, the results here obtained are vitiated by the failure of that part of the foundation. If when a portion of a home-produced commodity is displaced in the home market by importation from a

foreign country, the capital and labour thus set free cannot be employed in producing any other commodity for which there is a demand, the assumptions of our investigation fail.

(Whewell [5] p. 19)

It would seem that 130 years later Whewell's remarks are still very much to the point.

The consequence of the assumption of capital malleability can be brought into sharp relief by concentrating on the opposite case of complete non-malleability. In the following sections we use a simple numerical example to allow a comparison of the relevant consumption streams for an economy in which malleability is ruled out.

BASIC ASSUMPTIONS

(i) In autarky the economy produces two consumption goods by means of independent, fully integrated processes using labour and machines. The unit production flows for sector i ($i = 1, 2$) are as follows:

$$\beta_i(L) + \alpha_i(M_i) \rightarrow \text{one unit } (C_i)$$
$$b_i(L) + a_i(M_i) \rightarrow \text{one unit } (M_i)$$

where L is labour and M_i and C_i refer to the machine and consumption commodity appropriate to sector i. The technical coefficients are given and unalterable. Machines of type i can be converted into consumption goods of type i only through the process of production, while machines of type one cannot be converted either directly, or through production, into type 2 consumption goods (and *mutatis mutandis* for M_2 and C_1).

(ii) Machines are subject to 'radioactive' depreciation at rates δ_i in the production of C_i, and d_i in the production of M_i. (It is recognised that this method of introducing depreciation is unsatisfactory but, in the present context, where a simple means of introducing fixity of capital is required, it appears quite harmless.)

(iii) The rates of growth in both equilibria are, also for simplicity, assumed to be zero.

(iv) Labour is fully employed in the steady states.

(v) Trade takes place in consumption goods only. Exchanges of machinery, either in steady state or in transition, are ruled out by 'very high' transport costs and, for partly used machines, by 'very high' dismantling and re-erection costs.

134 *Fundamental Issues in Trade Theory*

(vi) The rate of profits is taken as exogenous and is the same in the autarky and free-trade equilibria, and is used as the rate of discount when comparing consumption streams. Note that during the transition the rates of return in the two sectors can be expected to differ. The appropriate discount rate is nevertheless assumed to remain equal to the equilibrium rate of profits.

(vii) Being 'small', the economy fully specialises with trade and world prices are unaffected by its participation.

(viii) The opportunity to trade arises unexpectedly. An announcement of trading possibilities is made shortly before the start of period 0, so that plans can be made in that period which are appropriate to a new (confidently held) set of expectations.

ALTERNATIVE CONSUMPTION STREAMS

Figure 12.1 shows the general nature of the time profiles of the autarkic (*A*) and free-trade (*F*) equilibrium consumption streams. The undiscounted difference between these streams is the vertically shaded area *X*.

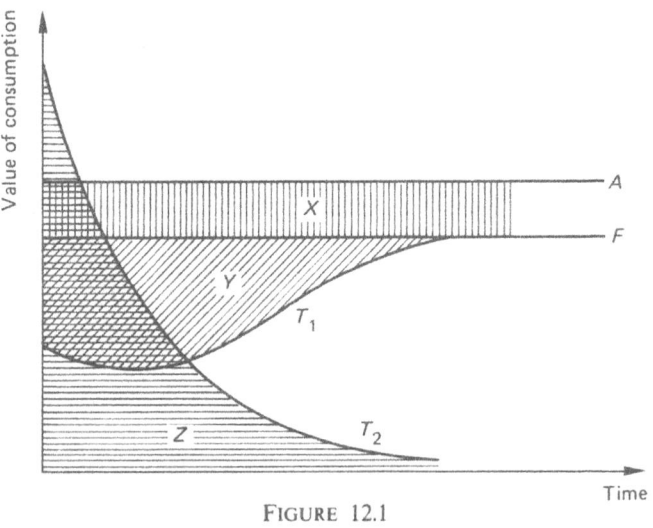

FIGURE 12.1

Suppose that, with trade, the country specialises in good 1. Then since during the transition sector 1 will be expanding, its output will be of less value than its free trade output, by an amount indicated by the diagonally shaded area Y. On the other hand, during the transition sector 2 will be producing in excess of its free trade level of zero. Since, moreover, there will be no further production of M_2 machines, those machines which were being used in the M_2 sub-sector will, in period 0, be transferred to the C_2 sub-sector giving, in the initial period of the transition an output in excess of its autarkic level. Thereafter the stock of machines and the value of consumption output will decline, as shown by the horizontally shaded area Z.[4] (It has been assumed here that production in sector 2 continues; see below for further discussion of this matter.)

If $X + Y > Z$ (all appropriately discounted) then the move to free trade involves a definite loss.

Example

The technical coefficients are as follows:

Sector 1		Sector 2	
$\beta_1 = 0.2$	$b_1 = 0.2$	$\beta_2 = 0.25$	$b_2 = 2.0$
$\alpha_1 = 1.0$	$a_1 = 1.0$	$\alpha_2 = 1.0$	$a_2 = 0.75$
$\delta_1 = 0.2$	$d_1 = 0.2$	$\delta_2 = 0.48$	$d_2 = 0.48$

In autarky, 40 units of each consumption commodity are produced so that the production flows are as follows:

Sector 1
$$2(L) + 10(M_1) \to 10(M_1)$$
$$8(L) + 40(M_1) \to 40(C_1) \qquad A_1$$

At the beginning of each period the stock of machines is 50. During the period one-fifth of this stock 'evaporates' and is replaced by the start of the next period by the new machine output. Similarly we have

Sector 2
$$60(L) + 22.5(M_2) \to 30(M_2)$$
$$10(L) + 40(M_2) \to 40(C_2) \qquad A_2$$

The economy employs a total of 80 units of labour.

In autarky, the wage and prices are determined by the following equations:

$$\pi_i = \beta_i w + \alpha_i p_i(r + \delta_i)$$
$$p_i = b_i w + a_i p_i(r + d_i) \qquad (i = 1, 2)$$

where r is the rate of profits, π_i the price of C_i, p_i the price of M_i and w the wage. Setting $\pi_1 = 1$, these four equations are sufficient to determine π_2, p_1, p_2 and w. At a rate of profits of 4% prices in our example are as follows:[5]

$$w = 3.8 \qquad \pi_1 = p_1 = 1 \qquad p_2 = 12.46 \qquad \pi_2 = 7.43$$

When the opportunity to trade arises the direction of specialisation depends on whether the free-trade price ratio is greater or less than π_2. If less, then specialisation in commodity 1 is profitable, and the consequent equilibrium production flow with full employment is

$$16(L) + 80(M_1) \rightarrow 80(M_1)$$
$$64(L) + 320(M_1) \rightarrow 320(C_1) \qquad\qquad F$$

In comparing the autarky (A_1 and A_2) and free-trade (F) consumption streams, outputs need to be valued in common prices. Since an arbitrarily small departure from autarky prices is sufficient to induce trade, we shall use autarky prices in valuation.

For the rest of this section we make the additional *assumption* that when trade begins (in period 0) sector 2 becomes unprofitable.[6] In this case losses are minimised if the capital stock carried over from autarky can continue to produce a value of net output in excess of wage costs. Since there is likely to be a degree of unemployment during the transition the assumption of unprofitable production may well imply that wages have a strong downward rigidity. Consideration of this issue is taken up in the final section.

A comparison of the equilibrium streams shows:

Value of $(A_1 + A_2) = A$	= 337.15
Value of F	= 320.0
Difference	= 17.15
D.p.v. of difference from 0 to infinity at $r = 0.04$	= 428.6

Next we need to consider the transitional paths T_1 and T_2. Consider first T_2.

Inspection of the production flows A_2 shows that there are 62.5 machines available for production at the start of period 0, all of which will be used to produce consumption goods. (There is clearly no problem

On the Transition from Autarky to Trade   137

in obtaining labour.) These machines then depreciate at a proportionate rate $\delta_2 = 0.48$. Since the machine:output ratio of the C_2 sub-sector is unity, the d.p.v. of the entire output stream to infinity is given by

$$\sum_{t=0}^{\infty}\left(\frac{1-\delta_2}{1+r}\right)^t 62.5\pi_2 = \sum_{t=0}^{\infty}(\tfrac{1}{2})^t 62.5\pi_2$$

which, conveniently, is equal to $2 \times 62.5\pi_2 = 928.6$. This is the d.p.v. of area Z. The d.p.v. of the difference $(Z - X)$ is

$$928.6 - 428.6 = 500$$

Thus if the d.p.v. of area Y exceeds 500 we can say that the move involves a loss. Consider then transitional path T_1. The shape of this path does, of course, depend on the rate of machine reproduction in the earlier periods. Whether or not the firms involved jointly choose that path which maximises the d.p.v. of the consumption stream does not matter since we need only investigate the first two transitional periods to reach a definite conclusion.

In period 0 production of C_1 cannot be greater, but may be smaller, than the autarky output of 40 as a result of machines being diverted to their own reproduction. Suppose, for example (for reasons given below), that the machines ordered to make good depreciation in the C_1 sub-sector are retained by the M_1 sub-sector in period 0. Then the production flows are:

$$18(M_1) \to 18(M_1)$$
$$32(M_1) \to 32(C_1)$$

There are still 50 machines in use but rather more are employed in subsector M_1 than was previously the case. The stock of machines at the start of period 1 is $(1 - d_1)50 + 18 = 58$. In this example the highest possible output of C_1 in period 1 (ruling out any *decrease* in machine outputs compared to autarky which would be incompatible with expansion) is given by the following pattern of production:

$$10(M_1) \to 10(M_1)$$
$$48(M_1) \to 48(C_1)$$

While the output of C_1 in period 0 was 8 less than the autarky output, in period 1 it cannot be more than 8 above the autarky level. In this example it appears then that there can never be more than a one-for-one trade-off between periods 0 and 1. This maximum trade-off, however, is quite independent of the particular example we have chosen here: it holds for whichever pattern of machine redistribution takes place (as may be readily verified and which is a consequence of the fact that $a_1 = \alpha_1 = 1$).[7] Even this one-for-one trade-off holds only in a physical sense since the d.p.v. of a unit of period 1's output is less than a unit of period 0's.

It follows from this that the transitional output of sector 1 in the first two periods inevitably falls short of the free-trade output level of 320 by *at least* $2 \times (320 - 40) = 560$ and this, in turn, is greater than the d.p.v. of the difference $(Z - X)$. This, moreover, seriously underestimates the loss involved because it neglects the short-fall of outputs in the remaining transitional periods.

DISCUSSION

Our considerations so far have been based on the additional assumption made in the previous section that the output of C_2 is constrained by the stock of machines left over from autarky. In other words, no production of M_2 occurs after period 0. At the same time it is clear that the closure of the M_2 sub-sector releases a large number of workers from employment, not all of whom find jobs in the expanding sector 1 for some periods to come. The consequence of this unemployment for the development of sector 2 depends on its effect on the real wage rate. If the wage rate does not fall then, at the new international prices, this sector is no longer profitable in the long run and its transitional path will be as described above. In circumstances in which the new price fails to cover wage costs, production will be terminated immediately.

It follows that *to the extent that* unemployment leads to a lowering of the wage the reduction in profitability is lessened. If the wage falls by a sufficient amount the long-run (equilibrium) rate of profits may continue to be paid in this industry until the slack in the labour market is taken up by the expansion of sector 1. In this way, the decline of sector 2 and the expansion of sector 1 may be more comfortably co-ordinated to avoid output losses.

There are, however, a number of points which need to be taken into account here. First, the outcome depends on the assumption that unemployment leads to a sufficient fall in real wages. One could just as well assume that wages are sticky during the transition and, *a priori*, there are no grounds for choosing one of these assumptions in preference to another. Secondly, even if wages do fall sufficiently, it is precisely because of unemployment; the transition will inevitably be characterised by the wastage of at least some resources.

The third point relates to the crucial role of expectations about which nothing has yet been said. If wages are perfectly flexible, then in the manner suggested above the transition could be visualised as a sequence of temporary equilibria over which the changes in production patterns are perfectly coordinated. (See Smith [3]). This way of viewing the transition, however, ignores the central problems by effectively sterilising the effects of uncertainty and expectations. Whilst these are undoubtedly difficult features of the world to model they should, nevertheless, be given some consideration. Whether or not sector 2 is earning the long-run rate of profits, its rate of return will always be less than that of sector 1 (provided the wage is the same in each sector). There will, therefore, always be an incentive for capitalists to transfer production from 2 to 1. It is true that sector 1's capacity is constrained at each stage in the transition. But does this mean that capitalists will continue to order old M_2 machines while they wait for new M_1 machines to become available? Capitalists are not omniscient; they cannot know the outputs of new M_1 machines for each succeeding period of the transition. But they do know that the M_2 machines have long lives and that as wages begin to rise they may well be caught with unprofitable machinery. Such expectations give further encouragement to the rapid termination of sector 2 production.

In our discussion so far it has been implicitly assumed that labour is homogeneous and, therefore, perfectly free to move from one sector to the other. In practice, it may be that workers have different skills so that the transfer of labour is conditional upon the acquisition of new skills, a process which may be both costly and time-consuming. In the numerical example we did not explicitly allow for the possibility of heterogeneous labour in order to avoid unnecessary complications, but some brief remarks will be sufficient to indicate the importance of skill differences in further undermining the presumption of a gain from trade. In the declining sector there will quickly emerge surpluses of the various types of labour skills specific to that sector. The effect of these surpluses on the rate of decline will depend on much the same factors as those which we discussed in relation to homogeneous labour. In the expanding sector, however, in addition to the costs of learning new skills, the short-run immobility of labour may have another important effect. If the expansion of sector 1 is constrained by the rate at which new skills are acquired, then the more prolonged is the retraining process the greater is the difference between sector 1's transitional output and the free-trade output (in other words, the greater is area Y in Figure 12.1). This additional constraint on the development of the expanding sector suggests that anyone wishing to argue *for* a gain from trade must take as much account of 'non-malleable' labour as of non-malleable capital. With homogeneous labour the assumption of wage rigidity is sufficient to establish the possibility of a welfare loss from trade. Without this assumption the outcome is not clear, but the existence of heterogeneous labour and of uncertainty about the transitional path may still mean that the movement from one equilibrium to another will feature unemployment, capital redundancy and consumption losses.

CONCLUSION

The difficult issues which have just been referred to notwithstanding, we can perhaps claim to have shown in this essay that there is no *presumption* that the gain from trade is positive once the transition is taken into account.

NOTES

*This paper has benefited enormously from the many improvements suggested by Ian Steedman. I should also like to thank David Evans and Alasdair Smith for helpful discussions.
1. It is interesting to note that the transitional arguments have come to prominence only since the possibility of steady-state losses was clearly established. This prompts the question whether equilibrium comparisons are not, after all, what the orthodox welfare theory has been concerned with. Indeed, there are good reasons for adopting the view that comparisons are the correct procedure for investigating the efficiency of capitalism under free trade, though we shall not enlarge on this matter here.
2. The transformation occurs either directly, or through employment of the capital in consumption goods industries still operating, or through its exchange for foreign consumption goods.
3. For further details of the argument, see Essay 4. With more than one primary factor the gain is equal to the increase in total primary income.
4. Note that because of radioactive depreciation Z continues to infinity. If the transition is completed in finite time then obviously Z will be cut short at some point. But since the 'tail' of Z is likely to be very small this consideration is neglected. (An addition of an extra amount of transitional output only serves to make our contention *more* difficult to demonstrate).
5. Some of the figures presented in this example are subject to very minor rounding.
6. 'Unprofitable' in the sense of being unable to secure the equilibrium rate of profits which may also be taken as the rate of interest on borrowed finance.
7. To allow a continued expansion of this sector, the one-period trade-off would

have to be even less favourable. Thus the production pattern in period 1 may be

$$14(M_1) \to 14(M_1)$$
$$44(M_1) \to 44(C_1)$$

Since $14/58 > d_1$ more machines are now being produced than are required to make good depreciation and so further expansion is possible, but only 4 more units of C_1 are being produced, as compared to autarky.

REFERENCES

[1] J. S. Metcalfe and I. Steedman. 'A note on the gain from trade'. *Economic Record*, 1974, pp. 581–95. See Essay 4 in this volume.
[2] P. A. Samuelson. 'Trade pattern reversals in time-phased Ricardian systems and intertemporal efficiency'. *Journal of International Economics*, 1975, pp. 309–63.
[3] M. A. M. Smith. 'The evaluation of intertemporal gains from trade'. London School of Economics, mimeo, 1977.
[4] J. E. Stiglitz, 'Factor price equalisation in a dynamic economy'. *Journal of Political Economy*, 1970, pp. 456–88.
[5] W. Whewell. *A Mathematical Exposition of Some Doctrines of Political Economy; Second Memoir*, 1850 (Reprinted 1974 by Gregg International Publishers, Farnborough).

13 The von Neumann Analysis and the Small Open Economy*

IAN STEEDMAN

While the available, common theories of trade perhaps capture some aspects of the significance of natural resource availabilities for patterns and volumes of trade, few would argue that they focus well on the role of produced means of production and of their accumulation. Yet, without denying the importance of natural resources for trade – which it would be difficult to do in the 1970s – it must be recognised that growth, produced means of production and trade in the latter are major features of contemporary world trade.[1] It is therefore natural to ask whether these aspects of trade can be captured in a reasonably simple analysis.

The most powerful tool available for the analysis of a growing, capital good producing and using closed economy is clearly that provided by von Neumann (and further discussed by subsequent writers), so that one is inevitably led to consider whether the von Neumann analysis can be applied to an open economy. This essay is intended to suggest that it can be so applied, in a reasonably simple way, to the case of a small open economy, making use, in particular, of Fujimoto's recent, powerful linear programming presentation of the von Neumann analysis.[2] It is not intended to suggest, of course, that such an analysis provides a complete or realistic picture of growth and trade. It is not necessary to rehearse here all the various special and rigid simplifying assumptions built into the von Neumann analysis, especially when used in its simplest form, as it will be here. It may simply be remarked that the respective emphases and silences of the von Neumann analysis—with respect to produced means of production, growth, scarce resources and consumer demand patterns—are neatly complementary to those of much modern trade theory.

The von Neumann Analysis and Trade   143

The following analysis contains no surprising or exciting conclusions. (As is to be expected, given the various background assumptions, the results obtained lie within the Ricardo–Taussig–Graham–McKenzie–Jones family of trade theorems.) It is to be hoped, nevertheless, that it does suggest an interesting line of approach to basic trade theory, along which standard results may be derived in a multi-commodity, growing economy framework.

THE SMALL ECONOMY

Only a single, small economy, facing given world prices, will be considered and it will be assumed throughout that its commodity trade is balanced, in terms of domestic currency; international capital flows, and their counterpart interest, etc. flows, will be assumed away. Since the economy considered will be growing at a positive rate, the 'small economy' assumption involves the further implicit assumption that the world economy is growing at least as fast as the particular economy examined. No attempt will be made to close the system by, say, presenting a theory of the growth rate, or a theory of the real wage; rather, one or the other will be treated as a given parameter. Nor will the analysis of paths of transition be undertaken, the analysis being confined to 'comparative dynamics'.

The number of commodities allowed, whether tradeable or non-tradeable, is arbitrarily large. It will be assumed to be known *a priori* which products are tradeable and which not. Whilst it would certainly be desirable to explain this division endogenously – in terms perhaps of transport costs, the costs of dismantling and re-erecting partially used fixed capital, and so on – to attempt such an explanation here would probably make the analysis unduly complicated. (It may be noted in passing that many of the non-tradeable products would, in reality, be partially used machines, buildings, etc. This fact cannot reasonably be ignored in analyses of the transition from, say, free trade to restricted trade. Changes in the structure of production typically involve the scrapping of plant and this cannot be dealt with by assuming that changes in the 'capital value' of means of production can be converted into transitional gains or losses in the value of consumption: see Essay 12 in this volume.)

THE EXISTENCE OF TRADE EQUILIBRIUM

Let the rectangular matrices A^+ and B be matrices of material inputs to and outputs from the various processes, where A^+ includes the elements of the given real wage bill, expressed as a physical bundle of products. The jth columns of A^+ and B refer to the jth productive activity, operated at some (arbitrary) unit level. Let the products be so numbered that A^+ and B may be partitioned horizontally as

$$A^+ \equiv \begin{bmatrix} A_1^+ \\ A_2^+ \end{bmatrix} \quad \text{and} \quad B \equiv \begin{bmatrix} B_1 \\ B_2 \end{bmatrix},$$

where A_1^+ and B_1 refer to non-tradeable and A_2^+ and B_2 to tradeable products. If $\underline{x}$ is the semi-positive column vector of activity levels, g the growth rate and $\underline{f}$ the strictly positive row vector of *world* prices of tradeables (expressed, say, in gold) then:

$$(1+g)A_1^+ \underline{x} \leqq B_1 \underline{x} \tag{1}$$

and

$$(1+g)\underline{f} A_2^+ \underline{x} \leqq \underline{f} B_2 \underline{x}. \tag{2}$$

Relation (1) states that the output of each non-tradeable is at least $(1+g)$ times the input of that product. Relation (2) states that the *total* gold value of output of tradeables is at least $(1+g)$ times the *total* gold value of the input of tradeables: this is equivalent to stating that exports at the end of a production period can at least pay for the imports of next period's inputs. It is to be noted that (2) is essentially different from (1). No reference is made in (2) to any *commodity by commodity* constraint; all that matters is that the aggregate gold value of exports should be growing at a rate not less than g. An alternative way of putting this is to say that, given $\underline{f}$, the important properties of any process, with respect to tradeables, are not the specific physical quantities of inputs and outputs but only the aggregate gold value of inputs and of outputs. Tradeables are, in effect, collapsed into a single product – gold.

Now let $\underline{p}_1$ be the semi-positive row vector of non-tradeables prices, expressed in domestic currency, let 'e' be the exchange rate, expressed as a number of domestic currency units per unit of gold, and let r be the rate of profit. The condition that no process should yield a rate of return greater than r may be written as:

$$(1+r)(\underline{p}_1 A_1^+ + e\underline{f} A_2^+) \geqq \underline{p}_1 B_1 + e\underline{f} B_2. \tag{3}$$

Turning now to the complementary slackness conditions – that any product in surplus has a zero price, while any unprofitable process is not used – one sees from (1), (2) and (3) that:

$$(1+g)\underline{p}_1 A_1^+ \underline{x} = \underline{p}_1 B_1 \underline{x} \qquad (4)$$

and
$$(1+g)e\underline{f} A_2^+ \underline{x} = e\underline{f} B_2 \underline{x} \qquad (5)$$

$$(1+r)(p_1 A_1^+ + e\underline{f} A_2^+)\underline{x} = (\underline{p}_1 B_1 + e\underline{f} B_2)\underline{x} \qquad (6)$$

Relation (4) ensures that any non-tradeable produced in 'surplus' will be a free good, (5) that gold will be a free good if the trade balance is in surplus and (6) that unprofitable processes are unused.

Now conditions (1)–(6) are merely a particular version of the standard von Neumann model conditions. Thus on making certain standard and reasonable assumptions, one can say at once that an equilibrium exists. The activity and price vectors, $\underline{x}$ and $\underline{p}$, may not be uniquely determined but r and g will be uniquely determined (see the following section). Furthermore, the unique values of r and g are equal – comparing the sum of (4) and (5) with (6), one sees that if the domestic currency value of aggregate input and output is to be positive, $r = g$. Thus the existence of a trade equilibrium is established in a small, growing economy, with an arbitrary number of tradeable and non-tradeable goods, which include fixed capital goods of various ages.

(It may be noted, in passing, that since the trade equilibrium considered above is merely a special case of the von Neumann equilibrium, it must follow at once that Morishima's 'Generalized Fundamental Marxian Theorem'[3] can be applied perfectly well in a small, open economy with balanced trade. It is not at all clear, by contrast, how traditional Marxist 'labour value' accounting could be applied to an open economy; how could the labour used in producing exports be allocated amongst the various commodities produced by means of imported commodities?)

FUJIMOTO'S ANALYSIS

Fujimoto has recently presented a beautiful linear programming formulation of the von Neumann analysis. He shows, amongst other things, that the equilibrium value of $r = g$ is *unique*, provided that equilibria with a total wage bill of zero value are ignored, and that, except at possible discontinuities, the unique equilibrium value of $r = g$ is inversely related to the level of the real wage rate. Fujimoto's approach will be used below; zero wage bill equilibria will be ignored, as will any discontinuities in the inverse, monotonic relation between $r = g$ and the wage level.

Fujimoto retains the traditional von Neumann assumption, accepted above, that wages are paid in advance but here they will be assumed to be paid *ex post*. Subject to this inessential change, which serves to simplify the relevant relations slightly, his analysis may be presented as follows for the closed economy. As before, let B be the output matrix; let A be the input matrix *not* including real wages. Let $\underline{p}$ be the semi-positive row vector of labour-commanded prices and $\underline{a}$ be the strictly positive row vector of labour input to each activity at unit level. (Fujimoto requires $\underline{a}$ only to be semi-positive but this complication is not our focus of attention.) Then if the semi-positive column vector $\underline{w}$ shows, at an arbitrary scale, the proportions in which products enter the real wage bundle, consider the following problems:

$$\text{Minimise } E = \underline{a} \cdot \underline{x} \qquad \text{Maximise } L = \underline{p} \cdot \underline{w}$$
$$\text{subject to } \begin{cases} B\underline{x} \geqq (1+g)A\underline{x} + \underline{w} \\ \underline{x} \geqq \underline{0} \end{cases} \qquad \text{s.t. } \begin{cases} \underline{p}B \leqq (1+r)\underline{p}A + \underline{a} \\ \underline{p} \geqq \underline{0} \end{cases}$$

The solution to the minimum problem minimises the total employment required to produce the bundle $\underline{w}$ and maintain growth at a rate not less than the given level g. It thus *maximises* the real wage *rate*. The solution to the maximum problem maximises the labour commanded by the bundle $\underline{w}$ subject to no process yielding a profit rate exceeding the given rate r. It thus *minimises* the real wage *rate*. Of course, if $r = g$ then the problems are dual and $E^{\min} = L^{\max} =$ the reciprocal of the real wage *rate*. As stated above, Fujimoto uses this framework of analysis to show that growth equilibrium is unique, with respect to $r = g$, if the value of the wage bill is positive, and that $r = g$ is inversely related to the level of the real wage rate.

TRADE EQUILIBRIUM AGAIN

Setting the domestic currency money wage rate equal to unity, so that labour-commanded prices equal money prices (numerically), defining $C \equiv [B - (1+g)A]$, taking $r = g$ as read from now on and partitioning commodities into non-tradeable (1) and tradeable (2) as before, one may represent the autarky equilibrium as the solution to:

The von Neumann Analysis and Trade

$$\text{Min } E = \underline{a}\underline{x} \qquad \text{Max } L = \underline{p}_1\underline{w}_1 + \underline{p}_2\underline{w}_2$$

$$\text{s.t. } \begin{cases} C_1\underline{x} \geq \underline{w}_1 \\ C_2\underline{x} \geq \underline{w}_2 \\ \underline{x} \geq \underline{0} \end{cases} \qquad \text{s.t. } \begin{cases} \underline{p}_1 C_1 + \underline{p}_2 C_2 \leq \underline{a} \\ \underline{p}_1, \underline{p}_2 \geq \underline{0} \end{cases} \qquad (7)$$

The free trade equilibrium can be represented in more than one way. A formulation obviously reminiscent of our earlier presentation of trade equilibrium is:

$$\text{Min } E = \underline{a}\underline{x} \qquad \text{Max } L = \underline{p}_1\underline{w}_1 + ef\underline{w}_2$$

$$\begin{cases} C_1\underline{x} \geq \underline{w}_1 \\ fC_2\underline{x} \geq f\underline{w}_2 \\ \underline{x} \geq \underline{0} \end{cases} \qquad \begin{cases} \underline{p}_1 C_1 + efC_2 \leq \underline{a} \\ \underline{p}_1 \geq \underline{0} \\ e \geq 0 \end{cases} \qquad (8)$$

(Note that the exchange rate, e, here has the dimensions 'labour commanded per unit of gold'.) A more explicit formulation can be presented, however, in which $\underline{m}$ and $\underline{e}$ are semi-positive column vectors of imports and exports, respectively. One then has:

$$\text{Min } E = \underline{a}\underline{x} \qquad \text{Max } L = \underline{p}_1\underline{w}_1 + \underline{p}_2\underline{w}_2$$

$$\text{s.t. } \begin{cases} C_1\underline{x} \geq \underline{w}_1 \\ C_2\underline{x} + \underline{m} \geq \underline{w}_2 + \underline{e} \\ f\underline{e} \geq f\underline{m} \\ \underline{x}, \underline{m}, \underline{e} \geq \underline{0} \end{cases} \qquad \text{s.t. } \begin{cases} \underline{p}_1 C_1 + \underline{p}_2 C_2 \leq \underline{a} \\ \underline{p}_2 = ef \\ \underline{p}_1, \underline{p}_2 \geq \underline{0} \\ e \geq 0 \end{cases} \qquad (9)$$

It is to be noted that the fact that, in the maximum problem, $\underline{p}_2 = ef$ is necessarily an *equality*, is reflected in the minimum problem by the presence of what is, in effect, the single, unsigned vector, $(\underline{e} - \underline{m})$, of net exports.

THE GAIN FROM FREE TRADE

Compare the minimum problems in (7) and (8), for some given (feasible) value of $r = g$. Any feasible $\underline{x}$, and thus the optimal $\underline{x}$, in (7) will necessarily satisfy the constraints in (8) but the converse is not true. Therefore E can be made at least as *small* in (8) as in (7), i.e. the real wage rate can be made at least as *large* in (8) as in (7). For any (feasible) growth and profit rate, free trade yields *at least* as high a real wage rate as does autarky. (Consumption per worker is here the same as the real wage rate, of course.)[4] Thus the gain from free trade is non-negative.

Under what conditions is that gain zero? Denote solutions to the autarky problem (7) by A superscripts and those to (8) by F superscripts. If $\underline{p}_2^A$ is *proportional* to $\underline{f}$ then, since $\underline{p}_2^A C_2 \underline{x} = \underline{p}_2^A \underline{w}_2$ in (7) by complementary slackness, $\underline{x}^F = \underline{x}^A$, $\underline{p}_1^F = \underline{p}_1^A$ and $e^F =$ the proportionality factor between $\underline{p}_2^A$ and $\underline{f}$ is a solution to (8), with $E^F = L^F = L^A = E^A$. The trade gain is zero if the autarky prices of tradeables are proportional to world prices. ($\underline{x}^F$ will not be uniquely determined, of course, $\underline{x}^A$ being merely a *possible* solution.) Alternatively, if $\underline{p}_2^A = \underline{0}$, so that all tradeables are 'free goods' under autarky, then $\underline{x}^F = \underline{x}^A$, $\underline{p}_1^F = \underline{p}_1^A$ and $e^F = 0$ is a solution to (8), again with $E^F = L^F = L^A = E^A$. Not surprisingly, trade brings no gain if all tradeables are 'over-supplied' under autarky. Thus if $\underline{p}_2^A = k\underline{f}$, where $k \geq 0$, the gain is zero. That the converse also holds may be shown by examining $\underline{p}_1^A, \underline{p}_2^A$ as a solution to the trade maximum problem. Thus the gain is zero if and only if $\underline{p}_2^A = k\underline{f}$, where $k \geq 0$.

If the scalar w denotes the level of the wage rate (the reciprocal of $E = L$) then the gain from trade may be depicted as in Figure 13.1. With either free trade or autarky, w is inversely related to $r = g$ but the free trade frontier never lies inside the autarky one and, indeed, only touches it (if at all) at points where $\underline{p}_2^A = k\underline{f}$, $k \geq 0$.

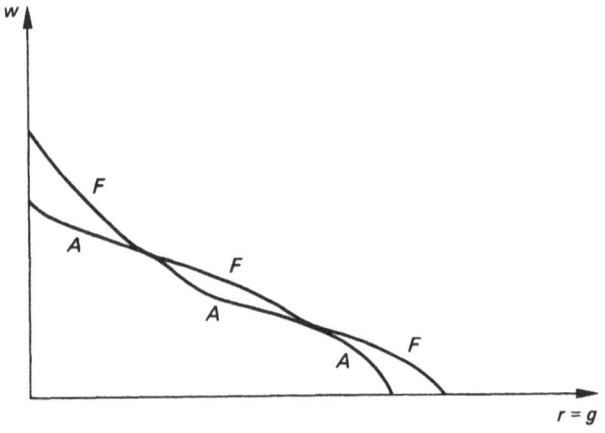

FIGURE 13.1

It may be noted that, although the frontiers in Figure 13.1 were determined above by taking $r = g$ as given, if the real wage level, w, is in fact exogenously determined, as in the original von Neumann model, then that figure still holds and the 'gain from trade' appears in the form of a higher rate of profit and accumulation for a given real wage level. It should also be remarked that varying the (parametrically) given value of either g or w, the processes used under free trade, shown by $\underline{x}^F$, and the pattern of exports and imports, shown by $(\underline{e}^F - \underline{m}^F) = (C_2\underline{x}^F - \underline{w}_2)$, will change, in general, even for fixed A, B, $\underline{a}$ and f. The present analysis can therefore not be identified with the so-called 'Ricardian' analysis of the textbooks, in which world prices and domestic conditions of production suffice to determine the patterns of output and trade in a small, open economy.

SOME OTHER PROPERTIES OF TRADE EQUILIBRIUM

Suppose that wage goods are all tradeables, so that $\underline{w}_1 = \underline{0}$ (non-tradeables might all be old machines and other producer goods); a number of properties of the equilibrium exchange rate follow at once. First, since $L^F = e^F(f\underline{w}_2)$ and L^F is positively related to $r = g$, one finds that

$$\frac{de^F}{dg} > 0.$$

(Alternatively, of course, $\dfrac{de^F}{dw} < 0$ where w is a given wage level.) A notional *increase* in the given growth rate increases e^F, that is it *devalues* the domestic currency relative to gold (revalues gold relative to domestic labour).

Now let the real wage be kept constant as between autarky and trade, so that $L^A = L^F$ and thus

$$\underline{p}_2^A \underline{w}_2 = e^F f\underline{w}_2$$

or

$$e^F = \left[\frac{\underline{p}_2^A \underline{w}_2}{f\underline{w}_2}\right] \tag{10}$$

Of course, $(\underline{p}_2^A \underline{w}_2)$ is also equal to the money wage rate in domestic currency; if the latter is m, rather than unity as elsewhere in this essay,

150   Fundamental Issues in Trade Theory

(10) may be written as

$$e^F = \left(\frac{m}{\underline{f}\cdot \underline{w}_2}\right) \quad (11)$$

Relation (11) shows, not surprisingly, that e^F is directly proportional to the domestic money wage rate and inversely proportional to the general level of world gold prices *for those tradeables which enter the real wage*. (If $w_{2j} = 0$ then e^F is independent of f_j.) e^F is positive provided that $(p^A_{2j} w_{2j})$ is positive for at least one j.

It follows from (10) that, since e^F is, in effect, a weighted average of the (p^A_{2j}/f_j),

$$\min_i [p^A_{2i}/f_i] \leqq e^F \leqq \max_i [p^A_{2i}/f_i], \quad (12)$$

where i runs over only those tradeables which enter the real wage bundle $(w_{2i} > 0)$.

While it might be tempting to leap from (12) to a 'chain rule' according to which all exports had a (p^A_{2i}/f_i) ratio less than that for all imports, such a leap is, of course, *illegitimate* unless the C matrix has a very special structure. (A structure which reduces, in effect, to that of the textbook 'Ricardian' model, though the labour cost of each commodity is here the 'growth augmented' labour cost.) This was pointed out, for example, by McKenzie.[5] The impossibility of such a jump does not even depend on the presence of non-tradeables or of joint production; the use of traded goods as inputs is sufficient.

Thus, holding g constant now, suppose that there are no non-tradeables, that

$$C_2 = \begin{bmatrix} 3 & -1 & -1 \\ -1 & 8 & -1 \\ -1 & -6 & 3 \end{bmatrix}$$

and that $\underline{w}_2 = (2, 3, 1)'$. Then $\underline{x}^A = (2, 1, 3)'$, $\underline{p}^A = (1, 1, 1)$ and $w^A = 1$. If $\underline{f} = (3, 2, 1)$ then $\underline{x}^F = (0, 6, 0)'$, $e^F = 1/42$ and $w^F = 3.2\overline{3}$. Commodity 2 is exported, while commodities 1 and 3 are imported, even though $(p^A_1/f_1) < (p_2{}^A/f_2) < (p^A_3/f_3)$. (Since g, not w, is held constant in this example, the fact that $e^F < \min [p^A_i/f_i]$ does *not* contradict (12) above. With g constant and $\underline{w}_1 = \underline{0}$, $e^F (\underline{f}\underline{w}_2) = L^F < L^A = (\underline{p}^A_2 \underline{w}_2)$.)

(It would be of interest to investigate whether the above points can be generalised to the case $\underline{w}_1 \neq \underline{0}$ but the question will not be pursued here.)

While the ratios of autarky to world prices for tradeables do not obey a chain rule, they do satisfy an aggregate inequality. It can be shown that

$$\underline{p}^A_2 \underline{m}^F \geqq \underline{p}^A_2 \underline{e}^F;$$

at autarky prices, the bundle of goods imported under free trade is at least as valuable as the bundle exported. (This, of course, is an expression of the gain from trade.) Now since $\underline{f}m^F \leq \underline{f}e^F$, it follows that

$$\left[\frac{p_2^A e^F}{\underline{f}e^F}\right] \leq \left[\frac{p_2^A m^F}{\underline{f}m^F}\right].$$

'Overall', (p_{2j}^A/f_j) is lower for exports than for imports, even though the rule does not hold commodity by commodity. (The reader may check that this inequality is indeed satisfied for the numerical example given above – and that e^F is *less than* the left hand member of the inequality.) It may be remarked that we have here a good example of the dangers of intuitive generalisation from the 2 (tradeable) commodity case. In that case, the 'aggregate' rule just given necessarily takes the form of a (two term) chain, thus inviting the unwary guess that a commodity by commodity chain rule holds with more than two commodities, whereas the proper generalisation is the 'aggregate' rule stated above.

We may now consider the question how 'specialisation' is to be interpreted in the joint production context. Let the *numbers* of non-tradeables and tradeables be n_1 and n_2 respectively and consider the minimum problem of (7) and (8). The number of processes used (the number of positive x_j's) will be less than or equal to $(n_1 + n_2)$ in (7) and $(n_1 + 1)$ in (8), if only basic solutions are considered. Now if e^F is positive and if not all tradeables are in surplus under autarky ($\underline{p}_2^A \neq \underline{0}$), it follows that 'the number of autarky processes *plus* the number of surplus non-tradeables under autarky *exceeds* the number of free trade processes *plus* the number of surplus non-tradeables under free trade'. Yet one cannot deduce, it seems, that fewer processes will be used under free trade than under autarky. Even when trade *is* 'more specialised' in terms of processes, however, it does not follow immediately that fewer commodities are produced under trade than under autarky – consider the (extreme) case in which every process produces every commodity (gross), so that $B > 0$.

CHANGES IN WORLD PRICES

It is clear from the minimum problem of either (8) or (9) that a strictly *proportional* change in all world prices will leave the solutions to those problems quite unaltered. Consequently, the dual variables, $\underline{p}_1^F$ and

152   *Fundamental Issues in Trade Theory*

$\underline{p}_2^F = e^F \underline{f}$, will be unaffected. All that changes is the exchange rate, e^F, which alters in inverse proportion to world prices so as to keep $\underline{p}_2^F$ constant. From now on, a 'change in world prices' therefore means a *non-proportional* change. The obvious effects of such a change to examine are the effects on the wage/growth rate frontier, on the exchange rate and domestic prices, on the structure of production and on the pattern and volume of trade. Some results on each of these issues will now be noted but none should occasion any surprise.

Consider first the minimum problem in (9). Starting from any given value of $\underline{f}$, an increase in any element f_j will relax the third constraint if j is an export but violate it if j is an import (holding $\underline{x}^F$, $\underline{e}^F$, $\underline{m}^F$ unchanged). Thus a *ceteris paribus* increase in a world price does not lower the wage/growth rate frontier, at given g, if that price is the price of an export and does not raise it if it is the price of an import. This result is not only obvious but is of a very partial nature, first because whether j is an export or an import will depend on the initial $\underline{f}$, secondly because j may change from being an import to being an export as f_j increases (though not vice-versa) and thirdly because the effect on the real wage level of an increase in f_j may vary with the given level of g (since the export/import status of j may so vary). Slightly more generally, if $(\underline{\Delta f} \underline{e}^F) > (\underline{\Delta f} \underline{m}^F)$ then the real wage cannot fall at the given g, and so on; this result could be expressed in terms of a 'terms of trade' index.

Suppose now that $\underline{w}_1 = \underline{0}$ and that the real wage (and thus L^F) is held constant, at unity say; as seen above, one may write

$$e^F = \left(\frac{1}{\underline{f}.\underline{w}_2}\right) \qquad (13)$$

and

$$\underline{p}_2^F = \left(\frac{1}{\underline{f}.\underline{w}_2}\right)\underline{f} = e^F \underline{f}. \qquad (14)$$

From (13), an increase in f_j will lower e^F if and only if j is a wage good. From (14), if $i \neq j$ then

$$\left[\frac{\partial p^F_{2i}}{\partial f_j}\right] = \left[\frac{\partial e^F}{\partial f_j}\right] f_i \leq 0.$$

An increase in the *world* price of a tradeable will lower the *domestic* price of every *other* tradeable if and only if the world price increase relates to a wage good. (If it does not, then no change results.) In any case, of course, the *relative* domestic prices of *other* tradeables will be unaffected. Again from (14).

$$\left[\frac{\partial p^F_{2j}}{\partial f_j}\right] = \left[\frac{(\underline{f}\underline{w}_2) - f_j w_{2j}}{(\underline{f}\underline{w}_2)^2}\right],$$

so that

$$0 \leqq \left[\frac{\partial p^F_{2j}}{\partial f_j}\right] \leqq e^F. \tag{15}$$

In (15), there is equality 'on the left' only if j is the *only* wage good and equality 'on the right' only if j is *not* a wage good. Thus if j is a wage good but not the only one then an increase in f_j leads to a *fall* in e^F, a *rise* in p^F_{2j} and a *fall* in the domestic price of every other tradeable, the *relative* prices of these latter being unchanged. Note that it is irrelevant whether j is exported or is imported.

Consider now the effect of a change in f on the pattern of activities, net outputs and trade flows. ('Net output' here means $C\underline{x} \equiv [B - (1+g)A]\underline{x} \equiv \underline{y}$ say.) It may be noted first that if $\underline{c}_{2j}$ is the jth column of C_2 then

$$(\Delta f \underline{c}_{2j})\Delta x_j \geqq 0.$$

A change in world prices which increases (decreases) the *net* gold output of process j will not lead to a smaller (greater) use of that process. It follows that

$$\underline{\Delta f} C_2 \Delta x \geqq 0$$

or

$$\underline{\Delta f} \cdot \Delta \underline{y}_2 \geqq 0. \tag{16}$$

If only f_j changes then (16) naturally becomes

$$\Delta f_j \cdot \Delta y_{2j} \geqq 0;$$

the *net* output of any tradeable is (weakly) positively related to its world (gold) price.

Now the second constraint of the minimum problem in (9) may be written as:

$$\underline{y}_2 + \underline{m} \geqq \underline{w}_2 + \underline{e}.$$

Suppose that, in a solution,

$$y_{2j} + m_j > w_{2j} + e_j \tag{17}$$

for any j. This would mean that $p_{2j} = 0$ by complementary slackness. Thus either (17) must be replaced by the equivalent equality, or $e^F = 0$, so that *every* $p_{2i} = 0$. Thus, ignoring the latter case,

$$\underline{y}_2 = \underline{w}_2 + (\underline{e} - \underline{m})$$

and (16) may be re-written as

$$\Delta \underline{f} \Delta (\underline{e} - \underline{m}) \geq 0. \tag{18}$$

Suppose that only f_j changes and that j is an export; then, from (18),

$$\Delta f_j \Delta e_j \geq 0.$$

If, on the other hand, j is an import then

$$\Delta f_j \Delta m_j \leq 0.$$

As might be expected, the export of a commodity will be 'increased' by a rise in its gold price, while the import of a commodity will be 'reduced' by such a rise. (A 'large' increase in the gold price of an import – large being defined tautologically – may, of course, turn it into an export if it provokes a change in $\underline{x}^F$.) Since, for either an export or an import, a change in f_j moves E^F in the opposite direction to the magnitude of the trade flow, the results also hold in per worker terms.

RESTRICTED TRADE

Consider the following problem:

Minimise $E = \underline{a}\underline{x}$ Maximise $L = (\underline{p}_1\underline{w}_1 + \underline{p}_2\underline{w}_2) - (\underline{y}\bar{\underline{e}} + \underline{z}\bar{\underline{m}})$

subject to
$$\begin{cases} C_1\underline{x} \geq \underline{w}_1 \\ C_2\underline{x} + \underline{m} \geq \underline{w}_2 + \underline{e} \\ \underline{fe} \geq \underline{fm} \\ \underline{e} \leq \bar{\underline{e}} \\ \underline{m} \leq \bar{\underline{m}} \\ \underline{x}, \underline{e}, \underline{m} \geq \underline{0} \end{cases} \quad \text{s.t.} \quad \begin{cases} \underline{p}_1 C_1 + \underline{p}_2 C_2 \leq \underline{a} \\ \underline{ef} - \underline{y} \leq \underline{p}_2 \\ \underline{p}_2 \leq \underline{ef} + \underline{z} \\ \underline{p}_1, \underline{p}_2, \underline{y}, \underline{z} \geq \underline{0}, e \geq 0 \end{cases} \tag{19}$$

If $\bar{\underline{e}} \geq \underline{e}^F$ and $\bar{\underline{m}} \geq \underline{m}^F$ then obviously (19) just has the free trade solution; otherwise it represents a situation of restricted trade. The trade restrictions are shown explicitly in the minimum problem as physical controls on export and import quantities. Given that at least one of them is binding, the trade controls clearly lower the real wage rate corresponding to a given growth rate, g.

Consider the constraints $\underline{e} \leq \bar{e}$ and $\underline{m} \leq \bar{m}$, when $\underline{e}$ and $\underline{m}$ take their optimal values, $\underline{e}^R$ and $\underline{m}^R$, and suppose that $e_i^R > 0$ ($m_i^R = 0$) while $m_j^R > 0$ ($e_j^R = 0$). For commodity i, we may set $\bar{m}_i > 0$, so that $m_i^R < \bar{m}_i$ and thus $z_i^R = 0$. Consequently $p_{2i}^R \leq e^R f_i$. For commodity j, similarly, assume that $e_j^R < \bar{e}_j$; then $y_j^R = 0$ and therefore $p_{2j}^R \geq e^R f_j$. Thus

$$(p_{2i}^R/f_i) \leq e^R \leq (p_{2j}^R/f_j), \tag{20}$$

where i is any exported commodity and j any imported commodity.

Now suppose that $e_i^R = \bar{e}_i$ and $m_j^R = \bar{m}_j$, so that the $\bar{e}_i$ and $\bar{m}_j$ trade restrictions are binding in the restricted trade solution. Binding constraints do not, of course, *entail* positive corresponding dual variables. However, if one leaves aside those (marginal) cases in which a binding constraint has associated with it a zero 'shadow price', it may now be said that

$$p_{2i}^R = e^R f_i - y_i^R \tag{21}$$

and

$$p_{2j}^R = e^R f_j + z_j^R, \tag{22}$$

where y_i^R and z_j^R are both positive. Define t_i and t_j by $y_i^R \equiv t_i(e^R f_i)$ and $z_j^R \equiv t_j(e^R f_j)$, so that (21), (22) may be re-written as:

$$p_{2i}^R = (1 - t_i)(e^R f_i) \tag{23}$$

and

$$p_{2j}^R = (1 + t_j)(e^R f_j). \tag{24}$$

The binding physical quantity restriction on the export of i is equivalent to an *ad valorem* export tax at the rate t_i (23); the effective import quota on j is equivalent to an *ad valorem* tariff at the rate t_j (24).

The physical trade controls are also equivalent, in principle, to a multiple exchange rate system. For example, from (21) and (22) it may be seen that the exchange rates for exports of i and imports of j, e_i and e_j, would be given by

$$p_{2i}^R = e_i f_i$$

or

$$e_i = [e^R - (y_i^R/f_i)]$$

and

$$p_{2j}^R = e_j f_j$$

or

$$e_j = [e^R + (z_j^R/f_j)].$$

Somewhat more generally than in (19), one could consider the problem in which $\underline{e} \leq \bar{e}$ and $\underline{m} \leq \bar{m}$, in the minimum problem of (19), are replaced by

$$0 \leq \underline{e}^- \leq \underline{e} \leq \underline{e}^+$$

and

$$0 \leq \underline{m}^- \leq \underline{m} \leq \underline{m}^+;$$

the maximum problem then has variables $\underline{p}_1, \underline{p}_2, \underline{y}^-, \underline{y}^+, \underline{z}^-, \underline{z}^+$ and e, such that

$$\underline{ef} + \underline{y}^- - \underline{y}^+ \leq \underline{p}_2$$

and

$$\underline{p}_2 \leq \underline{ef} - \underline{z}^- + \underline{z}^+.$$

Analogous arguments to those used above would then show how various kinds of physical trade controls are equivalent to trade taxes and subsidies, to multiple exchange rates and so on.

The above arguments could perhaps be extended to consider many traditional issues in the theory of restricted trade – for example, nothing has been said here about the use (financing) of trade revenues (subsidies). It should, however, have been made apparent how such issues might be investigated.

SOME TRIVIAL GENERALISATIONS

Merely to hint at some possible extensions of the above analysis, it will be indicated briefly how three traditional issues might be considered within the present framework; no attempt will be made at a full discussion.

(i) Transfers

If the small country in question were obliged to transfer, free of charge, a vector of commodities, $\underline{t}$, and a sum of gold, t, each period, the minimum problems of (8) and (9) would become

Minimise $E = \underline{a}x$ (8')   Minimise $E = \underline{a}x$ (9')

s.t. $\begin{cases} C_1 x \geq \underline{w}_1 \\ \underline{f}C_2 x \geq \underline{f}w_2 + (\underline{ft} + \underline{t}) \\ x \geq \underline{0} \end{cases}$ s.t. $\begin{cases} C_1 x \geq \underline{w}_1 \\ C_2 x + \underline{m} \geq \underline{w}_2 + \underline{e} + \underline{t} \\ \underline{fe} \geq \underline{fm} + t \\ x, \underline{e}, \underline{m} \geq \underline{0} \end{cases}$

With $f > \underline{0}$, it will be clear that any increase in t, or in any element of $\underline{t}$, lowers the domestic real wage/growth rate frontier. Since there will be minimal w/g combinations below which the economic and social order would collapse, there are maximal combinations of t and $\underline{t}$ (given $\underline{f}$) which can be imposed on the country in question.

(ii) *Wage differentials*

If the real wage *composition* is the same for workers operating all processes but the wage *levels* differ between processes, the effect will be the same as that of adjusting the elements of the labour input vector $\underline{a}$ in proportion to the wage rate differentials. Thus if the *relative* wage levels are represented by the relative sizes of the positive elements of the diagonal matrix $\hat{\underline{d}}$, then $\underline{a}$ must be replaced by $\underline{a}\hat{\underline{d}}$ in both the minimum and the maximum problems. The effects on trade of changing $\underline{a}$ to $\underline{a}\hat{\underline{d}}$ could then be investigated.

(iii) *Transport costs, etc.*

Let there be N other countries and suppose that the *effective* gold price vectors for imports from and exports to country j are f_j^m and f_j^e respectively, where $\underline{f}_j^m \geq \underline{f}_j^e$ because of fixed per unit transport costs (or for any other reason). The representative problem will, in an obvious notation, be:

Minimise $E = \underline{a}\underline{x}$ Maximise $L = \underline{p}_1\underline{w}_1 + \underline{p}_2\underline{w}_2$

s.t. $\begin{cases} C_1\underline{x} \geq \underline{w}_1 \\ C_2\underline{x} + \Sigma_1^N \underline{m}_j \geq \underline{w}_2 + \Sigma_1^N \underline{e}_j \\ \Sigma_1^N \underline{f}_j^e \underline{e}_j \geq \Sigma_1^N \underline{f}_j^m \underline{m}_j \\ \underline{x}, \underline{m}_j, \underline{e}_j \geq 0, \text{ for all } j \end{cases}$ s.t. $\begin{cases} \underline{p}_1 C_1 + \underline{p}_2 C_2 \leq \underline{a} \\ \underline{ef}_j^e \leq \underline{p}_2 \leq \underline{ef}_j^m \text{ for all } j \\ \underline{p}_1, \underline{p}_2 \geq \underline{0} \\ e \geq 0 \end{cases}$

In the solution each import will, of course, come from the cheapest source, while each export will go to the market with the highest net price. The effects of increasing transport (etc.) costs, of tariffs discriminating between countries, the implications for the small country's trade balance with each of the other countries, and so on could now be studied.

CONCLUDING REMARK

Just in case the reader should have become interested in the above arguments, it may be remarked finally not only that the above analysis is incomplete but that even a full analysis of the model used would leave many important trade theory issues completely untouched. It may be hoped nevertheless that an interesting line of enquiry has been pointed to.

NOTES

*I should like to thank S. A. Moore for much helpful discussion.
1. Cf. Maizels [2].
2. Fujimoto [1]. See also Morishima [5] and Morishima and Catephores [6], chapter 4.
3. Morishima [4].
4. With $r = g$, comparative dynamic 'losses from trade' cannot occur, of course.
5. McKenzie [3], especially pp. 177–9.

REFERENCES

[1] T. Fujimoto. 'Duality and the uniqueness of growth equilibrium'. *International Economic Review*, 1975, pp. 781–91.
[2] A. Maizels. *Industrial Growth and World Trade*, Cambridge University Press, 1971.
[3] L.McKenzie. 'Specialisation and efficiency in world production'. *Review of Economic Studies*, 1953–54, pp. 165–80.
[4] M. Morishima. 'Marx in the light of modern economic theory'. *Econometrica*, 1974, pp. 611–32.
[5] M. Morishima. 'Marx from a von Neumann viewpoint'. In M. Brown, K. Sato and P. Zarembka (eds.), *Essays in Modern Capital Theory*, North-Holland, 1976.
[6] M.Morishima and G. Catephores. *Value, Exploitation and Growth*. McGraw-Hill (U.K.), 1978.

14 Distribution, Growth and International Trade*

SERGIO PARRINELLO

This essay is concerned with certain relationships between the distribution of income, accumulation of capital and international trade. These relationships will be examined in the context of a two-country world, each economy being in long-run competitive equilibrium. Our method of analysis will be to consider paths of steady growth. This method will be used to examine certain relationships between distribution, growth and international trade which are independent of subjective elements, such as individuals' expectations and preferences. Moreover, this analysis will allow a critical examination of the foundations of the Heckscher–Ohlin–Samuelson approach;[1] foundations that are also at the basis of certain dynamic formulations of the neo-classical theory of international trade.

The result of the analysis presented below may be regarded as an extension of Ricardo's theory of international trade. As Professor Hicks[2] has pointed out, any analysis of steady growth requires the assumption of constant returns to scale in production and linear homogeneous consumption functions with regard to income, the latter assumption not being taken into account by Ricardo in his theory of comparative advantage. However, we would not claim that our attempt to reformulate the theory of comparative advantage for a growing economy is the only possible extension of Ricardo's work or even that it is the most 'Ricardian' extension.

Although the method of steady growth is consistent with alternative theories of distribution, the study of the relationships that exist between distributive variables, relative prices and the structure of international trade will be carried out within the limits of an incomplete theory of distribution. The incomplete nature of this theory is similar to that which is found in Sraffa's theory of value,[3] in so far as it derives from an exogenous determination of some distributive variables. The formulation of a complete theory regarding the division of the social product, therefore, will be left to a separate stage of the analysis and no simple causal interpretation will be given here concerning the choice of the independent distributive variables. As a result, even if it is assumed that real wages are fixed at a certain level and the purpose of the analysis is to show how the rates of profit and the pattern of international trade may vary as a result of changes in this level, it is not suggested that wages are at a subsistence level or that they are determined directly by collective bargaining. In the same way, if the rates of profit are taken as given, no simple relationship will be implied between central bank interest rate policies and those profit rates.

We shall therefore work with *open* models of international trade, these models each having a number of degrees of freedom equal to the number of countries; two in our case. The properties of the competitive equilibrium of the international economy will be examined, two distributive variables being taken as given. Since, as stated above, no causal significance will be attributed to the distinction between given and unknown distributive variables, we are free to choose any pair of such variables. It should be noted, however, that with more general assumptions than those made here, (for example, if there are joint products), a one-to-one correspondence between given and unknown variables does not necessarily exist for every possible choice of the given variables.

THE INTERNATIONAL MOBILITY OF COMMODITIES AND THE IMMOBILITY OF CAPITAL

As is well known, the hypothesis of the international mobility of products and immobility of the factors of production (land, labour and capital) has provided the basis for a pure theory of international trade as a distinct branch of neo-classical economics. This theory, in the contributions of Heckscher, Ohlin and others, analyses the causes and effects of trade among countries endowed with given quantities of factors of production. However, while the hypothesis of the international immobility of land and labour has a clear meaning, the immobility of capital is an ambiguous assumption as long as the movement of capital goods is not distinguished from the movement of financial capital. Therefore, hypotheses concerning different types of international transactions will be established, keeping this distinction in mind.

If the analysis were to refer to a short-run equilibrium, we could assume that each country was endowed with given stocks of capital goods at the beginning of the period. We could further assume that, in the face of international immobility of stocks, mobility would exist in the flows of newly produced capital goods during the period.[4] In the analysis of long-run equilibrium, however, it is necessarily the case that initial stocks of capital goods do not appear amongst the data. In fact, if such an equilibrium is to exist, the initial stocks of capital goods must be in the proportions consistent with steady growth and thus with the absence of quasi-rents and the existence of a uniform rate of profit on all capital goods. Thus in a theory of international trade which, like Ricardo's theory, is concerned with long-run equilibrium, the amounts of capital goods installed in each country must be excluded from the data and included as unknown variables. This property of stocks will be combined with the assumption of international mobility in the flows of newly produced capital goods. Hence we shall assume that, like consumption goods, all capital goods can be traded commodities (independently of their dimensions as stocks or flows).

With respect to financial capital, we shall assume, by contrast, complete international immobility. We shall therefore impose two distinct conditions of macro-economic equilibrium: balanced trade, i.e. equality between net saving and net investment, in each country.

Regarding labour, in the basic model it will be assumed that the levels of real wage rates in the two countries are given, and that, corresponding to these levels, the amount of labour available to the world economy does not set any limit to growth. There thus exists an inexhaustible reserve of labour, which can always supply the labour force required in the two countries. On the other hand, if the rates of profit were to be taken as exogenously given, whilst the wage rates were endogenous variables, then, since within each country it would be the propensity to invest of a specific class of capitalists which governed the increase in employment, it would not be necessary to assume the immobility of the labour force, in order to permit a wage difference as between the two countries. The hypothesis of a given labour supply for each country will be considered only in the part devoted to the examination of the foundations of the neo-classical theory of international trade.

As regards land, we shall assume that in each country it is sufficiently abundant to allow steady growth with land rent equal to zero.

THE BASIC MODEL

We shall use a model of international trade which is an extension of the type of two-sector model of growth used by Mrs Robinson,[5] Professor Hicks[6] and others for the study of a growing closed economy. We shall outline rather briefly those aspects of it which are common to this type of model, but consider more fully its international features.

Let us assume an economy where only one capital good exists, which is used to produce one consumption good or itself. Wages and profits are paid simultaneously at the end of successive, equal 'payment periods' and the capital good lasts exactly one period; i.e. it is circulating capital.

Since we wish to examine the relationships between distribution, growth and trade in isolation from the effects of international differences in technology, we shall confine our analysis to the case in which the two countries possess the same methods of production. We shall assume, furthermore, that there is only one fixed-coefficients technique available, defined by the capital and labour requirement per unit of output, for each of the two industries.

Within each country, capital and labour may be freely transferred from one industry to another and competition is sufficiently strong to assure a uniform rate of profit. Since there is free trade (no transport costs, tariffs, or other trade restrictions), the relative commodity price will, in equilibrium, be the same in both countries, while the rate of profit may differ as between the two countries, since financial capital is assumed to be internationally immobile. For the reasons set out above, an inter-country difference in real wages is consistent with equilibrium.

We may now present the basic model in formal terms, using the following notation, where the suffices (a, b) refer to the two countries a and b.

p : price of the capital good in terms of the consumption good;
Z^a, Z^b : outputs of the consumption good;
C^a, C^b : flows of consumption;
X^a, X^b : outputs of the capital good;
w^a, w^b : real wage rates in terms of the consumption good;
r^a, r^b : rates of profit;
g^a, g^b : rates of growth;
s^a, s^b : capitalists' average propensities to save;
u : capital coefficient ⎫ in the production of the
β : labour coefficient ⎭ consumption good;
v : capital coefficient ⎫ in the production of the
γ : labour coefficient ⎭ capital good.

The consumption good being taken as the standard of value, the following price equations must hold for country i:

$$(1+r^i)up + \beta w^i = 1 + \pi_1^i$$
$$(1+r^i)vp + \gamma w^i = p + \pi_2^i \quad (i = a, b); \tag{1}$$

where π_1^i, π_2^i are the potential losses per unit of output in country i, in the consumption and capital good industries respectively. Equilibrium requires that at least one of the two variables, output or unit loss, should be zero for each industry. It follows therefore that:

$$Z^a \pi_1^a = 0, \quad X^a \pi_2^a = 0, \quad Z^b \pi_1^b = 0, \quad X^b \pi_2^b = 0. \tag{2}$$

We define total employment in country i by:

$$L^i \equiv \beta Z^i + \gamma X^i, \quad (i = a, b), \tag{3}$$

and we define the value of capital in country i, in terms of the consumption good, by:

$$K^i \equiv (uZ^i + vX^i)p, \quad (i = a, b). \tag{4}$$

We shall assume classical savings functions in both countries: the workers do not save, while the capitalists save a given constant fraction of their profits; this fraction being different, in general, as between the two countries. Therefore we may write the consumption functions as follows:

$$C^i = w^i L^i + (1 - s^i) r^i K^i, \quad (i = a, b). \tag{5}$$

Macroeconomic equilibrium requires that capitalists' savings be equal to the value of net investment in each country; thus

$$s^i r^i K^i = g^i K^i, \quad (i = a, b);$$

from which we may derive:

$$r^i = \frac{g^i}{s^i}, \quad (i = a, b), \tag{6}$$

provided, obviously, that K^i is strictly positive. We shall make further assumptions below which assure the positivity of each K^i.

We turn now to the quantity equations. In equilibrium, total world output of the capital good must equal total world use of it in production, plus total world accumulation. Therefore, assuming a uniform rate of growth within each country, we have:

$$X^a + X^b = (1 + g^a)(uZ^a + vX^a) + (1 + g^b)(uZ^b + vX^b). \tag{7}$$

The system (1)–(7) implies that total world output of the consumption good must equal total world consumption:

$$Z^a + Z^b = C^a + C^b;$$

furthermore it implies that total world income be equal to total world net product:

$$w^a L^a + w^b L^b + r^a K^a + r^b K^b = Z^a + Z^b + p[g^a(uZ^a + vX^a) + g^b(uZ^b + vX^b)].$$

In addition the usual conditions of positivity must be satisfied:

$$p > 0, Z^i \geq 0, X^i \geq 0, C^i \geq 0, \pi_j^i \geq 0, w^i \geq 0.$$

Other restrictions on the unknowns r^i, L^i, will be imposed below.

The number of linearly independent equations and definitions is 17, the number of unknowns is 21. These are: $p, Z^i, X^i, C^i, L^i, K^i, g^i, w^i, r^i, \pi_j^i$ with $(i = a, b)$ and $(j = 1, 2)$.

Clearly no data exist in the basic model to render possible the determination of the scale of the two economies; i.e. the absolute quantities. On the other hand, the model can, once three degrees of freedom have been eliminated, determine the unknowns $(p, g^i, w^i, r^i, \pi_j^i)$ and a set of ratios among the unknowns $(X^i, Z^i, C^i, L^i, K^i)$. We shall assume the real wage rates as given in the two countries. The remaining degree of freedom in the system (1)–(7) may be eliminated by an additional condition. We shall specify this condition below but, in order to give it an economic interpretation, it is necessary to explain first in what sense the existence of different rates of growth in the two countries is consistent with the concept of steady growth.

THE DEFINITION OF STEADY GROWTH

We intend to argue that the definition of steady growth which is generally accepted for the description of a state of dynamic equilibrium in a closed economy, is too restrictive if extended to an international economic system. We shall therefore adopt a more general concept of steady growth, which appears to be appropriate when steady growth analysis is applied to the theory of international trade.[7]

We may note first that equilibrium, as discussed in the previous section, is of interest to the extent that it defines a state towards which a growth path, determined as a solution of a disequilibrium model, converges. It is possible that this path will converge towards a state characterised by rates of growth which are uniform within each country but different as between the two countries. In the long run we shall find a relatively 'large' country and a relatively 'small' country; so small indeed that trade has become insignificant with respect to the equilibrium of the large country. In the basic model the large country would then have the same composition of output, income distribution, relative prices and rate of growth as it would have had under autarky. It would thus produce both commodities and determine the terms of trade between the consumption good and the capital good independently of the small country. The small country, on the other hand, would remain in equilibrium specialising completely in the production of that commodity which, at the price fixed by the large country, would be more profitable. Three cases, and three corresponding equilibrium conditions, can be distinguished.

(a) $g^a = g^b$. This is the case of steady growth, strictly speaking.

(b) $g^a > g^b$. In this case a will be the large country and produce both goods; therefore $\pi_1^a = \pi_2^a = 0$. Since $\pi_1^a \geqq 0$, $\pi_2^a \geqq 0$, it is sufficient to write: $\pi_1^a + \pi_2^a = 0$.

(c) $g^a < g^b$. In this case: $\pi_1^b + \pi_2^b = 0$.

Therefore the solution of the basic model, according to the given notion of steady growth, must satisfy the equation:

$$(\pi_1^a + \pi_2^a)(\pi_1^b + \pi_2^b)(g^a - g^b) = 0. \tag{8}$$

In the case (a) no particular problems arise in the determination and interpretation of the equilibrium ratios between quantities. We can determine, for instance, the ratios between each of the quantities (L^a, Z^i, X^i, C^i) and the amount of labour L^b. In this case, if a positive solution to equations (1)–(8) exists, the equilibrium ratio (L^a/L^b) may be chosen to define the relative dimension of the two countries on the steady state path.

On the other hand, if either case (b) or (c) holds, the system (1)–(8) would admit some kinds of solution which will be excluded by the imposition of further restrictions. There is in fact the possibility that a country will produce both goods while the other country produces neither. If this state of equilibrium exists, the stability of equilibrium means that, starting from given initial conditions, the disequilibrium path would show the stock of the capital good and employment gradually decreasing in the second country; this will therefore lead to the disappearance of this country as an economic entity. It is possible that some models of trade and growth will have a solution of this type. Nevertheless, for simplicity we shall consider in the basic model only the case in which both levels of employment are strictly positive and the rates of profit are non-negative. Therefore, in addition to the non-negativity conditions already stated, the following limitations are imposed:

$$r^i \geqq 0, \; L^i > 0 \quad \text{with } (i = a, b).$$

WAGES AND THE STRUCTURE OF INTERNATIONAL TRADE

As is well known, the choice of techniques in the one country model satisfies the criterion of the maximum rate of profit, if the real wage rate is given. In this context, the maximisation of the rate of profit is not a behavioural hypothesis concerning firms but the outcome inferred from a behavioural hypothesis: that producers maximise extra-profits and therefore choose those techniques which minimise production costs. If one assumes a classical savings function, the same result, together with the savings-investment equation, implies the maximisation of the rate of growth of the economy. In our basic model, however, two distinct wage rates, two distinct rates of profit and two distinct rates of growth are admitted; one for each country. In this case it is necessary to consider, not the choice of technique relative to a given and uniform wage rate but rather the choice of the type of international specialisation, relative to two distinct wage rates, under the two macroeconomic conditions (savings = investment) and the requirements of positive employment. It may be helpful at this point to indicate the method we shall adopt in the following section to arrive at the choice of the type of international specialisation.

If a meaningful solution exists to the system (1)–(8), the corresponding outputs must satisfy one of the following sets of conditions, which define six possible trade systems $(AB, BA, A_1, A_2, B_1, B_2)$:

$$
\begin{array}{llllllll}
AB: & Z^a > 0, & X^a = 0, & Z^b = 0, & X^b > 0; \\
BA: & Z^a = 0, & X^a > 0, & Z^b > 0, & X^b = 0; \\
A_1: & Z^a > 0, & X^a > 0, & Z^b > 0, & X^b = 0; \\
A_2: & Z^a > 0, & X^a > 0, & Z^b = 0, & X^b > 0; \\
B_1: & Z^a > 0, & X^a = 0, & Z^b > 0, & X^b > 0; \\
B_2: & Z^a = 0, & X^a > 0, & Z^b > 0, & X^b > 0.
\end{array}
$$

Thus the basic model admits two systems of complete specialisation (AB, BA) and four systems of incomplete specialisation (A_1, A_2, B_1, B_2).

Linked to the systems (A_1, A_2) is a common system which we shall call A, which contains the consumption and capital good industries operating in the country a; similarly to the systems B_1, B_2 there corresponds a common system B, made up of the same industries operating in the country b. For each one of the systems (A, B, AB, BA) there is a corresponding system of price equations. Since, if a system of complete specialisation is chosen, the rates of growth in the two countries must be equal, as imposed by (8), we may say that the choice of any system (A, B, AB, BA) implies in equilibrium a uniform rate of growth within the industries of the same system. This rate of growth is fixed by the price equations together with equations (6); therefore it depends only on the technical coefficients, real wages, and the propensity to save relative to the chosen system. We shall show that, in equilibrium, the chosen system will be that which entails the highest rate of growth. Through the criterion of the maximum rate of growth applied to systems (A, B, AB, BA), we shall generally arrive at one of the following results: either the system superior to the others in terms of the rate of growth is one of the two systems of complete specialisation (AB, BA) or it is one of the systems (A, B) belonging to the systems of incomplete specialisation. In the first case we have determined the equilibrium trade system. In the other case we have still to choose between two systems of incomplete specialisation either of the (A_1, A_2) type or the (B_1, B_2) type. This last choice will satisfy the criterion of the maximum rate of profit, applied to the country which specialises completely and which will be the small country.

THE CRITERION OF THE MAXIMUM RATE OF GROWTH

Setting, in the price equations (1), alternatively

$$\pi_1^a - \pi_2^a = 0; \quad \pi_1^b = \pi_2^b = 0; \quad \pi_1^a = \pi_2^b = 0; \quad \pi_2^a = \pi_1^b = 0,$$

we form the four price systems corresponding to the systems (A, B, AB, BA). Substituting for the rates of profit from (6) and writing $g^a = g^b = g$, we obtain the following systems in the unknowns (g, p):

$$A \begin{cases} (u + g\dfrac{u}{s^a})p + \beta w^a = 1 \\ (v + g\dfrac{v}{s^a})p + \gamma w^a = p \end{cases} \qquad B \begin{cases} (u + g\dfrac{u}{s^b})p + \beta w^b = 1 \\ (v + g\dfrac{v}{s^b})p + \gamma w^b = p \end{cases}$$

$$AB \begin{cases} (u+g\dfrac{u}{s^a})p + \beta w^a = 1 \\ (v+g\dfrac{v}{s^b})p + \gamma w^b = p \end{cases} \qquad BA \begin{cases} (u+g\dfrac{u}{s^b})p + \beta w^b = 1 \\ (v+g\dfrac{v}{s^a})p + \gamma w^a = p \end{cases}$$

Given the real wages, each system determines p and g. Generally these systems may be ranked according to their respective values of g. *If there exists a positive solution then, in equilibrium, that system will be chosen which has associated with it the highest value of g.* In fact, from a purely logical point of view, the problem of the choice among the systems (A, B, AB, BA) is identical to the problem of the choice of techniques in the case in which the two countries were integrated as a single world economic system, where capital is completely mobile and g would be the uniform rate of profit. In this hypothetical case, the coefficients (u, v) and $(u/s^i, v/s^i)$ might be respectively interpreted as the flow-coefficients and the stock-coefficients of a capital good which depreciates according to rates of 'mortality' which are independent of the age of the capital good itself.

We observe that, in spite of the above mentioned formal analogy, the criterion of the choice of techniques applied to the integrated economy and the criterion of choice among systems (A, B, AB, BA) have essentially different economic meanings. In fact the choice of the trade system in the basic model is dependent not only on the technical coefficients and the level assigned to the exogenous distributive variables but also on the ratio between the average propensity to save in the two countries. Furthermore the order in which the unknowns are determined is different: whilst in a country where a uniform rate of profit rules, given the real wage, we determine the rate of profit first and then the rate of growth, in our case this causal succession is reversed. It could then happen that for a given pair of wage rates the order between the systems (A, B) in terms of g will be opposite to the order existing in terms of the respective rates of profit (r^a, r^b). In addition, in the special case in which the real wage rates are equal in the two countries the same rate of profit rules in the two systems. In this case, although A and B are equally profitable in terms of the criterion of the rate of profit, there will be an order of choice between A and B in terms of g, provided that the two propensities to save are different.

We shall consider in the next section the case in which $s^a \geqq s^b$ and the capital-labour ratio in the consumption good industry is higher than in the capital good industry; i.e. $\mu > 0$ where we define $\mu \equiv u\gamma - v\beta$. The analysis of the types of specialisation will be carried out for this case, whilst for $\mu \leq 0$ we shall simply establish the results without repeating the analytical procedure (which is in fact the same as we shall follow in the case $\mu > 0$).

THE CASE OF COMPLETE SPECIALISATION

The existence of a partial order among systems (A, B, AB, BA) in terms of g is proved in the appendix for each given pair of wage rates (w^a, w^b). The result is that the system BA is always dominated by at least one other system, which gives a higher value of g. It follows that for no pair of wage rates can the choice of complete specialisation imply country b producing only the consumption good and country a only the capital good. This conclusion derives from two hypotheses: the propensity to save in a is greater than that in b and the consumption good industry is more capital intensive than the capital good industry. Therefore, if the rates of growth in the two countries are to be equal, the equilibrium rate of profit will have to be higher in country b than in country a, whatever the levels of the fixed wage rates. It is indeed no surprise that in a fixed coefficients and one capital good model it is impossible for the country with the higher rate of profit to specialise in the more capital intensive good. The only possible type of complete specialisation is thus the opposite: country a may specialise in the consumption good and country b in the capital good. In the appendix we have proved that if and only if the wage rates are represented by points which are internal to the cone $\widehat{AB}$ (Figure 14.1), then the system AB dominates the other systems in terms of g and also satisfies the condition of positive employment in both countries. Therefore the cone $\widehat{AB}$ defines the only set of wage rates for which, in equilibrium, both countries specialise completely and grow at the same rate. In Figure 14.1, w_0 indicates the maximum wage rate admissible in each country without trade. Obviously the maximum wage rates coincide because equal techniques were assumed in the two countries.

In the particular case (interesting for its references both to the labour theory of value and to the neo-classical production function), in which the capital–labour ratio is equal in the two industries ($\mu = 0$), the cone $\widehat{AB}$ reduces to a straight line. This means that no system of complete specialisation dominates systems A and B. Thus in general (that is, except when the wage rates lie on the straight line, in which case A, B, AB, BA, may all be indifferently chosen) an equilibrium with equal rates of

170   Fundamental Issues in Trade Theory

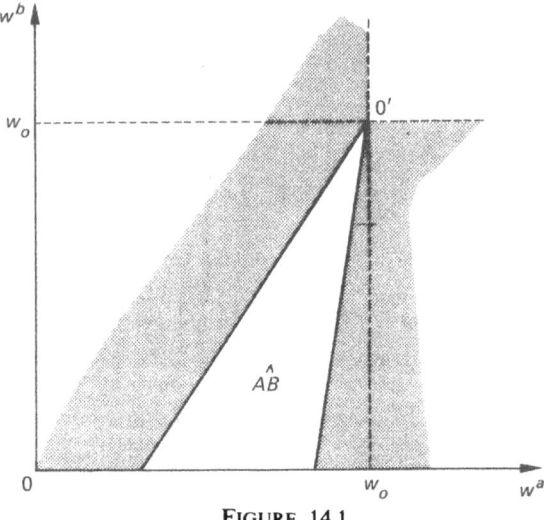

FIGURE 14.1

growth in the two countries cannot exist. It should be noted that the two edges of the cone $\hat{AB}$ define the switching points between system AB and other systems which imply an incomplete specialisation.

THE CASE OF INCOMPLETE SPECIALISATION

In the shaded region to the left of the cone $\hat{AB}$ (Figure 14.1) the dominant system in terms of g is A, whilst in the shaded region to the right, the dominant system is B. If the condition of positive employment in both countries had not been imposed, we would have found two new (unbounded) regions where the equilibrium solution may imply the extinction, from an economic point of view, of one of the two countries. However, since we assumed that in equilibrium both countries produce something, the latter type of solution must be excluded. Instead, states of equilibrium are admitted with incomplete specialisation and different rates of growth.

Let us consider the price systems associated with the trade systems A_1, A_2, B_1, B_2, which are obtained from equations (1), setting the appropriate combinations of unit losses equal to zero:

$$A_1 \begin{cases} (1+r^a)up + \beta w^a = 1 \\ (1+r^a)vp + \gamma w^a = p \\ (1+r^b)up + \beta w^b = 1 \end{cases} \qquad A_2 \begin{cases} (1+r^a)up + \beta w^a = 1 \\ (1+r^a)vp + \gamma w^a = p \\ (1+r^b)vp + \gamma w^b = p \end{cases}$$

$$B_1 \begin{cases} (1+r^b)up + \beta w^b = 1 \\ (1+r^b)vp + \gamma w^b = p \\ (1+r^a)up + \beta w^a = 1 \end{cases} \qquad B_2 \begin{cases} (1+r^b)up + \beta w^b = 1 \\ (1+r^b)vp + \gamma w^b = p \\ (1+r^a)vp + \gamma w^a = p \end{cases}$$

Each of the systems (A_1, A_2) and each of the systems (B_1, B_2) describes an incomplete specialisation in the countries a and b respectively. For every given pair of wage rates, the choice among the systems (A_1, A_2, B_1, B_2) determines the price p, the rates of profit (r^a, r^b) and, through equation (6), the rates of growth (g^a, g^b). In the appendix the complete order of choice has been established among the systems (A, B, AB, BA). Therefore we have a partial order of choice among the trade systems $(A_1, A_2, B_1, B_2, AB, BA)$: if a positive solution exists outside the cone $\widehat{AB}$, one of the systems A_1, A_2 will be chosen if system A dominates B (i.e. $g^a > g^b$); on the other hand, if B dominates A (i.e. $g^b > g^a$) one of the systems B_1, B_2 will be chosen. In the first case the country a will be the large one and the country b the small one; in the second case b will be the large country and a the small one. Furthermore, we know that in the cone $\widehat{AB}$, equilibrium implies complete specialisation, because the choice of any system of incomplete specialisation would involve the choice of one of the systems (A, B), both of which we have shown to be dominated by AB. Therefore two steps remain to complete the analysis of trade systems: to determine 1) the set of feasible wage rates; 2) the choice between the systems (A_1, A_2) or between the systems (B_1, B_2).

THE WAGES FRONTIER AND THE COMPLETE SPECIALISATION OF THE SMALL COUNTRY

Once the relative size of the two countries is known, outside the cone $\widehat{AB}$, the further choice between the two feasible systems of incomplete specialisation is reduced to the choice of the industry which is more profitable in the small country. This choice is made with respect to a relative price fixed by the production system of the large country. The criterion of choice for the small country will then be that of the maximum rate of profit. In this case, given the proportional relation between the rate of profit and the rate of growth, a maximum rate of profit implies a maximum rate of growth in the small country.

Given the above rule, we may proceed in the following manner. If, for instance, a is the large country, we obtain the equilibrium price in terms of w^a from its price equations,

$$p = \frac{v}{u} + \frac{\mu}{u} w^a. \tag{9}$$

Substituting (9) into the price equations for country b and setting $r^b = 0$, we obtain two linear equations in w^a, w^b. Both the lines which represent them (Figure 14.2) pass through point $0'$ and have positive intercepts with the axis w^b. The intercept $w_c^b = \dfrac{1-v}{\beta}$ corresponds to the price equation for the consumption good; the intercept $w_k^b = \dfrac{v(1-v)}{u\gamma}$ to that for the capital good. We know that $w_0 = \dfrac{1-v}{\beta + \mu}$ is the maximum wage rate for each country without trade. Therefore, since by hypothesis $\mu > 0$, it must be the case that $w_c^b > w_0 > w_k^b$.

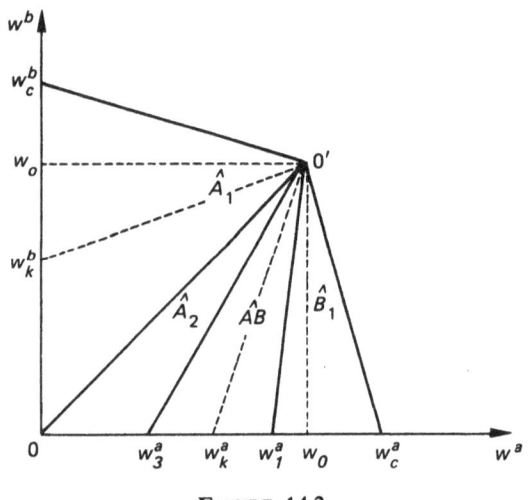

FIGURE 14.2

If the large country is b, we may by the same procedure determine two other straight lines in the plane (w^a, w^b); each line being the locus in which $r^a = 0$ with respect to one of the two price equations for country a. Since the production coefficients are the same in the two countries, these lines also pass through point $0'$ and have respectively w_c^a and w_k^a as intercepts with the w^a axis. Thus the bent line $w_c^b 0' w_c^a$ in Figure 14.2 defines, for every given wage rate in one country, the maximum wage rate attainable in the other country. It may be called the wages frontier in the following sense: beyond the frontier at least one of the rates of profit is negative; inside the frontier both rates of profit and the relative price are positive.

Regarding the choice among the systems (A_1, A_2, B_1, B_2) it should be noted that, if $w^a = w^b$, the system A dominates B, the line $w^a = w^b$ being to the left of the cone $A\hat{B}$. Along this line the choice between the systems (A_1, A_2) is indifferent, since these two systems (in the case $w^a = w^b$) give the same rate of profit in country b. In this special case, neither country will obtain any advantage from international trade, although for the large country a the choice between complete and partial specialisation will not be indifferent.

In order to determine the type of specialisation off the line $w^a = w^b$ and outside the cone $A\hat{B}$, it is sufficient to consider the relationship between wages and profits within each of the two systems A, B. From equation (9) it follows that, if $\mu > 0$, the equilibrium price rises if the wage rate rises. Hence, on the basis of the criterion of the maximum rate of profit applied to the small country, the most profitable trade systems in the cones $\hat{A}_1, \hat{A}_2, \hat{B}_1$ (Figure 14.2) are respectively (A_1, A_2, B_1). In fact, in the cone $\hat{A}_1$, the relative price of the capital good in system B is higher than in system A; while in the cones $\hat{A}_2$ and $\hat{B}_1$ the relative price is higher in A than in B. The country b therefore (which in the cones $\hat{A}_1, \hat{A}_2$ will be the small country) in the cone $\hat{A}_1$ will specialise completely in the consumption good and will import the capital good; in the cone $\hat{A}_2$ it will specialise completely in the capital good and import the consumption good. In the cone $\hat{B}_1$ a will be the small country; it will specialise completely in the consumption good and import the capital good.

By means of the same procedure as that followed for the case in which $\mu > 0$, we may repeat the analysis for the case $\mu < 0$. We shall again find a single cone of complete specialisation and three cones of incomplete specialisation. In the first cone the system BA will be chosen, whilst in the cones of incomplete specialisation, the systems will be alternatively A_1, A_2, B_2. In this case $w_k^i > w_c^i$ and the wages frontier will be represented by a new bent line $w_k^a 0' w_k^b$ corresponding to this second case.

THE EQUILIBRIUM QUANTITIES

In the case of complete specialisation, the choice of the trade system determines the uniform rate of growth, the two rates of profit, the relative price and the levels of two outputs (those which in equilibrium are zero). These equilibrium values may be substituted into the quantity equation (7), into the definitions of employment (3) and capital (4) and into the consumption function (5). We obtain a system which is completely determined with respect to the ratios between the unknowns

$(Z^i, X^i, C^i, K^i, L^i)$ with $(i = a, b)$. In the case of incomplete specialisation, by contrast, the choice of the trade system determines the two distinct rates of growth, the rates of profit, the relative price and *one* of the four output levels (that which in equilibrium is zero). In this case equations (3), (4), (5), (7) admit one degree of freedom with respect to the ratios between the unknowns $(Z^i, X^i, C^i, K^i, L^i)$. However, the equilibrium proportions among the quantities, corresponding to each country, may be uniquely determined as the following limits: in the case $g^a > g^b$, $L^a/L^b \to \infty$; in the case $g^a < g^b$, $L^a/L^b \to 0$.

THE CRITERIA USED FOR THE CHOICE OF THE TRADE SYSTEM

We have proved that the choice of the trade system may imply two distinct criteria which in some cases follow a causal order. The criterion of the maximum rate of growth determines an order among the systems (A, B, AB, BA). If a system of complete specialisation (AB or BA) is dominant, this system will be chosen in equilibrium. In this case the relative price and the uniform rate of growth are simultaneously determined; then the rates of profit. On the other hand, if no system of complete specialisation is dominant, the criterion of the rate of growth will establish which of the two countries does not specialise completely (the large country) and which will do so (the small country). In this second case, the relative price and the rate of growth of the large country are simultaneously determined; then its rate of profit follows. The criterion of the maximum rate of profit will however determine the commodity to be produced in the small country; here the country's rate of profit will be determined first and its rate of growth second.

If, instead of the wage rates, we take the rates of profit as given in the two countries, the rates of growth are fixed at once by means of the saving-investment equation (6). Therefore, in general, the rates of growth will be different in equilibrium and thus we know immediately which is the large country and which is the small one. The large country will produce both goods and determine the relative price; while the small country will specialise completely according to the criterion of the maximum wage rate.

If the rates of profit are fixed at such levels that their ratio (r^a/r^b) is equal to the inverse ratio between the propensities to save (s^b/s^a), the equilibrium rates of growth will be the same in the two countries. In this special case, the condition (8) becomes identically satisfied and the model

Distribution, Growth and International Trade 175

gains another degree of freedom. If we fix also one of the two wage rates (within a certain range, of course), it is possible to determine the choice of trade system. This choice will satisfy the criterion of the maximum wage rate: given the two rates of profit and the wage rate in one country, that trade system will be chosen which gives the maximum wage rate in the other country.

Having examined the choice-criteria in the basic model, we may ask if the same criteria would hold when certain assumptions in the basic model were replaced by other, more realistic ones.

If the basic model is extended to the case where many methods (not necessarily the same in the two countries) are available for the production of the same consumption good and the same capital good, the choice of techniques will be determined in each country simultaneously with the choice of the trade system on the basis of the double criterion established above, i.e. the maximum rate of growth and the maximum value of one distributive variable.

Finally, if the extension of the basic model consists in assuming any number of heterogeneous goods (consumption and capital goods) and a spectrum of techniques, the double criterion will again be applied both to the choice of the trade system and to the simultaneous choice of techniques. In this context, as long as we remain within the limits of classical savings functions and single product industries, a *weak* non-substitution theorem holds good for the trade model extended to many commodities: it means that the trade system, the techniques and the corresponding equilibrium prices are determined independently of the proportions in which consumption *within* each country is distributed among different goods.[8] In fact, if the real wages (or the rates of profit) are given in the different countries, relative prices are uniquely determined by technical conditions and by the savings coefficients.

THE GAINS FROM INTERNATIONAL TRADE

The analysis of the criteria behind the choice of the trade system has shown some of the advantages of international trade. It has been established in fact that, given the real wage rates, trading a wage-good against a good which is used to produce the wage-good allows an increase in the rate of profit in at least one country and, through an increase in the rate of accumulation, an increase also in the rate of growth of employment in that country. Furthermore, in both countries these rates are not lower than their values without trade. In a similar way, given the rates of profit, the employed workers in at least one country receive a higher real wage with trade; whilst in both countries the wage rates are not lower. It can however happen that in one country the net product (output of consumption good plus output of capital good, in value) per employed worker and the number of employed workers per unit of invested capital, fall with trade.

It is however impossible, so long as we remain within the method of balanced growth, to determine the effects of trade on income and employment outside the steady growth path. The method we have adopted, therefore, does not allow us to formulate any proposition concerning the properties of the transition path from one equilibrium, without trade, to an equilibrium with trade. Thus the gains from trade, which in the basic model come from an analysis of equilibrium dynamics, do not prove that trade is beneficial to every class of income earners and in respect to any time horizon. In this sense the analogy between the opening of international trade and the introduction of a new machine, which Ricardo underlines in the chapter of the *Principles* entitled '*On Foreign Trade*', and his argument about the possible effects of new machines on the working class, in the chapter '*On Machinery*', may be combined and carried to their logical consequences. In Ricardo's words:

> All I wish to prove, is, that the discovery and use of machinery may be attended with a diminution of gross produce; and whenever that is the case, it will be injurious to the labouring class, as some of their number will be thrown out of employment, and population will become redundant, compared with the funds which are to employ it.[9]

Since we cannot exclude the possibility that the opening of international trade also provokes a decrease in the gross national product of a country, we cannot exclude that the same effect, contrary to the interests of the working class, may derive also from trade. The possible lower employment in the short run is however consistent with the long run benefits, which were established by means of the steady growth method; in particular this effect is consistent with a higher rate of growth in employment, when the real wages are assumed to be fixed.

In our analysis of the relationships between distribution, growth and international trade we have not, however, considered all the possible pairs of exogenous variables whose choice allows the basic model to be logically closed. Amongst those choices not yet considered there are some which, although meaningful from the point of view of a theory of class-conflicts, do not permit one, without further hypotheses, to define the long run benefits of international trade. This is the case in which both distributive variables (the wage rate and the rate of profit) are assumed as independent variables in one country, and both distributive variables of the other country are treated as unknowns. It is indeed possible, by referring to an international economic system, to formulate a theory of value and distribution in which both profits and wages in one country are residual categories. Clearly, if this same choice between given and unknown variables is maintained in the definition of equilibrium for each country without trade, the price system associated with the first country is over-determined, while that of the other country is under-determined. Hence it would not be possible to determine the state of equilibrium without trade for either of the two countries; hence the terms of comparison needed for defining the benefits of trade would be lacking.

THE MODEL WITH HETEROGENEOUS CAPITAL: A NUMERICAL EXAMPLE

In this section we shall extend the basic model to the case of many capital goods and we shall examine, by means of a numerical example, some new cases which may arise in the choice of the trade system.[10]

Let us assume that two techniques are available to each country. To each technique there corresponds a specific capital good but the consumption good is the same for both. The two techniques are the same as between the two countries and are defined by the following capital coefficients (u, v) and labour coefficients (β, γ):

Technique I		Technique II	
$u' = 0.133$	$v' = 0.851$	$u'' = 0.075$	$v'' = 0.857$
$\beta' = 4.834$	$\gamma' = 1$	$\beta'' = 5.478$	$\gamma'' = 1$

For the sake of simplicity, let us consider the case in which the rates of profit are the independent distributive variables. For instance, suppose $r^a = 0.06$, $r^b = 0$. With given propensities to save, let us consider the case in which (since $g^a > g^b$) the large country is a and b is the small one. In order to determine the choice of the trade system, we apply the criterion of the maximum wage rate to the large country and, successively, to the small one.

The techniques I and II, used in country a, give respectively the wage rates $w^a_I = 0.159$ and $w^a_{II} = 0.158$. Therefore technique I is the more profitable for country a. Call capital good I and capital good II the two capital goods associated with the techniques I and II. In this case, country a, by the choice of technique I, determines the relative (i.e. in terms of the consumption good) prices of capital good I ($p_1 = 1.627$) and of capital good II ($p_2 = 1.722$). The price p_1 is an actual price, whilst the price p_2 is either actual or potential: if technique I is the more profitable (according to the criterion of the maximum wage rate applied to the country b) with regard to the prices fixed by country a, then p_2 remains a potential price; if instead the capital good II technique is more profitable, p_2 becomes effective. This latter case would imply a state of equilibrium in which, alongside the industries using the methods of technique I in country a, two other industries are working, each in a different country: country b specialises completely in the production of the consumption good, using the method of technique II; while country a, besides the consumption good and the capital good I, produces the capital good II, exports the net output of this capital good and imports the consumption good. Should this happen, in the country a three industries will exist, in equilibrium, which do not grow at the same rate. The consumption good and the capital good I industries will grow at the common rate of growth g^a, while the capital good II industry will grow at the rate g^b. In our numerical example, the following values of w^b, corresponding to ($r^b = 0$; $p_1 = 1.627$; $p_2 = 1.722$), make the prices of the various commodities equal to their respective costs of production in country b: $w^b = 0.162$ if country b produces the consumption good by means of the capital good I; $w^b = 0.242$ if it produces the capital good I; $w^b = 0.159$ if it produces the consumption good by means of the capital good II. Therefore the country b will specialise completely in the capital good I and will import the consumption good.

It is noteworthy that, in the model with heterogeneous capital, the same trade system may be chosen, then abandoned and then chosen again, when one of the two rates of profit changes monotonically. This means that a 'double-switch' of trade systems is admitted, in the same way as the double-switch of techniques is a well known property for a closed system.

The above mentioned cases indicate how the order of choice of the trade system must be formulated for the large country, when the basic model is extended to heterogeneous capital. In this more general version, it is convenient to distinguish the commodities as basics and non-basics (according to the concepts introduced by Sraffa) relative to each country. Basic commodities for one country are those commodities which enter, directly or indirectly, as inputs in the production of all the commodities that, in equilibrium, are produced in the same country. Some commodities may be basic for one country and non-basic for the other country. Thus in the case where the country a produces the consumption good by means of technique I and both types of capital goods, while country b produces only the consumption good by means of technique II, the capital good II would be basic for country b but non-basic for country a.

As regards the commodity classification into basics and non-basics in reference to each country, we can state that, if a is the large country and b the small one, then country a, for every given value of its rate of profit, determines its wage rate, the effective relative prices of its basic commodities, the potential relative prices of those commodities which are non-basic for country a and basic for country b; and the proportions among the quantities of its basic commodities. On the other hand, the quantity ratios of those commodities which are non-basic for country a and basic for country b, are dependent on the trade system, wherever they are produced; therefore they will depend also on the distribution of income ruling in the small country.

A CRITICAL NOTE ON THE NEO-CLASSICAL THEORY OF INTERNATIONAL TRADE

The Heckscher-Ohlin theorem states that, given an economic system constituted by two countries, two commodities and two factors of production, the commodity exported by a country is that requiring the relatively more intensive use of the factor which is more abundant, relatively to the other factor, in that country, by comparison with the other country. It has been proved that this theorem is true under a set of sufficient conditions.[11] If now we examine the evolution of the neo-classical theory of international trade, from the static Heckscher-Ohlin theory to the recent dynamic models of growth and trade, we find that its main stream continues to follow the lines imposed by the basic hypothesis of the original model: the two factor hypothesis. In the static theory the factor of production which is not labour has not always been specified, whilst this factor is explicitly called *capital* in recent models of growth and trade.[12] It is against this specification – and the models of trade in which it appears – that the critical content of the present section is addressed.

For the purpose of our argument, it is necessary to transform the basic model into a neo-classical growth model. Let us assign a given supply of labour to each country; each supply being inelastic with respect to the wage rate and growing at a given percentage rate. We may close the basic model by treating as endogenous all the distributive variables and imposing equality between the rate of accumulation and the rate of growth of the labour force in each country.[13] In order to isolate the cause of trade which corresponds, in the modified basic model, to the cause of trade in the Heckscher-Ohlin theory, let us assume that the capitalists have the same propensity to save in the two countries. In this case, the only possible cause of trade would be a difference between the rates of growth of the labour force; this difference implying a difference of equal sign between the rates of profit in the two countries. It follows, from the analysis carried out in the previous sections, that in equilibrium a system of incomplete specialisation will be chosen.[14] The country with a labour force growing at the lower rate (the small country) will have a lower rate of profit and will specialise completely in that commodity whose production requires the higher intensity of the capital good; whilst the other country (the large one) will produce both commodities.

Let us denote by the 'relative factor endowment' of a country, the ratio between the total quantity of the capital good and the total quantity of labour available in that country. We have shown that in equilibrium the country which possesses the larger relative endowment of one factor exports the commodity which uses the higher relative intensity of the same factor.[15] This proposition, however, does not state that the difference in relative factor endowments is the cause of trade; in fact the different rates of growth of the labour force explain both the relative factor endowments and the trade system.[16] Therefore the Heckscher-Ohlin theorem is true (although it does not establish a causal relationship) also for the basic model, where one factor and one product are the same commodity, i.e. the capital good.

Certainly a theory of international trade which is valid only within a two products – two factors model, is of very limited empirical interest. However, it has been said, in support of the neo-classical theory of trade, that the Heckscher-Ohlin theorem, under appropriate conditions, allows one to explain trade between two countries even for the multi-commodity case. Indeed Professor Bhagwati presents the following argument:

> [The Heckscher-Ohlin theorem] ... is valid for a multi-commodity model as well*: as Jones[17] has demonstrated, commodities can still be ranked, from technological and factor-supply data, in terms of factor ratios, and are thereby uniquely ranked also in terms of comparative

Distribution, Growth and International Trade 181

advantage, with demand being introduced (as in the Ricardian system) to 'break the chain' into exports and imports. . . .
* (Bhagwati's note) The definitions of 'factor abundance' and 'factor intensity' in a multi-factor model, however, are not so intuitive; but one can always adopt a convention.[18] The results, however, are both more restrictive and less intuitive.[19]

Therefore, the crucial condition which must be satisfied by means of some 'convention', if the Heckscher–Ohlin theorem can be extended in a meaningful way to the multi-commodity case, is the following: assuming tastes and technology as given, a unique order of commodities in terms of relative factor intensities and in terms of comparative advantages must correspond to each relative factor endowment.

On the other hand, an effective extension of the theorem would require that the capital goods also be included among the many commodities. Now, if we assume labour as one of the two factors of production and adopt the neo-classical 'convention' which defines the second factor as *capital*, the above stated condition is satisfied only if a unique pair of rates of profit and a unique system of equilibrium relative prices correspond to each pair of capital–labour ratios associated with the two countries. In this case, capital will be the *value* of the capital goods in terms of some standard of value; this value will generally change when distribution changes. On the basis of this dependence of the value of capital on distribution, it has been proved,[20] for a closed economy, that the same equilibrium ratio between the value of capital and total employment of labour may correspond to different rates of profit; hence to different systems of relative prices. From this it follows that, in a two-country world economy, the same capital–labour ratios in the two countries may correspond to different pairs of rates of profit and to different systems of relative prices.[21] This possibility entails that the order among commodities, in terms of relative factor intensities and in terms of comparative advantage, may not be uniquely determined by means of the relative factor-endowments. It has already been demonstrated that the cases in which a one-to-one correspondence between the relative factor endowment, within a single country, and its rate of profit does not exist are not exceptional at all. We may conclude, therefore, that a theory of international trade which, like the neo-classical one, postulates such a one-to-one correspondence cannot, in general, be extended beyond a world with only one capital good.

APPENDIX

THE ORDER OF THE PRODUCTION SYSTEMS IN TERMS OF g

Using g^A, g^B, g^{AB}, g^{BA} to indicate the values of g which are solutions respectively of the systems (A, B, AB, BA), let us determine the values of (w^a, w^b) for which we have:

$$g^{AB} = g^B$$
$$g^{BA} = g^A$$
$$g^{AB} = g^A$$
$$g^{BA} = g^B.[22]$$

We may solve the systems (A, B, AB, BA) with respect to g, substitute in the previous equations and write $\lambda = s^a/s^b$. Remembering that $\mu = u\gamma - v\beta$, we obtain:

$$g^{AB} = g^B \text{ for } [\beta - (\lambda - 1)\mu]w^b - \lambda\beta w^a + (\lambda - 1)(1 - v) = 0 \quad \text{(i)}$$

with $w^b > 0$; and for each value of w^a with $w^b = 0$.

$$g^{BA} = g^A \text{ for } \beta w^b - [(\lambda - 1)\mu + \lambda\beta]w^a + (\lambda - 1)(1 - v) = 0 \quad \text{(ii)}$$

with $w^a > 0$; and for each value of w^b with $w^a = 0$.

$$g^{AB} = g^A \text{ for } u\gamma w^b - [v(\lambda - 1)(\beta + \mu) + u\gamma]w^a + v(\lambda - 1)(1 - v) = 0 \quad \text{(iii)}$$

with $w^a \neq \dfrac{1}{\beta}$; and for each value of w^b with $w^a = \dfrac{1}{\beta}$.

$$g^{BA} = g^B \text{ for } [\lambda u\gamma - v(\lambda - 1)(\beta + \mu)]w^b - \lambda u\gamma w^a + v(\lambda - 1)(1 - v) = 0 \quad \text{(iv)}$$

with $w^b \neq \dfrac{1}{\beta}$; and for each value of w^a with $w^b = \dfrac{1}{\beta}$.

The equations (i)–(iv) are represented in the plane (w^a, w^b) by straight lines which all pass through the point $w^a = w^b = \dfrac{1-v}{\beta+\mu}$. Write $w_o = \dfrac{1-v}{\beta+\mu}$. If we replace (w^a, w^b) by w_0 in the systems (A, B), w_0 results as the maximum wage rate attainable in the two countries without trade. Let us assume $v < 1$. If $w^a = w^b = w_0$, both the rate of profit and the rate of growth are zero in the two countries. If the wage rate lies in the interval $(0, w_0)$, an equilibrium will exist for each country with a positive relative price and a non-negative rate of profit. The point which represents w_0 in the positive orthant of the plane (w^a, w^b), is crossed also by the straight lines which represent equations $g^A = 0$ and $g^B = 0$. Setting $w^b = 0$ in the equations (i)–(iv), we may determine the respective intercepts with the w^a axis:

$$g^{AB} = g^B \text{ if } w^a = \frac{(\lambda - 1)(1 - v)}{\lambda \beta} = w_1^a;\text{[23]}$$

$$g^{BA} = g^A \text{ if } w^a = \frac{(\lambda - 1)(1 - v)}{(\lambda - 1)\mu + \lambda \beta} = w_2^a;$$

$$g^{AB} = g^A \text{ if } w^a = \frac{v(\lambda - 1)(1 - v)}{v(\lambda - 1)(\beta + \mu) + u\gamma} = w_3^a;$$

$$g^{BA} = g^B \text{ if } w^a = \frac{v(\lambda - 1)(1 - v)}{\lambda u \gamma} = w_4^a.$$

Furthermore we assumed $\lambda \geqq 1$ without any loss of generality. Given the restrictions imposed on the coefficients, the intercepts w_1^a, w_2^a, w_3^a, w_4^a all have non-negative values. The order among these intercepts depends on the sign of μ. In our case $\mu > 0$ by hypothesis; it follows that $w_1^a \geqq w_2^a \geqq w_3^a \geqq w_4^a$.

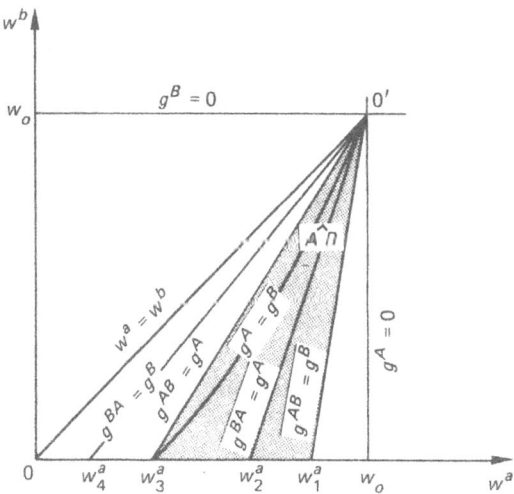

FIGURE 14.3

In Figure 14.3 the straight lines represent equations (i) – (iv) and the equations $g^a = 0$, $g^b = 0$. Since we know that g^A and g^B are monotonic decreasing functions of the respective wage rates and, in general,[24] also g^{AB} and g^{BA} are monotonic decreasing with respect to each wage rate, it is possible to determine distinct regions in the plane (w^a, w^b) where different (partial) orders of the production systems hold in terms of g. We obtain:

a) To the left above the line $g^{BA} = g^B$ and to the left of the line $g^A = 0$
$$\begin{cases} g^B < g^{AB} < g^A \\ g^B < g^{BA} < g^A \end{cases}$$

b) In the cone contained between the line $g^{BA} = g^B$ and the line $g^{AB} = g^A$
$$\{ g^{BA} < g^B < g^{AB} < g^A$$

c) In the cone contained between the line $g^{AB} = g^A$ and the line $g^{BA} = g^A$
$$\begin{cases} g^{BA} < g^B < g^{AB} \\ g^{BA} < g^A < g^{AB} \end{cases}$$

d) In the cone contained between the line $g^{BA} = g^A$ and the line $g^{AB} = g^B$
$$\{ g^A < g^{BA} < g^B < g^{AB}$$

e) To the right of the line $g^{AB} = g^B$ and below the line $g^B = 0$
$$\begin{cases} g^A < g^{AB} < g^B \\ g^A < g^{BA} < g^B \end{cases}$$

In Figure 14.3 we have shown, for completeness, the economically relevant stretch of the curve which represents the equation $g^A = g^B$. The values of (w^a, w^b), for which we have $g^A = g^B$, are solutions of the equation:

$$[v(\lambda-1)(\beta+\mu) - \lambda u \gamma]w^b + [v(\lambda-1)(\beta+\mu) + u\gamma]w^a$$
$$+ (\lambda-1)(\beta+\mu)\mu w^a w^b - v(\lambda-1)(1-v) = 0.$$

This equation is satisfied by $(w^a = w_o, w^b = w_o)$ and by $(w^a = w_3^a, w^b = 0)$. Hence the hyperbola which represents this equation passes through the points $0'$, w_3^a. We have shown that to the left, above the line $g^{AB} = g^A$ and to the left of the line $g^A = 0$, $g^B < g^A$, whilst to the right of the line $g^{BA} = g^A$ and below the line $g^B = 0$, $g^A < g^B$. Therefore, if the orders established above are not to be contradicted, the stretch of the hyperbola which is meaningful, must lie in the cone delimited by the line $g^{AB} = g^A$ and the line $g^{BA} = g^A$.

NOTES

* This is a revised version of the author's article: 'Distribuzione, Sviluppo e Commercio Internazionale', *Economia Internazionale*, 1973. The author would like to thank P. Garegnani and I. Steedman who made helpful critical observations on an earlier draft of that article. However he accepts all responsibility for any possible errors that remain.
1. Heckscher [3], Ohlin [10], Stolper and Samuelson [20], Samuelson [15].
2. Hicks [4].
3. Sraffa [18].
4. In certain neo-classical contributions to the theory of international trade (e.g., Samuelson [17]) the immobility of new capital goods is sometimes assumed, by contrast with the mobility of consumption goods, without, in our opinion, providing any adequate justification for this distinction. The fact that in the real world a given commodity may be used both as a consumption good and as a capital good, makes it impossible to draw a useful distinction between traded and non-traded goods on the basis of their final use.
5. Robinson [14].
6. Hicks [4], chapter XII and following.
7. The definition of steady growth, which we shall use in the version of the basic model presented in the last section of this essay (as a basis for a critique of the neo-classical theory of international trade), coincides with that already used in some neo-classical dynamic models of international trade. C.f. Kemp [8], Khang [9].
8. As long as we maintain the hypotheses of classical savings functions and single product industries, it is possible to obtain a system of price equations in the trade model extended to many commodities, which belongs to the class of systems for which the non-substitution theorem has already been proved. C.f. Parrinello [11].
9. Ricardo [13], p. 390.
10. Parrinello [11].
11. These sufficient conditions have been reviewed by J. Bhagwati in the following passage: '(1) international identity of production functions; (2) non-reversibility of factor-intensities, such that a given commodity is factor x intensive in relation to another at *all* relevant factor price-ratios; (3) constant returns to scale and diminishing returns (along isoquants) in each production function; and (4) identity of the consumption pattern between countries at each relevant commodity price ratio'. (Bhagwati [1], p. 174.)
12. It is interesting, in this respect, to compare the different specifications of the factors of production which Professor Kemp presents in his two books [6], [7]. Both these works start by illustrating a simple model of a closed economy, where two commodities are produced by means of two factors of production. However, while in the first book these factors are '... two homogeneous primary factors of production say labour (L) and land (T), the latter broadly conceived to embrace durable capital instruments of all kinds' ([6], pp. 9–10), in the second one they become 'two homogeneous primary

factors of production, say labour and capital, in quantities L and K, respectively' ([7], p. 5). Therefore the factor of production which, in the first and rather ambiguous specification, we may call 'assisted' land, in the second becomes homogeneous capital.

13. In the particular case in which the supplies of labour in the two countries both grow at the same percentage rate, the system (1)–(8) acquires one degree of freedom. In fact, in this case equation (8) becomes identically satisfied. In the neo-classical theory this degree of freedom disappears once the ratio between the supplies of labour in the two countries is given. In this case, applying the rule of 'zero prices for free goods' to the labour force, the basic model becomes determined by the addition of the following equations:

$$g^a = g^b = n; \quad \frac{L^a + \pi_L^a}{L^b + \pi_L^b} = \eta;$$

$$w^a \pi_L^a = 0; \quad w^b \pi_L^b = 0;$$

where n is the uniform rate of growth of labour, η is the ratio between the supplies of labour and π_L^a, π_L^b are two new unknowns which indicate the amounts of unemployed labour in the two countries.

14. If $s^a = s^b$, then $\lambda = 1$. In this particular case, the cones A_2 and AB (Figure 14.2) reduce to the bisecting line.

15. If, on the other hand, we consider each country i without trade, in equilibrium the following relationship holds between the relative factor-endowment (capital/labour), F^i, and the rate of growth g^i:

$$F^i \equiv \frac{uZ^i + vX^i}{\beta Z^i + \gamma X^i} = \frac{u}{\beta + \mu(1 + g^i)}$$

Therefore, if we compare the steady growth paths of the two countries without trade, we shall find that, with $g^a > g^b$, $F^a \lesseqgtr F^b$ according as $\mu \lesseqgtr 0$.

16. With regard to the problem of the equalisation of the prices of the factor services, we observe that in our model international trade leads to an increase in the difference between the wage rates in respect to the wage levels without trade.

17. Jones [5], quoted by Bhagwati [1].
18. Pearce and James [12]; Samuelson [16], quoted by Bhagwati [1].
19. Bhagwati [1], pp. 174–5.
20. Garegnani [2].
21. The demonstration is given in I. Steedman and J. S. Metcalfe [19].
22. For the purpose of determining the equilibrium system of specialisation, it would be superfluous to consider the equations $g^{AB} = g^{BA}$ and $g^A = g^B$.
23. One must interpret w_1^a as the value of w^a which satisfies (i) when w^b *tends* to zero.
24. g^i is a monotonically decreasing function of the wage in the consumption good industry if the wage in the capital good industry is strictly positive. If the latter wage were zero, g^i would be independent of the wage in the consumption good industry.

REFERENCES

[1] Bhagwati, J. 'The pure theory of international trade: A survey', as reprinted in A.E.A., *Surveys of Economic Theory*, vol. II, New York, 1968.
[2] Garegnani, P. 'Heterogeneous capital, the production function and the theory of distribution'. *Review of Economic Studies*, 37, 1970, pp. 407–36.
[3] Heckscher, E. 'The effects of foreign trade on the distribution of income'. *Ekonomisk Tidskrift*, 1919, pp. 497–512.
[4] Hicks, J. R. *Capital and Growth*. Oxford University Press, 1965.
[5] Jones, R. 'Factor proportions and the Heckscher–Ohlin model'. *Review of Economic Studies*, 24, 1956–57, pp. 1–10.
[6] Kemp, M. C. *The Pure Theory of International Trade*. Prentice-Hall, 1964.
[7] Kemp, M. C. *The Pure Theory of International Trade and Investment*. Prentice-Hall, 1969.
[8] Kemp, M. C. 'International trade between countries with different natural rates of growth'. *Economic Record*, 1970, pp. 467–81.
[9] Khang, C. 'Equilibrium growth in the international economy, the case of unequal rates of growth'. *International Economic Review*, 1971, pp. 239–49.
[10] Ohlin, B. *Inter-regional and International Trade*. Harvard University Press, 1935.
[11] Parrinello, S. 'Introduzione ad una teoria neoricardiana del commercio internazionale'. *Studi Economici*, 1970, 267–321.
[12] Pearce, I. F. and James, S. F. 'The factor price equalization myth'. *Review of Economic Studies*, 19, 1951–52, pp. 111–20.
[13] Ricardo, D. *On the Principles of Political Economy and Taxation* (Sraffa edition). Cambridge University Press, 1951.
[14] Robinson, J. V. *The Accumulation of Capital*. Macmillan, London, 1956.
[15] Samuelson, P. A. 'International factor-price equalization once again'. *Economic Journal*, 1949, pp. 181–97.
[16] Samuelson, P. A. 'Prices of factors and goods in general equilibrium'. *Review of Economic Studies*, 21, 1953–54, pp. 1–20.
[17] Samuelson, P. A. 'Equalization by trade of the interest rate along with the real wage'. In Baldwin, R. E. *et al.*, (eds.), *Trade, Growth and the Balance of Payments* (*Essays in Honor of Gottfried Harberler*), Rand McNally, Chicago, 1965.
[18] Sraffa, P. *Production of Commodities by Means of Commodities*. Cambridge University Press, 1960.
[19] Steedman, I. and Metcalfe, J. S. 'Heterogeneous capital and the Heckscher–Ohlin–Samuelson theory of trade'. In Parkin, J. M. (ed.), *Essays in Modern Economics*, Longman, London, 1973. (See Essay 5 in this volume.)
[20] Stolper, W. and Samuelson, P. A. 'Protection and real wages'. *Review of Economic Studies*, 9, 1941, pp. 58–73.

15 Exchange Rate Changes and the Choice of Technique*

L. MAINWARING

Shortly after the appearance of his 'absorption' approach to the effects of devaluation, S. S. Alexander [1] was criticised by Fritz Machlup [3] for conducting his argument in terms of the overall price level rather than in terms of relative prices and, therefore, failing to take account of resource allocation effects resulting from relative price changes. In this essay we consider a dynamic absorption model (dynamic in the sense of steady growth) which is of a rather more disaggregated variety than usual. Since it is set in a Sraffa-Leontief framework relative prices are of central importance, but not merely because of straightforward consumer substitution effects. Because of production interrelationships, relative prices exercise an influence on the choice of technique appropriate to any exchange rate. This, in turn, may lead to modifications of the traditional absorption conclusions.

THE CLOSED ECONOMY

The argument is, in part, an extension of some standard capital theory to an open economy. For that reason it may be useful to state at the beginning some of the properties of the Sraffa–Leontief, single-products, circulating capital model. For any particular technique the set of long-period equilibrium prices is given by the equations

$$\underline{p} = (1+r)\underline{p}A^* + w\underline{a} \quad (1)$$

where r is the rate of profits, w the wage, $\underline{p}$ the row vector of prices, $\underline{a}$ the row vector of labour inputs per unit of output, and A^* the matrix of unit input-output coefficients. (Equation (1) involves the assumption that the wage is paid at the end of the production period.) For any technique, equations of this type describe a negative monotonic relationship between w and r, the w–r frontier. To these price equations can be added a set of quantity equations: if $\underline{Z}$ is the column vector of gross outputs, $\underline{C}$ the column vector of consumption quantities, and g the rate of growth, then in equilibrium

$$\underline{Z} = (1+g)A^*\underline{Z} + \underline{C}. \qquad (2)$$

If the proportions in which commodities enter consumption are fixed, and are the same for wage and non-wage consumption, then, for any particular technique, equation (2) describes a relationship between g and consumption per worker which is the exact dual of the w–r frontier. As is well-known, the existence of many techniques may allow the possibilities of reswitching and capital reversing.

A SMALL OPEN ECONOMY

In this section we set out a prices-quantities model which is similar in structure to equations (1) and (2) but which applies to a small open capitalist economy. Our purpose is to analyse, in the following sections, interrelationships between the exchange rate, the trade balance and the growth rate. For this purpose it is of considerable convenience to maintain duality between the price and quantity equations, and to do so a number of simplifying assumptions are made:[1] (i) the wage is advanced at the beginning of the production period; (ii) in addition to consumption, imports and exports also consist of single (possibly composite) commodities; (iii) all profits are saved while all wages are consumed. A further assumption which is required for duality is noted below.

The small capitalist economy with which we are concerned exports a manufactured commodity and imports raw materials, food and similar primary commodities (in fixed proportions). The manufacture is differentiated from its competitors so that the volume of exports is a decreasing function of their foreign currency price. On the other hand, imports are of an undifferentiated nature so that, being small, the country has no influence on the world price, q, of this composite commodity.

Under these assumptions a new set of price equations may be written:

$$\underline{p} = (1+r)[\underline{p}(A^* + \underline{w}\underline{a}) + vq(\underline{b}^* + u\underline{a})]$$

where v is the exchange rate (defined as the domestic currency price of a unit of foreign currency), $\underline{b}^*$ is the row vector of imported input coefficients, $\underline{w}$ the column vector of the quantities of domestic commodities in the wage, and u the quantity of imported commodity in the wage. The wage payments can be incorporated into the domestic input-output matrix and imported input vector so that we can write

$$\underline{p} = (1+r)\underline{p}A + s\underline{b} \tag{3}$$

or
$$\underline{p} = s\underline{b}[I - (1+r)A]^{-1} \tag{4}$$

where $s = (1+r)vq$ and A and $\underline{b}$ refer to the modified (augmented) coefficients.

Gross outputs of domestic goods must now be sufficient to cover replacement and growth of wage and non-wage capital, plus exports:

$$\underline{Z} = (1+g)(A^*\underline{Z} + \underline{w}a\underline{Z}) + \underline{E}$$

where $\underline{E}$ is the column vector of export commodities (with non-varying proportions). This can be condensed into

$$\underline{Z} = (1+g)A\underline{Z} + \underline{E} \tag{5}$$

or
$$\underline{Z} = [I - (1+g)A]^{-1}\underline{E}. \tag{6}$$

The model is summarised by equations (3) and (5). Although the treatment of imports and exports remains at a highly aggregated level, results of interest arising out of our analysis do not hinge on this but on the disaggregation of domestic production relationships. The mathematical similarity between this model and the Sraffa-Leontief closed economy model can now be used to advantage in deriving dual relations between key variables in the price and quantity systems. Consider first the price system.

Equations (1) and (3) are identical in form so that there exists an s–r frontier possessing the same mathematical properties as the standard w–r frontier: if, for example, the exchange rate is fixed then so is the rate of profits (together with a unique set of positive prices). An increase in s leads to a reduction in the equilibrium r. Since $v = [s/(1+r)q]$, and q is constant by assumption, this implies an inverse relationship between v and r.

Equations (2) and (5) are also of the same form, so that we should expect to be able to derive an 'exports-growth' frontier identical to the consumption-growth frontier of the closed economy. However, we also desire that the 'exports-growth' frontier and the s–r frontier exhibit duality. This requires that the standard of value, in terms of which the

Exchange Rates and Choice of Technique

price equations are written, be a (composite) commodity in the same proportions as the vector $\underline{E}$. It is, therefore, convenient to take a representative commodity bundle $\underline{E}^o$ (in these proportions) as the standard of value:

$$\underline{p}\underline{E}^o = 1.$$

Duality may then be demonstrated as follows;[2] post-multiplying (4) by $\underline{E}^o$

$$\underline{p}\underline{E}^o = 1 = s\underline{b}[I-(1+r)A]^{-1}\underline{E}^o$$

so that $\qquad s = 1/\underline{b}[I-(1+r)A]^{-1}\underline{E}^o \qquad (7)$

which is the s–r frontier. Before deriving the 'exports-growth' frontier it should be noted that the quantity of goods imported in the present period, denoted by M, is not the same as the quantity *used up* in this period. The latter is equal to the quantity imported in the previous period, $m = M/(1+g)$. The value, X, of exports is the number of standard bundles $\underline{E}^o$, of price unity, so that

$$\underline{E} = X\underline{E}^o.$$

Now $\underline{b}\underline{Z} = m$; thus on pre-multiplying (6) by $\underline{b}$ and replacing $\underline{E}$ by $X\underline{E}^o$, we find

$$m = \underline{b}[I-(1+g)A]^{-1}X\underline{E}^o$$

or $\qquad x = 1/\underline{b}[I-(1+g)A]^{-1}\underline{E}^o, \qquad (8)$

where $x \equiv X/m$.

Relation (8), the x–g frontier, relates the value of exports *per unit of previous period's imports*, to the rate of growth. It is easily seen to be the exact dual of (7), (Figure 15.1).

THE NATIONAL ACCOUNTS

Points on the dual frontiers in Figure 15.1 represent steady growth equilibria and, initially, the analysis must be understood in terms of equilibrium comparisons. While it would clearly be desirable to investigate the out-of-equilibrium properties of this model it would also be prohibitively difficult. Nevertheless it is possible to qualify the comparative analysis by taking account of some consequences of a transition between equilibria on the implicit understanding that such a transition is always possible.

192   Fundamental Issues in Trade Theory

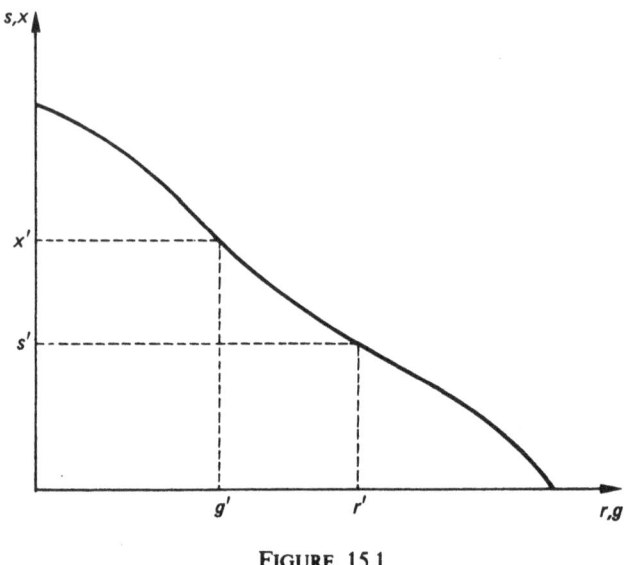

FIGURE 15.1

It has been shown (Metcalfe and Steedman [6]) that steady full-employment growth in an open economy normally requires unbalanced trade with the deficit or surplus growing at a proportionate rate equal to the growth rate of the economy. Here, however, we do not wish the trade balance to be constrained by steady growth requirements so that, to avoid the consequences of a deficit or surplus being accumulated indefinitely at an 'inappropriate' rate, we shall proceed on the assumption that such an imbalance is financed by accommodating capital on which the interest rate is zero.[3]

We can now proceed to the national accounts of our open economy, mindful that our last (somewhat forced) assumption removes any distinction between 'national' and 'domestic' items in these accounts. Looking first at the expenditure items, and abstracting from government spending and taxation, national income is the sum of consumption, investment and the trade balance. Because all profits are saved, consumption is entirely in the form of wages which are advanced as capital. We shall use a concept of national income which is neither gross nor net since consumption (that is, the replacement of wage capital) is included but the replacement of non-wage capital is excluded. In the following, the subscripts d and f are used to distinguish between expenditures on domestic and foreign goods. The value of imports in the

present period is
$$vqM = (1+g)vqm = (1+g)(W_f + K_f) \qquad (9)$$
where W_f and K_f are the values of wage and non-wage capital imported in the previous period. The values of current period consumption and investment are
$$C = W_d + W_f$$
$$I = g(K_d + W_d + K_f + W_f)$$
Subtracting (9) from the sum of C, I and X yields national income:
$$Y = W_d + g(K_d + W_d) + X - K_f$$
Dividing through by m (writing $y \equiv Y/m$, etc.) and rearranging,
$$y - w_d + k_f = i_d + x \qquad (10)$$
where i_d is investment expenditure on domestic goods (per unit of imports of the previous period).

Turning, now, to the income items, national income is the sum of wages and profits
$$Y = (1+r)(W_d + W_f) + r(K_d + K_f).$$
Adding K_f to both sides, dividing through by m, and rearranging
$$y - w_d + k_f = r(k_d + w_d) + (1+r)(w_f + k_f)$$
or, since $(w_f + k_f) = vqm/m = vq$,
$$y - w_d + k_f = p_d + (1+r)vq \qquad (11)$$
where p_d is profit on domestically produced capital.

The relationship between the accounting identities (10) and (11) is shown in Figure 15.2 (in which all items on the vertical axis are in terms of the imported good).

THE EFFECTS OF DEVALUATION

From Figure 15.2 we can recognise three possibilities relating to the state of the trade account and the relationship between the rate of profits and the rate of growth. Recalling that $(1+g)vq$ is the value of current imports (divided by m), we see that

(i) $r = g$ implies $x = (1+g)vq$ or balanced trade

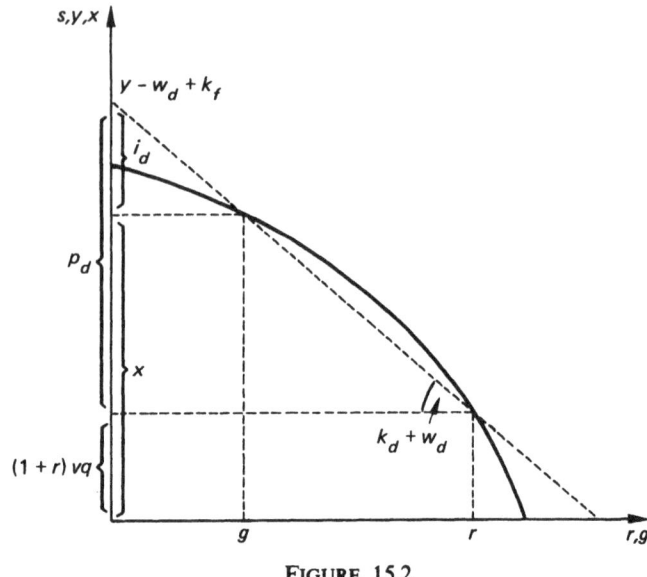

FIGURE 15.2

(ii) $r > g$ implies $x > (1+g)vq$ or a trade surplus
(iii) $r < g$ implies $x < (1+g)vq$ or a trade deficit.

The interpretation of these possibilities is straightforward: (ii) implies that an excess of savings (via profits) over domestic investment requirements must, in equilibrium, find an outlet in 'external investment' or exports; while (iii) implies that an insufficiency of domestic savings must be made up for by an excess of imports over exports.

Consider now the effects of a devaluation (an increase in v), on the assumption that there is just a single technique, represented by the frontier in Figure 15.2. Starting from a given point on the s–r frontier, a devaluation must lower the rate of profits on account of the inverse relationship between v and r. However, the impact of a devaluation is not confined to the s–r frontier. The foreign currency price of exports will, of course, change. Indeed, since a unit export bundle is taken as the standard of value, the foreign currency price of a unit of exports is $1/v$. With a downward sloping demand curve for exports, the volume of exports will increase with devaluation, as will their value in terms of domestic currency. (Their value in foreign currency may increase, decrease, or stay the same depending on the elasticity of demand with respect to $1/v$.) Devaluation thus implies an increase in x which can only be accommodated by a reduction in the growth rate.

Exchange Rates and Choice of Technique   195

On the import side there is no room for substitution since the input coefficients are fixed while the wage bundle is specified in constant proportions. On the other hand, the fall in the growth rate will lead to a reduction in the demand for imports, though whether the home currency value of these imports falls depends again on the usual elasticity considerations, which are themselves dependent on the sensitivity of the growth rate to the change in v.

These results, which appear to be a mixture of those obtained from the 'elasticities' and 'absorption' analyses of the balance of payments tend to be rather pessimistic, especially in their implications for the growth rate. In a more general analysis this pessimism would be tempered on at least two counts: (i) by allowing the possibility of import substitution; and (ii) by recognising that in the short run, there will often be spare capacity available for increasing the output of export or investment goods. These are accepted (and valid) qualifications. Another one, suggested by Machlup [3], is that substitution effects will give rise to favourable resource allocation changes. In the following section we look at resource allocation from a slightly different viewpoint: the adoption of the most profitable technique.

A CHOICE OF TECHNIQUE

We now allow the economy a choice of technique. The frontiers for two techniques, a and b, are drawn in Figure 15.3, in which the possibilities of reswitching and capital reversing are shown. In the present context capital reversing means that a devaluation, or increase in v, (resulting in an increase in the domestic price of the imported good) is associated with the adoption of a technique employing a *lower* value of domestic capital per unit of imported capital.[4] While this in itself is an unexpected result, our main concern is to show that with technical choice the growth rate may become extremely sensitive to small changes in the exchange rate.

With an exchange rate v_1 the profit rate is r_1, whichever technique is in use – they can operate together at this rate. Consider, now, two rates of profits, r'_1 and r''_1 which are, respectively, marginally smaller and marginally greater than r_1, so that at r'_1 technique a is used, at r''_1 technique b is used. If, then, there is a marginal increase of v about v_1 there is a switch in technique from b to a. The effect of such a marginal change in v on the volume and domestic value of imports is negligible so that x is unchanged. The result is a substantial reduction in the growth rate, from g'' to g'. We appear to have here a sort of 'super-absorption'

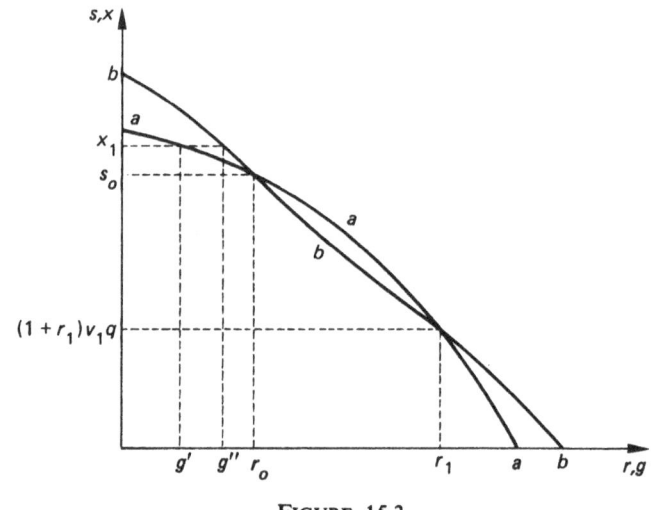

FIGURE 15.3

outcome. But consideration of the effect of a marginal devaluation about the *other* switchpoint, s_o, r_o (technique b replacing technique a), shows that the growth rate may *increase* substantially – an 'anti-absorption' outcome.

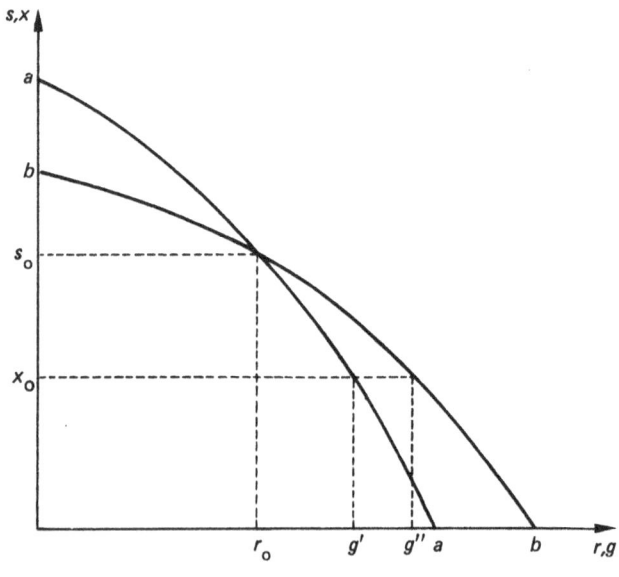

FIGURE 15.4

The first of these possibilities, a large reduction in g, seems to be associated with capital reversing. But this is only so when $g < r$, for which there is no necessity in an open economy. That capital reversing is not necessary for this result can be seen in the example illustrated in Figure 15.4, in which $g > r$. A small devaluation about v_0 produces a switch from b to a and, again, a substantial fall in the growth rate. This time, however, the value of domestic capital per unit of imported capital increases.

The concentration on marginal changes around a switchpoint has been deliberate. It is very doubtful in such cases that full allowance for output expansion or for substitution and its resource allocation consequences would affect the conclusions in any but the most marginal way, since the price changes arising out of depreciation *per se*, rather than through technical change, are insignificant.

TRANSITIONS

Our conclusions, reached on the basis of equilibrium comparisons, are: (i) with a single technique and assuming sufficiently high demand elasticities, devaluation improves the trade balance only at the cost of reducing the growth rate; (ii) with a choice of technique, devaluation may produce either an increase or a decrease in the growth rate (although increases only come about with 'small' devaluations about *some* switchpoints).

Analyses conducted in terms of equilibrium comparisons need careful interpretation. To take one example, Ricardian models in which comparative analysis suggests the possibility of a loss from trade[5] have to be qualified when actual transitions from no-trade to with-trade equilibria take place. The argument is that steady state losses only occur where the autarkic capital stock is of greater value than the with-trade capital stock. The actual transition would thus involve disinvestment and this freeing of resources might give rise to a transitional consumption boost. It can then be shown under particular assumptions (Metcalfe and Steedman [5]; see also Samuelson [8]) that the discounted value of the 'transition plus trade' consumption stream is greater than that of the autarky stream.

This example, at least, suggests that any conclusions be considered in the light of a comparison of capital stocks in any two equilibria. Let us reconsider the cases discussed above. Devaluation with a single technique (Figure 15.2) leads to a reduction in both r and g so that there is a fall in the value of domestic capital per unit of imports. Since imports also fall, the absolute value of domestic capital is lower. The resources so freed *may* be convertible into (say) consumption goods. Thus although the growth rate and hence future output in the new equilibrium are lower, nevertheless the move may be desirable once the additional (transitional) consumption is brought into consideration. Precisely the same considerations apply to the marginal devaluation in Figure 15.3 associated with capital reversing (that is, a fall in the value of domestic capital), while the argument is reversed for the case of a devaluation around the switch point s_o, r_o: here the attainment of a higher growth rate equilibrium requires the investment of additional domestic capital during the transition.

Needless to say, these transitional considerations are themselves dependent on certain critical assumptions. In particular they imply that the transition occurs without capital redundancy and unemployment of labour which, in turn, requires some naive assumptions relating to expectations, capital malleability, labour skills, etc.[6] The importance of the last case discussed (Figure 15.4) is that a move to a lower growth rate equilibrium involves *increased* investment of domestic capital. Thus even if one has every faith in the transitional argument referred to above, the conclusion reached on the basis of equilibrium comparisons is not offset but, rather, strengthened by the transitional considerations. It may also be noted that this case, involving as it does a trade deficit, is probably the most relevant to a discussion of devaluation.

CONCLUSION

We have attempted in this essay to analyse some effects of devaluation in the context of a steady growth model. It is recognised that a devaluation implies a transition from one steady state to another (though, in this respect, the comparative static nature of the analysis is essentially no different from standard approaches) and the conclusions must be appropriately qualified to allow for this. Such qualifications may weaken or strengthen the initial conclusions. It should be stressed, however, that our intention is not to provide a general theory of devaluation but merely to emphasise one hitherto neglected aspect of the problem. In this respect it may be useful to draw a distinction between the short and long-run effects of exchange rate changes. The short-run impact of a devaluation is likely to depend heavily on substitution and standard absorption effects. But it is often argued that a further consequence is to bring about appropriate structural changes in the economy. Clearly, such structural changes will not reflect day-to-day fluctuations of the exchange rate but, rather, its more permanent long-run trend.

The usual presumption is that these structural changes will be desirable in the sense of restoring the international competitiveness of the economy. In the dynamic analysis presented here, however, we have seen that such changes may imply adverse effects on the rate of growth. The significance of this is that one can no longer hold to the presumption that the structural adjustments which occur as a result of profit-motivated changes in techniques, responding to long-run movements in the exchange rate, will be the appropriate ones. The widely held view that free international adjustment necessarily promotes desirable long-run changes thus comes under question.

Finally, consider a more general implication of the analysis, related to the concept of 'export-led growth'. The concept appears to be valid only in the short run when the increase in effective demand is able to take up slack resources. In the long run, an increase in exports, if it takes place without reducing consumption, will generally require the reduction of investment (as implied by the negative relationship between exports and the growth rate). Changes in the level of exports can only be used for internal policy as a means of short-run demand management. But an improvement in the growth rate cannot (other things being equal) be sustained over time by a continuous increase in exports.

NOTES

*This essay is a substantially revised version of an article of the same title which appeared in *Economic Record*, 1977. I am grateful to Ian Steedman for drawing my attention to an important contradiction in the original paper and for suggesting many other improvements. I should also like to thank J. S. Metcalfe and two referees of the *Economic Record* for their helpful comments.
1. A discussion of the importance of some of these assumptions can be found in section VII of the original article.
2. Our argument follows that of Weizsäcker [9].
3. Such an assumption was implicitly made by Harrod [2] in a steady-growth context (see Metcalfe and Steedman [6] who, together with Neher [7], provide useful treatments of capital flows in steady growth).
4. Having demonstrated the direct correspondence of our equations to those of standard capital theory, we simply state the possibility of reswitching and capital reversing without further proof.
5. See, for example, Mainwaring [4] and Metcalfe and Steedman [5].
6. See Essay 12 in this volume for further discussion of capital malleability, etc., and transitions.

REFERENCES

[1] Alexander, S. S. 'Effects of a devaluation on a trade balance'. *IMF Staff Papers*, 1952, pp. 263–78.
[2] Harrod, R. F. *Towards a Dynamic Economics*. Macmillan, London, 1948.
[3] Machlup, F. 'Relative prices and aggregate spending in the analysis of devaluation'. *American Economic Review*, 1955, pp. 255–78.
[4] Mainwaring, L. 'A neo-Ricardian analysis of international trade'. *Kyklos*, 1974, pp. 537–53. (See Essay 9 in this volume.)
[5] Metcalfe, J. S., and Steedman, I. 'A note on the gain from trade'. *Economic Record*, 1974, pp. 581–95. (See Essay 4 in this volume.)
[6] Metcalfe, J. S., and Steedman, I. 'Growth and distribution in an open economy'. (See Essay 16 in this volume.)
[7] Neher, P. A. 'International capital movements along balanced growth paths'. *Economic Record*, 1970, pp. 343–401.
[8] Samuelson, P. A. 'Trade pattern reversals in time-phased Ricardian systems and intertemporal efficiency'. *Journal of International Economics*, 1975, pp. 309–63.
[9] Weizsäcker, C. C. von. *Steady State Capital Theory*. Springer-Verlag, Berlin, 1971.

16 Growth and Distribution in an Open Economy*

J. S. METCALFE and IAN STEEDMAN

Several of the previous essays in this book have in common the assumptions of an arbitrarily fixed rate of growth and rate of profits, the links between the two magnitudes remaining unspecified. In this final essay our purpose is to begin to bridge the gap between growth and distribution with an explicit analysis of accumulation in an open economy. In so doing, we shall develop relations between the wage-profit and consumption-growth frontiers in an open economy and between the volume of net foreign lending and the distribution of domestic product between wages and profits. The distributional relations we develop provide a basis, we would argue, for a macro economic alternative to the H–O–S theory of income distribution in open economies. The essay is divided into four main parts. Part I develops an analysis of the wage–profit and consumption–growth frontiers in an open economy, to demonstrate their dependence on the terms of trade and the influence of the trade balance on the consumption–growth frontier. Part II is concerned with the external constraint for a small open economy in steady growth and explores the links between the volume of foreign lending and the trade balance. Part III introduces this external constraint into the Harrod growth scheme and shows how a value of the trade balance can be found which reconciles natural and warranted growth rates, despite the assumptions of a constant saving:income ratio and a constant capital:output ratio. Part IV, the most important part, brings the various strands of the analysis together to investigate the links between growth and distribution in an open economy. In particular, we show how the trade balance, terms of trade, rate of profits and real exchange rate (the labour commanded price of foreign currency) are linked together under conditions of steady growth. However, before we turn to our substantive analysis, some preliminary points must be established.

SOME UNDERLYING CONCEPTS AND ASSUMPTIONS

We consider first the assumptions upon which the analysis is based, assumptions which are formulated to emphasise the macro economic nature of the argument.

Following a well established tradition in international economic theory, we shall consider the case of a small, open economy with a rate of growth no greater than that of the rest of the world with which it trades. The foreign currency prices of the commodities it trades (and thus the terms of trade) are fixed independently of the volume of commodities traded by it. The domestic currency prices of traded commodities are, of course, equal to their foreign currency prices multiplied by the nominal exchange rate.

The economy we discuss is a capitalist economy in which the decision to invest in real capital assets is taken in the light of their anticipated profitability. To be more precise, the volume of real investment depends on the comparison of the 'marginal efficiency of investment', adjusted for the appropriate risk premium, with the money rate of interest. Investment decisions are taken by *entrepreneurs*, who must be distinguished from *financiers* who buy and sell money and other financial assets in the domestic and in the international money and bond markets. We shall assume that the only form of placement which enters international exchange is a perpetual bond and that domestic bonds and foreign bonds are perfect substitutes. It is further assumed that the country is also small with respect to international movements of financial capital and that the arbitrage operations of financiers ensure that the domestic money rate of interest is always equated with the given 'world' money rate of interest, it being assumed that the domestic rate of inflation is always equal to the 'world' rate of inflation. Although the investment horizons of financiers are international, the investment horizons of entrepreneurs are strictly domestic; we do not allow direct international investment to enter the argument.[1] It should be noted that we do allow for international trade in capital goods, which trade flows must not be confused with, or treated as equivalent to movements of money capital, i.e. finance.

It is important in our analysis to distinguish between the money rate of interest, the rate of profits and the expected rate of profit. The rate of interest is defined as the annual coupon on the perpetual bond divided by the price of the perpetual bond. The rate of profits, however, is a macro economic concept, which relates to the current state of the economy and which is defined as the ratio of current profits to the total of invested capital valued at replacement cost. By contrast, the expected rate of profit is a forward looking concept, which only makes sense in the context of the entrepreneurial planning of a given investment programme. It is only in the conditions of steady growth discussed in this essay that the expected rate of profit will coincide with the rate of profits. In such conditions, the rate of profits cannot be less than the money rate of interest if investment in real capital assets is to take place. For simplicity, we shall consider the domestic and 'world' rates of inflation to be zero and to be fixed independently of the variables discussed in this essay; we merely note that the argument can be readily extended to take account of non-zero and fully anticipated rates of change of all money prices.

In discussion of the open economy one must also keep in mind the following distinctions. First and foremost, it must be recognised that domestic product no longer coincides, in general, with national income, but falls short of or exceeds national income by the volume of interest receipts or payments related to the net external assets or liabilities of the economy. Second, one must distinguish three separate items in the balance of payments. By the trade balance, we shall mean the excess of the money value of commodity exports over commodity imports; by the current account balance, we shall mean the trade balance plus the net inflow of interest income on net external assets; and, finally, by the basic balance we shall mean the current balance minus the net outflow of foreign lending. Of course, a country can only engage in net foreign lending to the extent that it simultaneously has a current account surplus, i.e. an excess of national income over national expenditure.

The sole concern of this essay is the analysis of equilibrium growth situations in which the basic balance is zero, any imbalance in the current account being exactly matched by an equivalent volume of foreign lending or borrowing. Another way of putting this is to state that any discrepancy between domestic saving and investment is exactly covered by borrowing or lending on the perfectly competitive international capital market. We therefore eliminate any possibility of financing a disequilibrium in the current balance through changes in holding of foreign exchange reserves, with the added implication that the domestic supply of money is independent of the state of the balance of payments.

It should be noted, finally, that the method of analysis utilised in this essay is one of the comparison of equilibrium steady growth paths in which we make use of three distinct concepts of the growth rate. By the warranted rate of growth, we mean that rate of expansion of output which maintains aggregate saving equal to aggregate investment with a fully utilised stock of capital goods. By the desired rate of growth, we mean that rate of expansion of output which leaves entrepreneurs content to maintain the existing rate of capacity expansion in the future. Finally, by the equilibrium growth rate, we mean that rate of growth of output at which warranted and desired growth rates coincide. We do not attempt the more difficult analyses which are involved in treating disequilibrium situations, although by treating equilibrium growth paths we generate the appropriate reference paths for any subsequent treatment of disequilibrium.

It will prove useful at this stage to outline some notation and some useful identities and inequalities which our argument relies upon at various stages.

NOTATION, IDENTITIES AND INEQUALITIES

We denote absolute magnitudes, measured in terms of home currency, by the following capital letters:

Q Domestic product (it is assumed that all physical assets are everlasting so that any net/gross distinction is superfluous)
Y National income
W The wage bill
P Profits generated in domestic production
K Value of the domestically located stock of means of production
S Domestic saving
I Domestic investment – the increment to the value of K
F Inflow of income on net holdings of foreign assets (bonds)
Z Net foreign bond holdings (assets minus liabilities)
B Balance of trade (exports minus imports)
D Current account balance
L Net balance of foreign lending[2]

The following lower case letters represent rates and ratios:

r Rate of profits generated in domestic production
r_e The expected rate of profit
i Money rate of interest
e The real exchange rate, i.e. the ratio of the nominal foreign exchange rate to the domestic money wage rate
n Natural rate of growth

Growth and Distribution in an Open Economy

- g_w Warranted rate of growth
- g_D Desired rate of growth
- g Actual rate of growth
- v Capital: output ratio
- s Ratio of saving by domestic residents to national income
- s_w Ratio of saving out of wages to the wage bill
- s_p Ratio of saving out of profit and interest income to the total of profit and interest income accruing to domestic residents.

Identities

$$Q \equiv W + rK$$
$$Y \equiv Q + F$$
$$D \equiv B + F$$
$$v \equiv K/Q$$

Inequalities

From the beginning it is important to rule out as economically meaningless certain relationships between the above variables and parameters. We shall only discuss economic systems in which the following inequalities hold:

1. $\qquad\qquad\qquad r \geqq i$

In conditions of steady capital accumulation, the rate of profits must not be less than the money rate of interest.

2. $\qquad\qquad\qquad 1 > vi$

Since we are only concerned with economies in which real wages are positive, it must be the case that $1/v > r$. Using inequality 1 then leads immediately to inequality 2.

3. $\qquad\qquad\qquad 1 > nv$

Unless this inequality holds, full employment growth is impossible.

4. $\qquad\qquad\qquad g > si$

This condition is important for all our results. It states that real investment must be greater than the savings which would flow from national income, if the rate of profits happened to equal the money rate of interest.[3]

Combining inequalities (2) and (4) we obtain

5. $$0 < i < \min\left[\frac{g}{s}, \frac{1}{v}\right]$$

as a restriction on the feasible values of i, g, s and v.

6. $$B < Q - nK$$

Only if this condition is satisfied will the increase in aggregate net wealth of domestic residents, on a full employment growth path, be less than the national income.

7. $$K + Z > 0$$

The aggregate net wealth of domestic residents must be positive.

PART I FOUNDATIONS: WAGE-PROFIT AND CONSUMPTION–GROWTH FRONTIERS FOR AN OPEN ECONOMY

Prices and Distribution

A straightforward analysis of the production and distribution aspects of the open economy can be made by assuming three distinct commodities, each of which has a dual role as productive input and consumption commodity. Two of these commodities, the export commodity (commodity one) and the non-tradeable commodity (commodity two) are produced domestically, in constant returns to scale production processes, in which labour is the only primary input. Commodity three, the imported commodity, is not produced domestically, and it therefore plays a role logically equivalent to a second primary input in our analysis. Let A^* denote the commodity input-output matrix for a given technique for producing the two commodities, let $\underline{m}$ denote the vector of direct inputs of the imported commodity in the production of the domestic commodities, and let $\underline{a}$ denote the vector of direct labour inputs. With labour as the standard of value and under competitive conditions, $\underline{p}$, the vector of labour commanded prices of commodities one and two (expressed in domestic wages) is given by

$$\underline{p} = \underline{p} A^* r + p_3 \underline{m} r + \underline{a} \tag{1}$$

where p_3 is the labour commanded price (in domestic wages) of the imported commodity. (All three commodities have infinite lives when used as capital goods.) Define

$$\underline{M}(r) = r\underline{m}[I - A^*r]^{-1} = [M_1(r), M_2(r)],$$

a vector of direct and indirect inputs of the imported commodity compounded up at the ruling rate of profits, and

$$\underline{A}(r) = \underline{a}[I - A^*r]^{-1} = [A_1(r), A_2(r)],$$

the corresponding vector of compounded total labour inputs.

Each element of $\underline{M}(r)$ and $\underline{A}(r)$ is an increasing function of r.

The labour commanded prices of domestic commodities can now be written as

$$p_1 = p_3 M_1(r) + A_1(r) \qquad (2)$$
$$p_2 = p_3 M_2(r) + A_2(r)$$

In this small open economy, of course, we have the two additional conditions,

$$p_1 = e\pi_1 \text{ and } p_3 = e\pi_3, \qquad (3)$$

where e is the real (labour commanded) exchange rate and the π_i are the foreign currency prices of the two tradeable commodities. From equations (2) and (3) we can derive each of the labour commanded commodity prices solely as a function of the technical coefficients, the terms of trade $\pi = \pi_1/\pi_3$, and r. (The exchange rate also depends on π_3.) Thus:

$$p_1 = \left[\frac{\pi A_1(r)}{\pi - M_1(r)}\right] \qquad p_2 = \left[\frac{A_1(r) M_2(r)}{\pi - M_1(r)}\right] + A_2(r)$$

$$p_3 = \left[\frac{A_1(r)}{\pi - M_1(r)}\right] \qquad e = \frac{1}{\pi_3}\left[\frac{A_1(r)}{\pi - M_1(r)}\right] \qquad (4)$$

It will be clear, from (4), that in any open economy in which real wages are positive, the terms of trade and r must jointly satisfy the condition $\pi > M_1(r)$. From equations (4) we can see that each of these labour commanded prices is an increasing function of r and a decreasing function of π. An improvement in the terms of trade is therefore unambiguously associated with an improvement in real wages for given r. It is interesting to note that r and e are related in a positive fashion; this is because an increase in r raises the domestic currency price of exports in relation to the domestic money wage and so requires an offsetting depreciation in the exchange rate to maintain the condition $p_1 = e\pi_1$.

The relative price of the two domestically produced commodities is given by

$$\frac{p_2}{p_1} = \frac{[M_2(r)A_1(r) - M_1(r)A_2(r)] + A_2(r)\pi}{A_1(r)\pi} \tag{5}$$

Only in the special circumstances in which the proportions of imported inputs to labour inputs are the same for each domestic commodity is this relative price independent of π, and only with the further restriction of equal proportions of values of commodity inputs to labour inputs is it also independent of r.

To derive the wage-profit frontier we let the real wage, w, consist of elements of the three commodities in proportions given by the vector $\underline{\omega}$ for the first two commodities and by the scalar ω_3 for the third. Then

$$w = \frac{1}{\underline{p}\underline{\omega} + p_3\omega_3} = \frac{\pi - M_1(r)}{A_1(r)[\omega_3 + \underline{M}(r)\underline{\omega}] + [\pi - M_1(r)]\underline{A}(r)\underline{\omega}}$$
$$= f_1(\pi, r) \tag{6}$$

This relation is sketched in Figure 16.1.

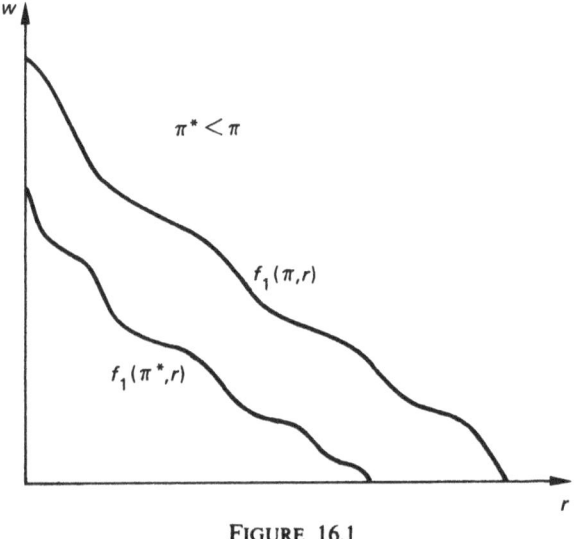

FIGURE 16.1

Since each labour commanded price is an increasing function of r, it follows that w is a decreasing function of r and that the maximum

Growth and Distribution in an Open Economy 209

feasible value for r is found from the solution to $\pi - M_1(r) = 0$. Furthermore, since each labour commanded price is a decreasing function of π it follows that a deterioration of the terms of trade (reduction in π) shifts the wage–profit frontier inward toward the origin and reduces the maximum value of r. Conversely, an improvement in the terms of trade increases the maximum feasible value of r and increases the real wage associated with any given value of r. (The maximum value of r will be independent of π if and only if the import enters neither directly nor indirectly into the production of the export commodity.) In an obvious sense, an improvement in the terms of trade is equivalent to technical progress and a deterioration in the terms of trade to technical regress.

Consumption and growth

It is a well known proposition in production theory that the wage–profit and consumption–growth frontiers are dual to each other, being the same technical relation between different pairs of variables.[4] In this section we show how this duality breaks down when the economy has a non-zero trade balance. Let $\underline{x}$ be a vector of gross outputs per worker of the two home produced commodities, let $\underline{y}$ be the corresponding vector of commodities consumed domestically and exported, and let $\underline{e} = (e_1, 0)'$ be the vector of exports per worker. We shall also assume that the proportions in which commodities enter total consumption are the same as the proportions in which they enter the wage bundle. Then the following quantity relations hold

$$\underline{x} = gA^*\underline{x} + \underline{y} \qquad (7)$$

$$\underline{y} = c.\underline{\omega} + \underline{e} \qquad (8)$$

where c is the level of consumption per worker.

Now define

$$\underline{M}(g) = g\underline{m}[I - gA^*]^{-1} = [M_1(g), M_2(g)],$$

a vector of the total import requirements to produce a unit of each commodity and allow for the increment in output associated with accumulation, and

$$\underline{A}(g) = \underline{a}[I - gA^*]^{-1} = [A_1(g), A_2(g)],$$

the corresponding vector of total labour inputs allowing for accumulation. Then, since $\underline{a}\underline{x} = \underline{A}(g)\underline{y} = 1$, we can obtain from (8) the relation between the level of exports per worker and the level of consumption per worker. Thus $\underline{A}(g)[c\underline{\omega}+\underline{e}] = 1$, that is,

$$e_1 = \left[\frac{1-c.\underline{A}(g)\underline{\omega}}{A_1(g)}\right]. \qquad (9)$$

Thus for a given growth rate, an increase in exports per worker requires a reduction in consumption per worker, while, for a given c, an increase in g requires a reduction in exports per worker.

To complete the system of quantity relations in this economy we need to specify the relation between exports per worker, imports per worker and the trade balance per worker. Let β be the trade surplus per worker expressed in foreign currency; then we have

$$\pi_1 e_1 = \pi_3 [c.\omega_3 + g\underline{m}\underline{x}] + \beta \qquad (10)$$

as the fundamental equation for the economy's external constraint. Since $\underline{x} = [I - gA^*]^{-1}\underline{y}$ we may write (10) as

$$e_1 = \frac{c[\omega_3 + \underline{M}(g)\underline{\omega}] + \beta/\pi_3}{\pi - M_1(g)}.$$

Combining this with (9) we can write the solution for c as

$$c = \frac{\pi - M_1(g) - A_1(g)\beta/\pi_3}{A_1(g)[\omega_3 + \underline{M}(g)\underline{\omega}] + [\pi - M_1(g)]\underline{A}(g)\underline{\omega}}. \qquad (11)$$

Now, in order to consider the (non-) duality of the relations (6) and (11), we may note that $\beta/\pi_3 \equiv b/wp_3$, where b is the trade surplus per worker valued in terms of the bundle $(\underline{\omega}, \omega_3)$. It then follows from (4), (6) and (11) that

$$c = f_1(\pi, g)\left\{1 - \left[\frac{A_1(g)}{\pi - M_1(g)}\right]\left[\frac{\pi - M_1(r)}{A_1(r)}\right]\left[\frac{b}{w}\right]\right\}. \qquad (12)$$

It is clear from (12) that if trade is balanced, $(b = 0)$, then $c = f_1(\pi, g)$, just as $w = f_1(\pi, r)$, so that we have dual consumption–growth and wage–profit frontiers. Equally clear, however, is the fact that if trade is *not* balanced, $(b \neq 0)$, then (6) and (12) entail that

$$c = f_2(\pi, r, g, b).$$

Not only is the $c-g$ relation different from the $w-r$ relation but c itself depends on r: duality has completely vanished, with a variable from 'the quantity side' (c) depending on a variable from 'the price side' (r).[5] (It may be noted that in the special case $r = g$, (12) collapses to $c = w - b$.)

Growth and Distribution in an Open Economy 211

Before we turn to the macro economic arguments of the following Parts, it may be helpful to show how certain macro quantities are related to the variables discussed in the present Part I. As is usual, we start with national accounting identities:

$$q \equiv w + rk \equiv c + gk + b,$$

where q is output per worker and k is capital per worker, q, w, k, c and b all being measured in terms of the standard of value (ϖ, ϖ_3). With $r \neq g$, it follows at once that

$$k \equiv \left(\frac{c+b-w}{r-g}\right)$$

$$q \equiv \left[\frac{r(c+b)-gw}{r-g}\right]$$

$$v \equiv k/q \equiv \left[\frac{c+b-w}{r(c+b)-gw}\right].$$

Taking account of (6) and (12) we see that, for *given* technical conditions,

$$k = f_3(\pi, r, g, b) \qquad (13)$$

$$v = f_4(\pi, r, g, b). \qquad (14)$$

It has frequently been noted, in the closed economy context, that ratios such as k, v depend not only on technical conditions but also on r and g: it is seen here that in an open economy they also depend, in addition, on the terms of trade and the trade surplus per worker. Nothing useful can be said, *a priori*, about the directions of change in k and v when π, r, g or b change.

PART II   THE BALANCE OF PAYMENTS IN CONDITIONS OF STEADY GROWTH

Like all post-Keynesian discussion of growth equilibrium, our analysis has its roots in Harrod's growth scheme, which extended Keynes's short-period conclusions – on the absence of any automatic tendency to full employment – to the long period. For full employment growth to be possible, the warranted rate of growth of output must equal the natural rate of growth of output and, as Harrod demonstrated, there is no economic reason why a capitalist economy, in which investment decisions are guided by anticipated profitability, should ever be in a situation in which natural and warranted rates of growth coincide, except by fluke.[6]

As is well known, this Harrod problem has stimulated two distinct attempts at its resolution. On the one hand, Solow, Swan and others have argued that a value of the capital:output ratio will exist which reconciles warranted and natural growth rates and that competitive forces will result in that particular capital:output ratio's being chosen by entrepreneurs.[7] On the other hand, certain post-Keynesian writers, in particular Kaldor, Kahn, Robinson and Pasinetti, have suggested that the reconciliation of warranted and natural growth rates can be achieved through variations in the aggregate saving ratio.[8] For present purposes, a significant feature of each of the above modifications to the original Harrod scheme is that they have been developed solely within the context of a closed economy, devoid of trading and financial links with other economies. What discussion of trade, foreign lending and growth there is, lies largely outside the mainstream of growth literature and refers to such questions as, for example, stagnationist fears of oversaving at full employment or, on the other hand, the converse problem of the role of foreign borrowing as a supplement to deficient domestic saving.[9] At the same time, the extensive developments which have recently occurred in the theory of balance of payments policy concentrate on the potential conflict between the attainment of a full employment *level* of output and the attainment of external payments equilibrium. International capital flows are treated extensively in this context but primarily in the form of portfolio adjustments of given stocks of financial assets, in response to interest rate differentials and anticipated changes in exchange rates. Such changes reflect short-period, once-for-all changes in liquidity preference, rather than continuous long period adjustments to a growing stream of saving and investment.[10] Even more rarely do these analyses take account of the interest flows associated with foreign asset holdings, which are entered in the current account.

As a preliminary step in the long-period analysis of the relations between warranted and natural growth rates in an open economy, we first consider the relationships which must hold between various balance of payments magnitudes in conditions of steady growth, irrespective of whether or not full employment is being maintained.

The central point is that in conditions of steady growth, the trade balance, the current account balance and the basic balance must each be a constant *proportion* of domestic product; as must the total stock of net external assets.

With long period payments equilibrium defined in terms of a zero basic balance, the net acquisition of foreign securities over any interval of time—the net capital export—must be equal to the current account surplus. But that surplus depends, in part, on the volume of past capital exports, through the relationship between the interest flow and the stock of net external assets. The net international flow of interest payments or receipts is thus endogenously determined and the fundamental external relation becomes one between the trade balance and the stock of external net assets. In terms of the previously outlined notation, the zero basic balance requirement can be written as $L = D = B + F$, that is, as

$$\Delta Z = B + iZ. \tag{15}$$

In steady growth, the stock of external assets will increase at the same rate as domestic product, so we have

$$\Delta Z = gZ. \tag{16}$$

Combining (15) and (16), we obtain the following external constraint

$$B = (g - i)Z. \tag{17}$$

The flow of capital export, i.e., the current account, is then related to the trade balance by the condition

$$L = gZ = \left(\frac{g}{g-i}\right)B; \quad (g \neq i). \tag{18}$$

The economic significance of (17) and (18) may be seen by considering the case of a country which is an international creditor, $Z > 0$. Clearly there are three possible sets of relations between B and Z and between B and L, which depend only upon the relative magnitudes of the growth rate of domestic product and the international money rate of interest.

(a) $g > i$. In this case, the increase in the stock of external assets (capital exports) exceeds the return flow of interest on the existing stock of external assets. In order to effect the transfer of the 'excess' capital export, $(L-F)$, a trade surplus is required.

(b) $g = i$. The increase in external assets is exactly matched by the return flow of foreign interest income, there is no problem of capital transfer and equilibrium in the basic balance requires a trade balance of zero. This is the only case in which external payments equilibrium coincides with balanced trade (leaving aside, that is, the trivial case of $Z = 0$).

(c) $g < i$. The increase in the stock of external assets is less than the return flow of interest income, so there is a transfer problem in reverse, the solution of which requires that the economy have a trade deficit.

Exactly similar conclusions apply to the international debtor, $Z < 0$, but with $B \gtreqless 0$ as $g \lesseqgtr i$.

The immediate conclusion we may draw from this is that although a capital exporting country must of necessity have a current account surplus, it need not simultaneously have a trade surplus to achieve the transfer of the capital export. Similarly, the capital importer need not of necessity be a net importer of commodities. This, of course, is a well-known proposition, which can be traced back at least to Cairnes's *Some Leading Principles of Political Economy* (1874), and which has found recent expression in discussions of the relationship between foreign aid and the capacity to import of the developing countries.[11]

PART III THE HARROD PROBLEM IN AN OPEN ECONOMY

In this section we shall investigate how the presence of trade and capital flows can influence the warranted growth rate and create an alternative means by which it can be reconciled with the natural growth rate; alternative, that is, to variations in the saving:income ratio or in the capital:output ratio.

In an expanding economy in which basic balance is always achieved in the external accounts, two modifications are needed to the relations which determine the warranted growth rate. First, the macro economic equilibrium condition $I = S$ must be modified to $I + D = S$, thus adding the trade balance and the flow of net foreign interest income to the determinants of aggregate demand. Second, even though the ratio of domestic saving to *national income* is constant by assumption, it is the ratio of saving to *domestic product* which is relevant for the warranted growth rate and this will vary with each variation in net foreign interest income. If, for the purposes of this section *only*, we treat the capital:output ratio as independent of balance of payments conditions, we can write the 'fundamental equation' as

$$g_w = \frac{1}{v}(sy - d) \tag{19}$$

where $yQ = Q + iZ$ and $dQ = B + iZ = D$. With balanced trade and zero external assets this reduces to the familiar Harrod formula for the closed economy.[12]

Growth and Distribution in an Open Economy

If we now introduce the steady growth constraints (17) and (18) which link together B, D and Z, we can write (19) either as

$$\frac{b_w}{v} = -\frac{(g_w - s/v)(g_w - i)}{(g_w - si)} \tag{20}$$

or as

$$g_w = \frac{s}{v}\left[\frac{1 + iz_w}{1 + z_w/v}\right] \tag{21}$$

where b_w and z_w are the values of B/Q and Z/Q, respectively, appropriate to the maintenance of growth at rate g_w. Of course, in a more complete analysis we would have to take account of the dependence of v on the trade balance, noted in Part I, but for the macro economic emphasis required in this section we may temporarily ignore this dependence.

In Figure 16.2, we sketch the relationship between b_w, z_w and g_w implied by equations (20) and (21).

It will be obvious from the above account that, in the open economy, the warranted growth rate is not uniquely determined by the values of s and v but depends in addition on the values of B/Q and i. Although we here treat the international interest rate as exogenously given, the possibility immediately arises that we may 'solve' the Harrod problem by finding that trade balance ratio, B/Q, which sets $g_w = n$. From equations (20) and (21) we can immediately obtain expressions for the full employment trade balance ratio and the associated external assets ratio. Setting $g_w = n$ we have[13]

$$b_n = \frac{(n - i)(s - nv)}{(n - si)} \tag{22}$$

and

$$z_n = \left(\frac{s - nv}{n - si}\right). \tag{23}$$

The total capital assets ratio of domestic residents, $(K + Z)/Q$, is then equal to

$$(v + z_n) = \frac{s(1 - iv)}{(n - si)} \tag{24}$$

which is necessarily positive from inequalities (2) and (4).[14-15] From this, we can deduce the following properties of the full employment equilibrium.

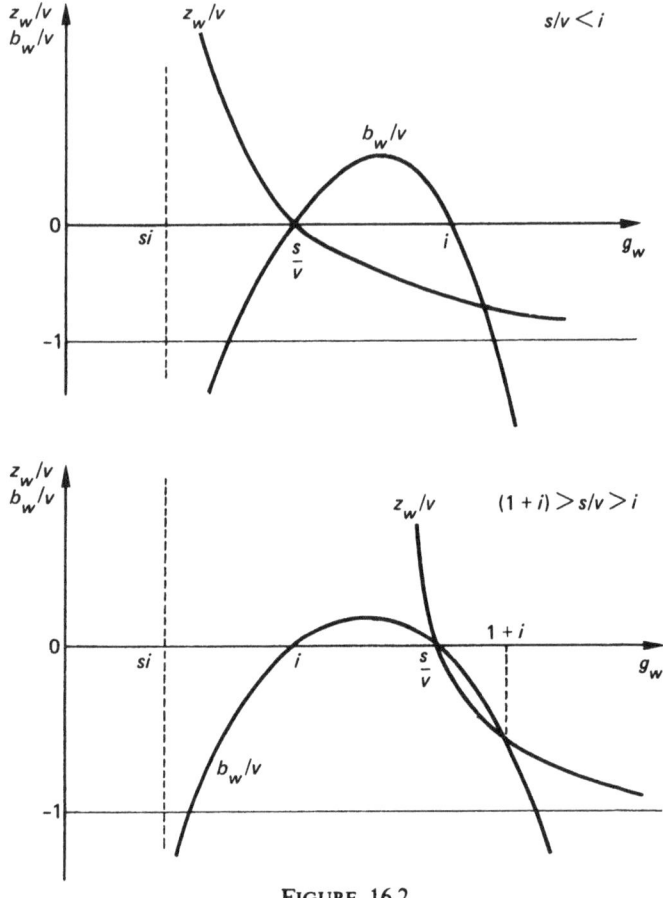

FIGURE 16.2

(i) Whether a country will be an international debtor or an international creditor in conditions of full employment growth depends only on the comparison of s/v with n, i.e., on the comparison of the warranted growth rate in conditions of balanced trade, with the natural growth rate. The oversaving country must always be an international creditor and the undersaving country must always be an international debtor. This result does not depend on the value taken by the international money rate of interest.

(ii) However, there is no presumption that the capital exporting country will have a trade surplus in full employment equilibrium or that the capital importing country will have a trade deficit. For, as shown in

Part II, the precise relation between trade balance and capital export does depend on the comparison of n with i.

It is at this point that our conclusions differ from those reached by Harrod in his original treatment of the relationship between the trade balance ratio and the warranted growth rate.[16] For Harrod implicitly assumed that the interest rate on foreign lending and borrowing is zero so that the current account is identical to the trade balance. Trade balance and warranted rate of growth are then inversely related. Once we drop this assumption, there is no presumption that a situation in which $g_w > n$, for example, is to be 'solved' through a greater trade surplus.

The above analysis, we would claim, is a logical development of the ideas contained in Harrod's original work on the relation between foreign lending, trade balance and warranted growth rate. We have demonstrated how warranted and natural rates of growth may be reconciled, even with constant s and v, by disposing of surplus full employment savings in foreign lending or by supplementing deficient savings through foreign borrowing.[17] Crucial to this conclusion is our assumption of a perfect international capital market, in which domestic and foreign securities are perfect substitutes and in which the arbitrage activities of financiers equate the domestic and the international rates of interest. We have also assumed that the requisite trade balance ratio can be attained to transfer completely the full employment international flow of capital. Further discussion of this point will follow an elaboration of the Harrod scheme to take account of the effects of the trade balance and capital exports on the distribution of domestic product. To this we now turn, without making the (arbitrary) assumption that v is independent of the trade balance.

PART IV TRADE BALANCE, FOREIGN LENDING, GROWTH AND DISTRIBUTION

The previous sections of this essay have provided us with the elements necessary for a macro economic treatment of distribution in an open economy. We take as our starting point the Kaldor theory of distribution which relates the share of profits in domestic product to the share of investment expenditure in domestic output, thus relating the functional distribution of income to the physical composition of output. To employ this as a long-period theory of distribution requires us to assume that output is limited by the physical capacity of existing capital equipment, that money prices are flexible relative to money wages and that the fraction of profits saved exceeds the fraction of wages saved.[18] To extend this theory to an open economy we shall assume that the saving ratio out of profits applies to domestically generated profits plus net foreign income. Equilibrium in the circular flow of income then requires that

$$I + D = s_w W + s_p(P + F)$$

from which follows the following formula for profits as a fraction of domestic product:

$$\left(\frac{P}{Q}\right) = -\left(\frac{s_w}{s_p - s_w}\right) + \left(\frac{1}{s_p - s_w}\right)\left[\left(\frac{I}{Q}\right) + \left(\frac{B}{Q}\right) + (1 - s_p)i\left(\frac{Z}{Q}\right)\right] \quad (25)$$

It is clear that (25) is of the same form as Kaldor's distribution equation for a closed economy and differs from the latter only in that the trade balance and consumption out of foreign property income must be added to domestic investment before the profit share can be stated. The greater is the trade surplus, or the greater is foreign property income, the greater is the equilibrium profit share. However, in conditions of steady growth we know that the trade balance and foreign assets are linked together, (17), so that we can rewrite (25) as

$$\left(\frac{P}{Q}\right) = -\left(\frac{s_w}{s_p - s_w}\right) + \left(\frac{1}{s_p - s_w}\right)\left[\left(\frac{I}{Q}\right) + (g - s_p i)\left(\frac{Z}{Q}\right)\right] \quad (26)$$

The profit share is determined by the total of home and foreign investment less the amount of saving out of the related stream of foreign property income.

From this it follows that any increase in the trade balance ratio is only favourable to the profit share if that increase is also associated with an increase in the foreign assets ratio, that is, trade balance ratio and profit share are only positively related if $g > i$.[19]

Referring now to the warranted growth path, it is convenient to express this distributional relationship in terms of the rate of profits, rather than in terms of the profit share, and to simplify by ignoring saving out of wages ($s_w = 0$). Remembering that $r \equiv (P/Q) \cdot (Q/K)$, we can now reduce (26) to

$$r = \frac{1}{s_p}\left[g_w + (g_w - s_p i)\left(\frac{Z}{K}\right)\right] \quad (27)$$

so that the rate of profits is positively related to the ratio of foreign assets to domestic capital stock. It will be clear from (27) that the simple Cambridge growth formula, $g_w = s_p r$, is not generally valid in the open economy. Instead, on re-arranging (27) we have

$$g_w = s_p \left[\frac{rK + iZ}{K + Z} \right] \tag{28}$$

which relates the growth rate to the *average* rate of return on *all* net assets owned by domestic residents.

We now have sufficient information to establish that the open economy has the following (*cet. par.*) equilibrium properties, relative to a given warranted growth path, with $s_w = 0$;

(a) The rate of profits is positively related to the rate of capital exports. For the capital exporter, the rate of profits is greater than that obtained in the absence of capital flows and, for the capital importer, the rate of profits is lower than that obtained in the absence of capital flows. Thus, for a given growth rate, capital exports are akin to domestic investment in their effect on the rate of profits;

(b) The relation between the trade balance and the rate of profits is ambiguous, depending as it does on the comparison of g_w with i;

(c) A lower value of the rate of interest is associated with a higher equilibrium rate of profits if $Z > 0$, and with a lower rate of profits if $Z < 0$. These differences reflect the condition that the *average* rate of return on domestically owned assets is always equal to g_w/s_p, irrespective of the external situation.

The above propositions have been specified in terms of external assets but in our economy these latter are determined, more fundamentally, by the trade balance. And since imports are endogenously determined, it is exports that are the major determinant of the trade balance. Thus the equilibrium properties of our economy apparently depend as much on the 'geographical horizons' of entrepreneurs as they do on their temporal horizons in making investment decisions. We can, therefore, add a fourth equilibrium property to our list.

(d) A greater 'propensity to export' is associated with a higher rate of profits if $g_w > i$ and with a lower rate of profits if $g_w < i$.

We are now in a position to pull together the various strands of this discussion and investigate the relations which hold in equilibrium between growth, distribution and the external characteristics of a small open economy. Our treatment is meant only to be suggestive, rather than final, so we propose to discuss only two of many possible cases. We first consider a 'classical' economy, in which the real wage is exogenously given; then we investigate the properties of a 'post-Keynesian' economy,

220 Fundamental Issues in Trade Theory

in which the relation between growth and rate of profits is governed by the propensity to accumulate of the entrepreneurs.

A Given Real Wage

In this 'classical' economy we treat the real wage as exogenously determined and we know, from the discussion of Part I, that the rate of profits and the relative prices of commodities are then given functions of the terms of trade. In particular, the more favourable are the terms of trade, the higher will be the equilibrium rate of profits.

If the economy were closed to trade and foreign capital flows then the rate of capital accumulation would follow immediately as $g = s_p r$. However, unless the current account of our economy is in exact balance this relation will not hold in the open economy. A current account surplus implies that a proportion of the volume of saving out of profits is invested abroad in the acquisition of foreign assets, so that the equilibrium rate of domestic capital accumulation must be correspondingly lower than that given by the Cambridge formula. Conversely, a current account deficit will be associated with net foreign borrowing and a higher equilibrium growth rate.

We may now ask what external characteristics of the economy are consistent with a given real wage and a given growth rate. Specifically, if the growth rate is to be the natural growth rate, what must the external position be if full employment growth is to be attained? To help with this, equation (27) is graphed in Figure 16.3, with $g_w = n$, and we see that r is an increasing, linear function of Z/K. A minimum value of $Z/K = -1$ corresponds to $r = i$ and the maximum value for Z/K is set by the associated maximum value of the rate of profits. Given the real wage and given the terms of trade there will be a particular value of the rate of profits; suppose this is given by r_o in Figure 16.3. This value of r is greater than that consistent with autarkic equilibrium growth at the rate n, $(r_o s_p > n)$, so that there is a lack of harmony between the warranted growth rate and the natural growth rate at the given real wage. In effect, the real wage is too low to be consistent with autarkic equilibrium growth. In our open economy, however, this 'problem' can be resolved by disposing of the surplus domestic savings on the international capital market, and acquiring external assets to generate the ratio $(Z/K)_o$ of foreign assets to domestic capital stock. Clearly this economy will have a current account surplus but whether it also has a trade surplus depends on the comparison of n with i. By contrast, if the real wage were too high for autarkic equilibrium growth, with $r_o < n/s_p$, then the economy would

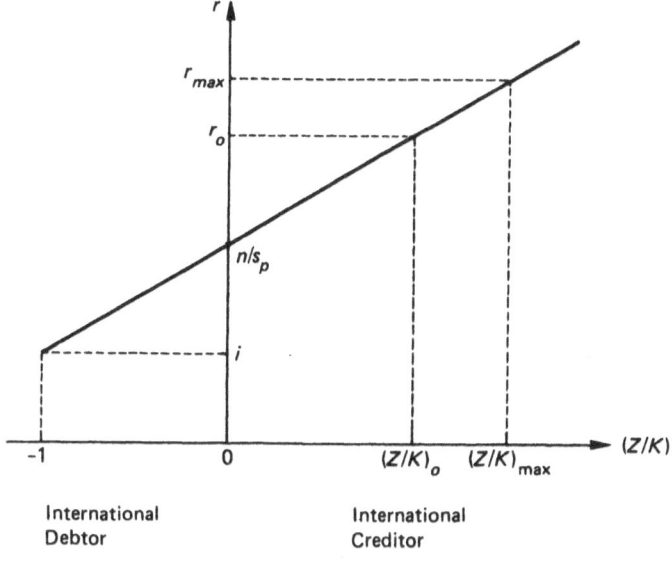

FIGURE 16.3

need to supplement domestic savings with foreign borrowing, to achieve growth equilibrium at the natural rate. This economy would be an international debtor with a current account deficit but with a trade balance which depended on the comparison of n with i. These conclusions, of course, mirror those found in the simple Harrod model discussed in the previous section – but note that the international creditor/debtor status of the economy is independent of the capital:output ratio and only depends indirectly on technical relations (through the relation between the real wage and the rate of profits).

Let us now compare this economy with a second economy, the two being identical in all respects except that the second is faced with a lower world price for its export commodity. Since both economies, by assumption, have the same real wage, we know from equation (6) and Figure 16.1 that the wage–profit frontier for the second economy will lie below the wage–profit frontier for the first economy, so that the equilibrium rate of profits must be lower in the second economy. It follows immediately that the second economy will have a smaller equilibrium ratio of Z/K to maintain macro economic equilibrium. In an obvious sense this notional deterioration in the terms of trade reduces the capacity to engage in foreign lending—and increases the capacity for foreign borrowing—if a given growth rate is to be maintained. A second difference between the two economies will be in their relative price structures and real exchange rates, but how these variables differ it is not possible to say, *a priori*, without a detailed specification of the production methods and the wage bundle. Since the two economies have different equilibrium price structures, different equilibrium rates of profit and different equilibrium trade balances per worker, it will also follow that they will have, in general, different equilibrium capital:output and capital:labour ratios, as given by (13) and (14). How these ratios differ it is not possible to say, but it is clear that any difference between the capital:output ratios, for example, will be associated with different shares of investment in output, different shares of profits in domestic product and different equilibrium values of the external assets ratio, Z/Q, and the trade balance ratio, B/Q.

Suppose now that the economies differ only in that they have different natural growth rates. Then, although they will have the same rate of profits, relative price structure and real exchange rate, the economy with the higher natural growth rate will have the smaller value of Z/K in growth equilibrium. Except in the special case of $n = i$, our small economy will not have a balanced trade account in growth equilibrium. From the analysis of Part I, we know that one implication of this will be that the wage–profit frontier and the consumption–growth frontier will no longer be dual relationships.

A 'Post-Keynesian Model': Given Propensity to Accumulate

As a second example, we consider a post-Keynesian world and introduce a relation between the rate of profits and the desired rate of accumulation of the entrepreneurs, a form of long-period 'investment function'. The central idea is that there is some minimum expected rate of profit, r_e, below which investment will not occur and that as the expected rate of profit is notionally increased, so the desired rate of accumulation will also increase. In growth equilibrium, the expected rate of profit will be equal to the actual rate of profits so that the relation becomes one between the desired rate of accumulation and the rate of profits, which we can write as

$$g_D = \phi(r_e, i), \; r_e = r > i \qquad (29)$$

When the rate of profits equals the rate of interest a floor to the rate of accumulation is reached, with only those investment projects carrying a zero degree of risk being undertaken. For any higher rate of profits the rate of accumulation will be greater and will be pushed to the point at which the gap between r and i equals the risk premium on the set of marginal investment projects. For any given value of the money rate of interest, the position of the accumulation schedule depends on entrepreneurial calculations of anticipated profit and their willingness to act on the basis of these estimates, i.e. their 'animal spirits'. In an important sense, the accumulation schedule captures the independent dynamic role of entrepreneurs in terms of their willingness to accumulate capital.[20]

In conditions of full employment growth we will have $g_D = n$, so that we can determine the rate of profits consistent with growth at the natural rate from the accumulation schedule (29). Comparison of this rate of profits with the ratio n/s_p immediately indicates the presence of surplus or deficient domestic savings and thus the necessity of foreign lending or foreign borrowing if full employment growth is to be possible. Foreign capital transactions may thus reconcile 'animal spirits' and thriftness conditions under conditions of full employment growth.

Suppose animal spirits are more active, in the sense that $g_D = n$ is consistent with a lower equilibrium rate of profits. Then, as with the case of a higher real wage in the 'classical' model, the economy now has a lower equilibrium value of Z/K in line with the reduction in the quantity of domestic saving. Furthermore, the equilibrium real wage is higher and the labour commanded price of foreign exchange is lower, as a result of the more active animal spirits.

If we now compare our post-Keynesian economy with one that differs only in that it receives a higher world price for the export commodity, then both will have the same rate of profits (provided we assume, rashly, that the accumulation schedule is independent of the structure of relative prices). However, from equations (6) and (4) we see that the economy with the inferior terms of trade will also have a lower equilibrium real wage and a higher real exchange rate. Unlike the 'classical' case, the difference in the terms of trade does not generate any corresponding difference in the external macro economic characteristics of the two economies, neither Z/K nor B/K being influenced by the difference in the terms of trade. However, the economies will have different relative price structures and different capital:output ratios, so that the ratios of investment to domestic output, profits to domestic output and trade balance to domestic output will each differ between the two economies, in a manner which cannot be specified *a priori*.

Finally, if the two countries differ only in their natural rates of growth, it is not possible to say (by contrast with the 'classical' case) whether the economy with the higher rate of growth will also have the greater or the smaller value of Z/K. The high natural growth rate makes for a reduction in Z/K, cet. par., but this may or may not be offset by the associated increase in the equilibrium rate of profits. The outcome clearly depends on the shape of the accumulation schedule, equation (29). Again the relative price structures and capital:output ratios will differ between the two economies, so that differences in macro-structure are associated with differences in micro-structure, as was seen in Part I.

Comment on the Comparisons

In the above comparative dynamics of the 'classical' and 'post-Keynesian' models we have shown how the warranted, natural and desired rates of growth might be brought into harmony through borrowing and lending on a perfect international capital market, to match the total supply of saving to a given growth requirement. We have not, however, provided any mechanism to ensure that such harmony can be actually attained. We only know that for an equilibrium Z/K there is a required value of the ratio B/K, which will transfer the necessary flow of saving. That is all. Whether this B/K ratio is achieved is outside the scope of our analysis; and if it is not achieved then it will not be possible for the economy to grow at the specified growth rate. We have demonstrated what equilibrium requires, not that equilibrium may be achieved.

Within this limited framework, however, we would argue that the above analysis contains the necessary elements of any macro theory of distribution relevant to an open economy. Our analysis does not require the existence of a factor 'capital', and it takes explicit account of accumulation of domestic capital assets and foreign capital assets. In this account, the geographical horizons of entrepreneurs turn out to be as important as their temporal horizons.

CONCLUDING REMARKS

The purpose of this essay has been that of developing relationships between external and internal equilibrium in the context of growing capitalist economies, where the wage bargain is struck in terms of money, which have developed financial markets, and in which entrepreneurs 'rule the roost' by making the crucial decisions relating to the proportions of domestic productive capacity which are devoted to the production of export and investment commodities. Within this framework, we have attempted a *preliminary* treatment of the Harrodian and

Cambridge growth theories and reached the general conclusion that, except by fluke, full employment growth is inconsistent with balanced trade. In general, the possibility of full employment growth requires that capital funds be exported or imported, according to circumstance.

It need hardly be added that much has been left unsaid. Long-period analysis rules out of court many of the most significant real world aspects of capital flows—e.g. their volatility—and we have nowhere attempted to abandon our small economy assumption. Nowhere do we treat direct foreign investment, a most important omission. That much remains to be done is obvious; we submit only that this essay may suggest a fruitful way of beginning to deal with the manifestly complex problems of trade and accumulation in open capitalist economies.

NOTES

*We should like to thank Richard Kahn, Jan Kregel, Paulo Pettanati and Joan Robinson for helpful comments on earlier versions of this essay.
1. For a valuable treatment of direct foreign investment and the difference between direct foreign investment and the foreign borrowing and lending discussed in this essay, see Arndt [1].
2. We shall use the terms 'foreign lending' and 'capital export' interchangeably. Both correspond to the excess of domestic saving over domestic real investment. Capital exports should not be confused with exports of capital goods; indeed it is perfectly possible for an economy to be simultaneously a net capital exporter, (in the sense defined) and a net importer of capital goods.
3. In a closed economy this is obviously the case, for $g > sr$ if real wages are positive, hence $g > si$. In an open economy, in which the financing of payments disequilibria leads to the acquisition of external assets or liabilities and in which the basic balance is always in equilibrium, the result may be proved as follows:

$$S = s[W + rK + iZ]$$

Now, as we show in the text, $S = I + D = g[K + Z]$ in conditions of steady growth. Hence

$$s[W + rK + iZ] = g[K + Z]$$

or

$$s[W + (r-i)K] = (g - si)[K + Z]$$

Now $W + (r-i)K > 0$ in any meaningful equilibrium, i.e. one with positive real wages. Hence

$$(g - si)[K + Z] > 0$$

in any such equilibrium.
Since $K + Z > 0$, inequality (7), it follows that $g > si$.

4. On duality, see Pasinetti [17], ch. 7.
5. Only if $\omega = Q$ is r not an argument of $f_2(.)$.
6. Harrod [5], ch. 3 and [6], ch. 2.
7. See, for example, Solow [21], ch. 2.
8. See, for example, Kaldor [10], Kahn [9], ch. 9, Robinson [19] and [20] and Pasinetti [16], chs. 5 and 6.
9. See Nurkse [15], pp. 127–9, and the paper by Kurihara referred to in Nurkse's discussion. Mention may also be made of a paper by Johnson [7], which contains an extended discussion of the relation between the warranted growth rate and the rate of growth of exports, without, however, treating the question of full employment growth.
10. For an up-to-date review, see Stern [22], ch. 10; also Borts [3], pp. 215–16.
11. For a discussion of Cairnes's analysis, see Iverson [8], pp. 53–6. More recent discussions can be found in Domar [4], Knapp [12] and Mikesell [13], ch. 4. The 'Reddaway Report' treats the relation between the volume of capital exports and the trade balance required for external equilibrium in terms of a constant flow of capital exports, i.e., a declining rather than a constant rate of growth of external assets–[18], ch. 18.
12. It may be noted that if all foreign interest flows are added to or subtracted from savings, or if $i = 0$, then equation (19) reduces to $g_w v = [s - b]$, where $b \equiv B/Q$.
13. For $s < 1$, equation (22) satisfies inequality (6), provided that inequality (2) is also satisfied.
14. The prior restriction imposed by inequality (7) is, therefore, satisfied on the full employment warranted growth path.
15. Expressions similar to (22) and (23) may be found in the work of Neher [14] and Borts [3]. It must be noted, however, that neither author derives these relationships within the context of a solution to the Harrod problem.
16. Harrod [5], pp. 101–15.
17. We leave it to the reader to show how notional variations in n, s, i and v influence the full employment values of B/Q and Z/Q, and how the outcome depends on the manner in which the change in parameter alters the difference between domestic saving and domestic investment.
18. Considerable controversy still surrounds the basis for the assumption that $s_p > s_w$. Without wishing to suggest that Kaldor's original treatment is definitive, it does appear to provide a valuable starting point for a consideration of the complications created by foreign trade. For further discussion see Kaldor [11], Pasinetti [16] and Wood [23].
19. Along an equilibrium growth path, we have

$$s_w W + s_p (rK + iZ) = g(K + Z)$$

or

$$s_w W + s_p (r - i)K = (g - s_p i)(K + Z)$$

In the economies we discuss, $K + Z > 0$, so that $g > s_p i$ if $r \geqq i$. Note that when we ignore saving out of wage income, $g > s_p i$ provided $r > i$.
20. Cf. Robinson [19], ch. 2, and Asimakopulos [2].

REFERENCES

[1] Arndt, H. W. 'A suggestion for simplifying the theory of international capital movements', *Economia Internazionale*, 1954, pp. 469–79.
[2] Asimakopulos, A. 'The determination of investment in Keynes's model'. *Canadian Journal of Economics*, 1971, pp. 382–8.
[3] Borts, G. 'Long-run international capital movements'. In J. Dunning (ed.), *Economic Analysis and the Multinational Enterprise*, Allen & Unwin, London, 1974.
[4] Domar, E. D. *Essays in the Theory of Economic Growth*, Oxford University Press, 1957.
[5] Harrod, R. F. *Towards a Dynamic Economics*. Macmillan, London, 1948.
[6] Harrod, R. F. *Economic Dynamics*. Macmillan, London, 1973.
[7] Johnson, H. G. 'Equilibrium growth in an international economy'. *Canadian Journal of Economics and Political Science*, 1953, pp. 478–500.
[8] Iverson, C. *International Capital Movements*. Oxford University Press, 1935.
[9] Kahn, R. F. *Selected Essays on Employment and Growth*. Cambridge University Press, 1972.
[10] Kaldor, N. 'Alternative theories of distribution'. *Review of Economic Studies*, Vol. 23, 1955–56, pp. 83–100.
[11] Kaldor, N. 'Marginal productivity and the macro-economic theories of distribution'. *Review of Economic Studies*, Vol. 33, 1966, pp. 309–19.
[12] Knapp, J. 'Capital exports and growth'. *Economic Journal*, 1957, pp. 432–4.
[13] Mikesell, R. F. *The Economics of Foreign Aid*. Weidenfeld & Nicolson, London, 1968.
[14] Neher, P. A. 'International capital movements along balanced growth paths'. *Economic Record*, 1970, pp. 343–401.
[15] Nurkse, R. *Problems of Capital Formation in Underdeveloped Countries*. Basil Blackwell, Oxford, 1953.
[16] Pasinetti, L. L. *Essays on Growth and Distribution*. Cambridge University Press, 1974.
[17] Pasinetti, L. L. *Lectures on the Theory of Production*. Macmillan, London, 1977.
[18] Reddaway, W. B and Associates. *Effects of U.K. Direct Investment Overseas: Final Report*. Cambridge University Press, 1967.
[19] Robinson, J. V. *Essays in the Theory of Economic Growth*. Macmillan, London, 1962.
[20] Robinson, J. V. 'Harrod after twenty-one years'. *Economic Journal*, 1970, pp. 731–6.
[21] Solow, R. *Growth Theory: An Exposition*. Clarendon Press, Oxford, 1970.
[22] Stern, R. M. *The Balance of Payments, Theory and Economic Policy*. Macmillan, London, 1973.
[23] Wood, A. *A Theory of Profits*. Cambridge University Press, 1975.

Index of Names

(Only the more significant references to names are listed.)

Acheson, K., 74n5
Alexander, S. S., 188
Arndt, H. W., 225n1

Batra, R. N., 13n10
Bhagwati, J., 12n3, 75n18, 180–1, 185n11
Bliss, C. J., 46n2, 75n17, 85, 88n19, 90–1, 94
Borts, G., 226n15
Bruno, M., 84–5
Burmeister, E., 46n2

Cairnes, J. E., 214
Caves, R. E., 12n3, 74
Champernowne, D. G., 36n13
Chipman, J. S., 12n3, 12n5

Fujimoto, T., 145–6

Garegnani, P., 87n4, 109n19

Harrod, R. F., 211, 217
Hicks, J. R., 130n5, 159

Iverson, C., 226n11

Johnson, H. G., 226n9
Jones, R. W., 5

Kahn, R. F., 212
Kaldor, N., 212, 217, 218, 226n18
Kemp, M. C., 88n16, 130n3, 185n12
Kenen, P. B., 74n3
Keynes, J. M., 211

Lancaster, K., 5

Leontief, W. W., 5, 66, 72–3

Machlup, F., 188, 195
McKenzie, L., 150
Marx, K. H., 87n8, 92, 111
Morishima, M., 145

Neher, P. A., 226n15
Neumann, J. von, 142
Nuti, D. M., 119, 121

Pasinetti, L. L., 119, 212, 226n18

Reddaway, W. B., 226n11
Ricardo, D., 7, 13n8, 73, 99–109, 110, 131, 132, 159, 161, 176
Robbins, L., 74n4
Robinson, J. V., 35n5, 212

Samuelson, P. A., 13n9, 35n5, 75n16, 85, 86, 90, 94, 97, 124–5, 131, 185n4
Smith, M. A. M., 131
Solow, R. M., 212
Spaventa, L., 130n5
Stiglitz, J. E., 130n5, 131
Swan, T. W., 212

Taussig, F. W., 12n8, 110

Vanek, J., 4, 46

Warne, R. D., 46n5
Whewell, W., 132–3
Wicksell, K., 74n6
Wood, A., 226n8

Index of Subjects

Balance of payments with steady growth, 212–14
Basic commodities, 78, 107, 178–9

'Cambridge' equation
  not generally valid in an open economy, 218–19, 220
Capital
  as a 'factor', vii, 10, 38, 181, 224
  as a set of physical goods, 7, 65–6, 74n3, 161
  as a sum of value, 5–6, 66, 74n3, 74n5
  in H–O–S theory, 4–6, 9–10, 64–75, 179–81
  and international investment, 9–10, 13n10
  malleability and transitions, 9, 132–40, 143, 198
Capital controversies, vii, 5–6, 64
Capital intensity
  depends on trade balance and on terms of trade, 211, 222, 223–4
Comparative advantage, 7, 12n6, 65, 102–5
Comparative statics results
  undermined by positive rate of profit, 30–2
Competitive 'imperfections', 8–9, 12, 13n9, 50–2, 157, 189
Consumption–growth frontier, see Wage–profit frontier

Devaluation, see Exchange rate
'Double-switching' of trade systems, 178

Effective protection, 12n4

Employment level, 109n19, 118, 176
  and wages, 35n5, 138–40
Exchange rate, 144–5, 147–56, 207
  devaluation and effects on capital and growth, 194–9
  inverse relation to profit rate, 190–7; the dual relation, 191–7
  and technique choice, 195–9
Expectations, 203, 222–3
  and transitions, 55, 60, 62, 139–40, 159, 198
Export-led growth, 199
Export tax, 155–6

Factor intensities
  alternative interpretations, 94–6
  'direct' and 'total' rankings identical, 35n7
  reversal ruled out, 16, 39, 50, 65
Factor price equalisation, 45, 186n16; see also Interest rate equalisation

Gain from trade, 8–9, 47–62, 103–5, 115–16, 127–30, 131–40, 147–9, 175–7
  can be negative, in comparative dynamic terms, 8, 53–5, 103–5, 109n25, 116–18, 127–30
  and discount and interest rates, 8–9, 60, 132, 134
  and transitions, 8–9, 55–61, 130n5, 131–40
Golden rule, 55, 119, 121, 127, 130n4, 158n4

Harrod problem, 211–12
  resolved in the open economy, 214–17

229

Heckscher–Ohlin–Samuelson theorem
  price form, 42, 44, 70–1
  quantity form, 41–2, 43, 70–1, 180–1
Heckscher–Ohlin–Samuelson theory
  basic assumptions, 2, 39, 65
  and capital, 4–6, 64–75, 179–81
  emphasis on 'scarcity', 1–3, 11
  and growth, 6, 179–80
  and international investment, 9–10
  and production, 3–6
  with land, labour and a positive rate of profit, 38–46
Heterogeneous labour and transitions, 139–40

Incomplete specialisation in Ricardian trade theory, 107–8, 165–7, 170–1, 174
  during a transition, 136–40
Interest rate equalisation, 72, 75n16, 75n17, 85–7, 90–7, 124–6
International investment, 9–10, 13n10, 212–14, 225n2
  need not involve a trade surplus, 213–14, 216–17

Joint production and trade theory, 142–58, 160

Kaldorian distribution formula, 217–24

Labour theory of value, 99–105, 110, 145, 169–70
Leontief paradox, 66, 72–3

Multiple exchange rates, 155–6

Non-substitution theorem, 123–5, 175
Non-traded commodities, 66, 109n14, 127, 143–5, 146–58, 185n4, 206–10
  and interest rate equalisation, 75n17, 85–7, 92–7

Offer curve, 44

Planned economy and trade, 118–21
Preferences, 11–12, 13n11, 16, 30–1, 39, 48, 65, 159
Primary inputs, 15–46
  distortions in markets for, 48–52
  and growth 11, 161
  relative use need not be inversely related to relative prices, 22–8, 40–1

Quotas, 154–6

Rate of profit (interest)
  compared with a distortion, 48–52
  differences in as a basis of trade, 114–15, 124–5, 177–8
  effects of positive rate on neoclassical theory, 15–46
  raised by trade, 100–2, 106–7
  rates of profit and of interest distinguished, 202–3
  relation to wages, see Wage–profit frontier
  relation to wages and rents, 18–21, 33–4
Relative prices
  conditions for their repetition, 77–85, 91–6
Relative supply of two commodities need not be positively related to relative prices, 26–8, 42–3
Restricted trade, 154–7
Ricardo's theory of trade, 99–105
  and gain from trade, 103–5
  and pattern of trade, 102
  and the profit rate, 100–2, 109n16
Rybczynski theorem, 62n6

Scarce factor can benefit from trade, 44
Steady growth, 10–11
  definition extended for trade theory, 164–6
Stolper–Samuelson theorem, 45, 71–2

Tariffs, 12n4, 45, 71–2, 155–6
Technical progress, 11, 13n11

Textbook 'Ricardian' theory, 7, 73, 110, 149
Transfers, 156–7
Transformation rate, 49, 51–2, 54, 62n6, 63n14
Transport costs, 157
Uniqueness of trade equilibrium
  no presumption of with a positive profit rate, 44
Von Neumann analysis, 142–58
  and changes in world prices, 151–4
  and existence of trade equilibrium, 144–5
  and restricted trade, 154–6
Wage differentials, 157
Wage–profit frontier, 68, 78, 82, 84, 86, 111–15, 117–18, 122n5, 148, 152, 189, 208–9, 221
  depends on terms of trade, 152, 208–9
  dual to consumption-growth frontier, 115, 117–18, 189; but not when trade is not balanced, 209–10
Wage–rent–profit frontier, 18–21, 33–4

GPSR Compliance
The European Union's (EU) General Product Safety Regulation (GPSR) is a set of rules that requires consumer products to be safe and our obligations to ensure this.

If you have any concerns about our products, you can contact us on

ProductSafety@springernature.com

In case Publisher is established outside the EU, the EU authorized representative is:

Springer Nature Customer Service Center GmbH
Europaplatz 3
69115 Heidelberg, Germany

www.ingramcontent.com/pod-product-compliance
Lightning Source LLC
LaVergne TN
LVHW040735250326
834688LV00031B/311